THE FERRY

Resistance and Rebellion
With Tax-based Representation

Jordan David Weisinger, M.S., M.A., M.B.A

DEDICATION

To all the people that make these opportunities possible. Their hard work and good decisions are a beacon of hope for all the ambitious and courageous authors in the world.

CONTENTS

	Acknowledgments	i
1	Language of Rebellion	1
2	Input Equals Output	16
3	Reciprocity and Retribution	27
4	Boundaries of Loyalty	39
5	Resisting Authoritarianism	55
7	Institutional Inequalities	67
8	Organizational Structure	84
9	Liability Simulations	103
10	Fiscal Median Partitions	124
11	Liability Coefficients	159
12	Engineering	187

FOREWORD

The Red Queen is an evolutionary hypothesis where organisms must constantly adapt to circumstances that are also in a constant state to change, in order to gain reproductive advantages and survive. The more they evolve to meet the demands of their current environment, the faster their environment evolves to overcome them. The organism must constantly adapt in order to preserve their current position. Hence, it appears to be running in place. The Red Queen rules over the domains of biology and politics. States and nations are living organisms subject to the same competitive evolutionary environments other animals are. They must ceaselessly work at survival or they will be overcome by wealth inequality, corruption, or predictably brutalized by a neighbor. Just like in biology where successful organisms pass on their genetics, the more successful states and nations will pass on their public policy. This is more evident in democracies where their governance systems are more adaptive and responsive. A more dominant political party will win more elections and pass more laws. Really successful nations export their public policy and preferences through negotiated trade agreements, nation building and coalition formation.

Political ideologies also evolve as time passes and new environments emerge. Socialism is dying. Its centrally controlled industry might be acceptable for healthcare, policing, and other sensitive government-based services but it is the worst way to organize the overwhelming majority the economy. Communism was the most abhorrent political system to be tested to date, affecting the lives of hundreds of millions of persons. The fixed and despotic political outcomes ensured the centrally managed economies were not reformed or delivered equitably. The evidence is in and Communism is an abject failure. However, the rhetoric and idealization of socialism persists because Capitalism produces wealth inequality and poor justice system outcomes. Like a virus or some other adaptive system, democracy must incorporate the more successful elements of socialism to make it immune to movements seeking equality in outcomes rather than equality in opportunities. Econometric representation accomplishes this by adopting the   language and organizational aspects of socialism within the machinery of democracy. Instead of the proletariat monopolizing political power, they are permanently incorporated in the electorate and bicameral process.

By separating and isolating the below median class within its own legislative chamber, it empowers them with better role identity, stronger collective bargaining, and more agency from wage restricted political representatives. The proletariat is thus elevated by democracy, and set equal to the leisure class and investors class in the above median chamber. Democracy is by far the dominant process, but it learns from it experiences like other social or biological organisms. Democratic Socialism is the belief that socialism can be acquired through the Democratic process. Economic Representation builds this belief system into the machinery of the political process. The electorate can be split evenly into two equal parts, with one group comprised of those paying below median tax liabilities and another group comprised from those paying above median tax liabilities. This is the highest form of democratic entitlements as it perseveres majority rule and a bicameral process, while imbuing vectorized class identity within the legislature. The more specialized electorates will produce more honest representatives and more accurate and efficient public policy. This is how more specialized labor produces value for firms and it will be the same result for a more evolved political market.

Human biology is remarkable because a billion years ago our simplest cells merged with a virus called mitochondria, and it is only from this incorporation that we are able to survive. This is equivalent to the role specialization in a median partition based on class. Communism is a virulent and dangerous ideology but when it is stripped bare of its violent tendencies and collared within the democratic process, it will act as a source of motivation and power for the nation, much like mitochondria does for our most fundamental cells. Democracy will be forever changed by the median partition. It will be stronger, smarter, and more adaptable than its ancestors. It only needs outcomes to support these conclusions. The evidence needs to be derived from real world models, that swim, leap, fly, and run in the same economic and political environments more conventional democracies are found.

This is no easy task, but if citizens of occupied nations are able to decide on the form of their own government during nation building exercises, many will choose a newer, more efficient, and more adaptable version of democracy. The other route is more tenuous, more tedious, and less certain. Contemporary democracies can reform their current institutions, or strike the older ones down to recreate a government closer to their own image, but this is more speculative and less certain. Both strategies require a leap of faith. Without prior examples, there will never be the pressing evidence needed to convince bureaucrats or activists that there exists a more perfect system.

Biology has performance measures for fitness such as reproduction rates, mortality rates, and longevity. Politics also has performance measures. They come in terms of GDP growth rates, satisfaction polls, electoral turnout. This is the science of politics. It can be captured in the discrete values that are recorded over time by individuals, firms, and governments. This does not capture all of the probabilities and possibilities inherent in a social organism like democracy. Some of it can be predicted from prior histories with known variables and unknown inputs, but a significant portion is never captured in the data. It is left to speculation and imagination.

The value of literature is in part evaluating and estimating outcomes that are possible but have not come to pass. There is value to predicting poor outcomes and then assessing the causes and presenting possible solutions. History tends to reoccur in predictable patterns. The same situation may arise with different outcomes possible. Literature is able to examine these alternate solutions to histories while they are still imaginary. The stated goal of this deliberation is to keep the worse outcomes imaginary by increasing the sanctions on behavior contributing to these poor outcomes. The intent is to develop a culture which recognizes or identifies these behaviors earlier and then commits to actions that avoid or change them. There will always be demonstrated value in assessing the inputs into an event, and then assessing the possible remedies to change output. This is why uncomfortable inquiries into the motives and consequences of events must continue to be scrutinized.

It is also the responsibility of government to investigate those outcomes which may not be preferable but where there is a statistically significant probability of occurring, despite any cultural or personal objections to the possibility. Government must assess the likelihood and then allocate resources to mitigate the threat. This includes low probability and high impact events. If a probability of just 2% was assigned to an event as catastrophic as a debt default or secession, the government should still investigate and prepare for the possibility, despite the lack of imminent danger. These calculations get more complicated when they depend on an electoral outcome that can vary wildly and oscillate from term to term. Although current conditions may not validate urgent concern, the loss of an election cycle may change the disposition of politicians and civil servants. Outside stimulus, like the business cycle, may also alter the trajectory of the nation, and this is hard to predict out from one term to the next.

This process becomes increasingly uncomfortable when it involves coworkers and neighbors, but when large numbers of voters support pubic policies like debt defaults and prolonged government shutdown, their preferences should not be discounted. These outcomes must not be underestimated because of the negative consequences but rather expected despite them. Populations usually pursue political outcomes which may contradict normative values or outcomes outside rational expectations, but this doesn't mean they are less likely, it only distributes incentives or outcomes less evenly. It is a lack of understanding or a deficit in perspective that contributes to the poor estimation of intent, when outcomes exceed the range of normal expectations.

Governments don't have the leisure to discount unproductive behaviors, they must immediately respond with public policy and preparation to mitigate the worst consequences of that behavior. This is easier to accommodate in federal systems, as states gain representational efficiencies with specific perspectives found within the electorate. Instead of relying on gross estimates of public perceptions or expectations on the federal level, states can specialize in a more precise interpretation of events or likelihoods. The states are more diverse and a larger number of possible outcomes or solutions can be considered. This will improve the quality of outcomes, especially if the consideration is priced into elections leading up to a possible event.

Predicting is often the easy part. Presenting solutions is the hard part. This book posits tax-based representation as the best means to protect against threats of debt default and government shutdowns. Tax-based systems of representation make democratic nations less susceptible to the threat of government shutdown and debt defaults by allocating more political representation to the states paying more federal taxes. This has two significant effects. The more populous and wealthier states generally prefer progressive taxes and this will result in lower deficits. Threats to shut down the government or default of its debt are less legitimate when the government takes on less accumulated debt and maintains smaller deficits. The states that generally pursue austerity measures and pursue government shutdowns most often will have significantly less representation in at least one of the legislature's chambers. This will reduce the number of attempts and seriously curtail the support for these dangerous policies. The combination of these two properties in tax-based representation will make nations more likely to survive into maturity, where higher per capita incomes and stronger labor rights, make the population far less susceptible to a culture of government shutdowns and debt default threats.

Despite the best laid out plans, it is impossible to predict the outcomes of elections held under a new system like income or tax-based representation. Not only are those electorates untested but each one will develop their own opposition party with different political preferences and voter turnout. Predicting Conventional elections are notoriously hard even with decades of histories to rely on. Econometric systems have no histories and predicting results is strictly speculative. However, certain themes are present in history and econometric system plays on those which tend to focus on those voters which are generally underrepresented in majoritarian democracies and conventional democracies. Form matters more than output, in respect to this book as it introduces a new paradigm derived from applying descriptive statistics and econometrics to institutions and electorates. It may change everything or nothing. Splitting the electorate into two adversarial parts may produce the same quality and frequency of laws in a majoritarian or conventional democracy.

However, the audacity of hope leads me to believe that improved role identity, a fiduciary duty, and the adversarial relationship between chambers will markedly improve the quality of labor laws for the poor and civil rights for minorities. This book Ileana expressly intended to improve the outcomes of demographic shifts and the plight of the poor and vulnerable citizens. Democracy is a living organism that must adapt new environments including demographic shifts, wealth inequality, and climate change. The old style of majoritarian politics will fail us in every respect. To have faith in the people is to understand they need support the support of institutions and rhetoric to explain the nuances of political power and economic advantage. Econometric systems of representation provide this extra benefit where conventional democracies languish.

Tax-based representation is intended to insulate the public from the most serious defects in due process by incentivizing a path towards progressive taxes and durable government. Debt default threats and government shutdowns are the most derisory risk to democracies and tax-based representation is the best protection against these insults.

The more insults a government suffers, the more short-term thinking dominates public policy and electoral outcomes. This threatens the democratic nation and their neighbors. Tax-based representation allows the public the time they need to address wealth inequality, demographic shifts, and climate change without the persistent threat of default or shutdown.

Democracy is not yet done evolving, and econometric systems of representation will prove themselves to be an effective offshoot of demographic-based systems. These competing political are less adversarial and more complementary. Tax-based systems are compatible with other forms of democracy requiring no explicit choice to exclude one or favor another. Econometric systems come in enough variety to satisfies the organizational demands of most constituencies and sovereignties. At the very least, they will push contemporary democracies to their boundaries when trying to accommodate the anti-discrimination and anti-corruption properties of econometric systems. The goal is always towards a more perfect union, with high quality democratic entitlements distributed to the adult age population, without exclusion or disproportionate representation.

THE FERRY: RESISTANCE AND REBELLION

1 THE LANGUAGE OF REBELLION

The smell of secession is in the air. The United Kingdom has successfully seceded from the European Union. Now Scotland and Northern Ireland want to secede from the UK. Spain also has a strong secessionist movement brewing in its Catalonia region. Rebellion is clearly percolating below the surface of the United States. A prior history of violence is important but there is other corroborating evidence. Not only does the United States suffer from rampant wealth inequality but it is in middle of historic demographic shift, where for the first time ever, a democracy will transfer majority political power from one demographic group to another. Most demographic shifts have resulted in pogroms or genocide, and the United States is presenting the telltale signs for the same risks. The nation is acquiring significant amounts of debt due to a relentless defunding of the federal government, and suffers almost yearly government shutdowns and debt default threats. These two political acts are the most effective way a political party can organize a revolt against a democratic government. As the number of insults increase, so does the likelihood of an event.

The United States federal government ran a $1 trillion deficit in 2019[1], it passed a $2 trillion stimulus bill in 2020[2], and can expect future deficits to be in excess of $1-2 trillion dollars after adjusted for higher unemployment and lower government revenues. The 2020 election will be contentious and the nation can expect more government shutdowns and possible defaults throughout the next Presidents 1st term. The threats started in 2011 with the refusal to raise the debt ceiling after agreeing to the Sequester Act[3]. In 2013, the nation almost defaulted on the debt again, and was only averted by the discretion of the Speaker who went against their parties' preferences[4]. After the 2013 shutdown, the nation suffered two other shutdowns, two in 2018 with one extending into 2019, clearly setting the trend for the next administration[5].

The last shutdown was the longest with the nation experiencing a 30-day shutdown which accounted for nearly 9% of all days in the year[6]. The nation has suffered 20 government shutdowns since the Civil Rights Act and Voting Rights Act passed in the 1960s[7]. The shutdowns are getting

---

[1] Alan Rappeport (Oct. 25 2019)."Federal Budget Deficit Swelled to Nearly $1Trillion in 2019". Retrieved from https://www-.nytimes.com/2019/10/25-/us/politics/us-federal-budget-deficit.html

[2] Jordain Carney (March 25 2020). "Senate unanimously passes $2T coronavirus stimulus package". Retrieved from https://thehill.com/home-news/senate/489590-senate-passes-2-trillion-coronavirus-stimulus-package

[3] Amanda Cox, Elaine HE, Alan Mclean, Karl Russel, Archie Tse, and Lisa Waananen (July 2011)"Charting the American Debt Crisis". Retrieved from http://archive.nytimes.com/www.nytimes.com/interactive/2011/07/28/-us/charting-the-american-debt-crisis.html

[4] Jonathan Weisman and Ashley Parker (Oct 16,2013). "Republicans Back Down, Ending Crisis Over Shutdown and Debt Limit". Retrieved from https://www.nytimes.com/2013/10/17/us/congress-budget-debate.html

[5] Infoplease staff (March 17 2020). "Timeline of U.S. Government Shutdowns", Retrieved from https://www.infoplease.com/history/us/timeline-of-us-government-shutdowns

[6] Infoplease staff (March 17 2020). "Timeline of U.S. Government Shutdowns", Retrieved from https://www.infoplease.com/history/us/timeline-of-us-government-shutdowns

[7] Infoplease staff (March 17 2020). "Timeline of U.S. Government

longer and the inhibitions against default are breaking down which is most likely attributed to the changing demographics and expectation of minorities acquiring majority demographic status in 2045[8]. The current demographic shift and wealth inequality are changing the political calculations the parties are making, we are in an outlier political market.

The political parties should not expect the same outcomes for recent disagreements, even if they are reminiscent of prior periods like the Labor movement and Women's Suffrage movements. Those were resolved when the electorate was almost entirely Caucasian and they were self-dealing by giving themselves more property rights and voting rights. It's a different political market after Civil Rights Act passed and Caucasians expect to the minority demographic group and fear the same abuse they are guilty of over the last 250 years. The recent public finance crises and nearly complete legislative obstruction must be viewed through the prism of the dominant political party and demographic group expecting to lose majority status.

Debt defaults and government shutdowns pose a persistent threat in most presidential democracies because they require interventions to avoid. If any part of the process fails to pass a debt ceiling measure, the nation defaults. Most legislatures are bicameral and in competitive elections the control will be split between two or more parties. In other democracies, a president may have veto power over the bills. Too many things can go wrong. A debt default may be a reaction to a criminal investigation, a compromised election, or a simple miscounting of votes. It only takes one chamber or one principle for the unthinkable to occur. Defaults may also occur as a result or intent or negligence. The motivation for a debt default is far less important than the consequences.

The shutdown itself may incite a default without any actual vote held on a debt ceiling measure. A government

---

Shutdowns", Retrieved from https://www.infoplease.com/history/us/timeline-of-us-government-shutdowns

[8] William H. Frey (March 14 2018). "The US will become 'minority white' in 2045, Census projects." Retrieved from https://www.brookings.edu/blog/the-avenue/2018/03/14/the-us-will-become-minority-white-in-2045-census-projects/

shutdown is effectively a boycott on new legislation and that may include debt servicing and debt ceiling measures. If the legislature isn't meeting to pass a budget, and the shutdown persists for longer than the commitment to the last debt servicing measure, a lack of dedicated funds will provoke a default even if not overtly intended. If the government shutdown causes a debt default, the parties and pubic may not be able to assign blame. It will be a partisan conflict with people relying on tribalism for support. Worse, if a party was perceivable at fault, it will introduce a moral hazard. They won't want to reconstitute the government because they will almost certainly lose the next election. They will have every incentive to maintain the shutdown and move their leadership to the regional governments. This is an optimal environment for secessions or usurpations.

Once a default has occurred, it changes the political calculations made by all of the elected officers and voters. What was once a viable relationship between states and citizens, now becomes a burden. The debt serving costs could double, causing a huge increase in taxes. The securities markets and economy could crash, requiring even more government intervention or subsidy. Worse, voters will examine which states make the most contributions to the nation, and which receive the greatest subsidies. The political union will be viewed primarily in financial terms. The cost benefits analysis will exclude intangibles and those hard to measure aspects. One demographic group or political party will blame the other and conflict may ensue. What may have been negligence could result in civil war or dissolution.

A debt default followed by a government shutdown is the most effective way one party or demographic group can start a rebellion and win a civil war. Imagine a scenario where the government defaults on its debt and debt servicing costs double. Also imagine a massive correction in the economy that cuts tax revenues by 20% or increases spending by 20%. The government will already be struggling with a 40% change in revenues and expenses in an environment where borrowing is no longer an option. In the chaos, half of the states secede, cutting revenues by another 40-50%. Costs would effectively double while revenues shrink by half with no prospect of raising capital through the bond markets. Wars are incredibly expensive and could effectively double the government's expenditures again.

A prolonged government shutdown could last as long as the full term of the representatives in the chamber that refused to pass a budget. In the United states, this is two years and more than enough time for the rebellious states to constitute a new interim government and raise an army from the national guard and local police forces. A federal government will be able to continue operating for a few weeks or months with emergency funds, but if the legislature refuses to pass a budget, the government will remain shut down. Eventually all borrowing authority will end and all funds exhausted. It is within these first two years, where the nation faces its most severe threat of secession or loss of democratic entitlements.

A few weeks into a prolonged government shutdown, the president will be reduced to a figurehead. They will have no means to enforce laws or fight wars. If the rebel legislators keep the government shutdown, the legislature cannot pass any new laws and pass any new budgets. The rebel legislators may remain in office and can obstruct any effort by the loyalists to reassert law and order over the Union. The legislature cannot act without them if no quorum can be met. The legislature cannot remove them. Nothing can compel a majority of legislators to pass any laws supporting the federal executive branch. This is true even if the rebel states are in open revolt against the government. The rebels can wait the full two years or until their interim government is established before declaring secession and retracting their representatives. If prosecuted in the correct order, there is virtually no recourse to a secession enforced by a government shutdown and debt default. Although, typically immoral and unpatriotic, this strategy is completely legal until the declaration of independence is made by the rebels.

Enlisted would start leaving the armed forces if the government could not pay their wages. It would also certainly be an incentive for less loyal soldiers to join the confederacy. The rebellious states will start diverting federal revenues back to their own balance sheets. Tax-holidays are more effective when state laws are passed, appropriating the payroll, sales, and income taxes collected by firms and large corporate businesses. This will allow them to staff up their local militias form from municipal police forces. Almost three quarters of an army may be support roles for front-line troops while police forces are almost entirely front-line operators. Often, the number of police officers employed by the local governments will be equal to the number of enlisted in a nation's standing army. They will be able to onboard the disaffected enlisted from the formerly federal government. In some nations, the state governments already manage veteran enlisted in National Guard units which can be up to 50% of the nation's front-line soldiers. These veteran troops will assume leadership over the veteran's police forces and effectively organize a formable force to defend territory or launch insurgency.

Whenever threats of debt default and government shutdowns are present, it requires a state-level response. In most simulations, the states will have priority to respond by resisting authoritarianism or by rebelling against the current administration. Federal systems of government include sovereignty for the state governments and they are granted full authority to act in all instances not covered by the constitution. A prolonged government shutdown is one of these circumstances. The federal government won't be able to marshal the financial resources, the labor resources, or good will it needs to put down a confederacy of states. If the government is shutdown, there is no appropriation authority to make purchases or meet payroll obligations. The federal government loses all borrowing authority and must rely on cash tax receipts. After the states start diverting revenues back to themselves, the federal government will be devastated financially and unable to enforce its laws.

The states will still have viable budgets and cash flows and the nation will depend on them to put down the rebellion or usurpation. Each state has its own borrowing authority and balance sheet, giving it access to the credit it needs to subsidize a war effort. The state government have significant veteran police forces and national guard armies to draw on, before they enact a draft or financial incentive to enlist. The states have to be aware of supply chains for military hardware, ensuring they have the arms and munitions to defend themselves. Supply chains will be disrupted, with many manufacturers using parts from other nations or states. Those states with ports have a huge advantage in that they can import new arms and munitions rather than build them. Every state should have an emergency plan in place should the federal government be shut down for an extended period. The states should have their own plans and not rely on plans determined by the defunct federal government. There is no downside to states maintaining these plans if the risk of default or shutdown is already present in the political environment.

States will have to fill the vacuum left by the incapacitated federal government and this presents its own risks. Without clear leadership, the states may break into geographic or ideological factions, unable to coordinate themselves in the defense of the nation. Worse, they may hesitate and patiently watch while the nation is dissolved. If the federal government has no borrowing or appropriations authority, it is more of a liability than a benefit, and when this is recognized, the state will invariably pursue their own interests instead of protecting and supporting each other. If the nation is in economic free fall, and there is no federal government to back stop, a larger portion of the population will view dissolution as safer and more equitable way to proceed. Fear, anger, and mistrust will encourage demagogues, increasing the likelihood of highly partisan and regional preferences dictating electoral outcomes. Institutional protests like government shutdowns and debt defaults promote populism and separatism in the electorate and there is little an establishment party can do.

Before any real violence started, the opposition party could sue for peaceful dissolution, and it would be a more reasonable outcome than destroying the nation's GDP with bombing campaigns, urban assaults, and occupation. The former union may be better off splitting into two new nations, discharging the debt acquired by the former government, and starting off in peace with a clean balance sheet and the benefit of a functioning economy. The two nations can then agree on immigration policies between them with trade resuming. It is not a best-case scenario but many nuclear armed nations will have no other recourse. They will have to accept a peaceful dissolution of face possible nuclear war with a nation sharing their border.

For non-nuclear armed nations, the combination of a debt default and economic ruin will greatly improve the effectiveness of local militia, veteran national guard armies, and defecting enlisted from the standing armies (air forces and navies included). The local sourcing of troops will allow the secessionists to deflect any attempt from the loyalist to forcibly preserve the territorial borders of the political union. Without nuclear annihilation to dissuade the two sides from violence, armed conflict is far more likely with a devastating effect on GDP and democratic institutions. Although the nation may have avoided secession or violence with more debate. Once the debt default and government shutdown occur, there will be fewer inhibitions to violence. Even if the right to secession is culturally accepted, the economy will already be in ruin and there will be less reason to avoid open warfare.

The use of institutional protests, like government shutdowns, provide another strategy for rebel parties. The opposition party can impeach the President if they step over Constitutional boundaries when responding to the rebellion. If the President provides law enforcement and military funding during the shutdown, the opposition party can impeach and possibly remove the President. Individual members of a political party could be convinced to support the impeachment on legal or constitutional grounds. These politicians may reside in the rebel states and be fearful of incarceration or loss of life. They may fear being removed from office for not supporting the impeachment, or secession. These politicians may also seek to avoid conflict at all costs, including removing their own President from Office. There are enough rationalizations or justifications for individual politicians to support impeachment that it can't be excluded. The possibility is certainly within the margin of error.

When successful, regime change could coerce a premature end to the war, earning a successful secession for the rebels. A new President may be more willing to make concessions to the rebels. They may be more likely to sue for peace. After the display of non-violent political force, the President may relent and consent to a peaceful dissolution. At the very least, it will discourage a sitting President from acting extra-judicially by continuing to fund the armed forces putting down the uprising. If the President can't act unilaterally, they will have to depend on the individual states to levy taxes and fund law enforcement and armies to engage the rebel states. This is far less effective than a unilateral response, meaning the rebel forces can a major advantage by pursuing impeachment during a secession supported by a lawful government shutdown. The rebel politicians have to have the willpower to resist vacating their offices during the buildup to conflict, but all of the advantages are earned by the opposition party the refrains from violence, to coerce a peaceful dissolution through institutional protests and patience.

Government shutdowns pose the most significant risk to democratic governments for three reasons. First, they are the most effective method to divert funds away from the federal government back to the state governments. Most taxes are collected on the state and firm levels and can be easily redirected. Second, they prime the electorate to support the rebellion by coercing them into public commitments of support. Public declarations of support make the rebellion far more effective than any secretive coups or spur of the moment movement. Third, when rebellions are fomented on due process, it limits the options another party has to counteract it. On the surface, the rhetoric and policies are legitimate, serving the interests of their constituencies, which makes it more effective than outright declarations. Without historical references, this strategy for rebellion is less recognizable and nearly impossible to dispel or prevent. During this period neither the military nor the federal law enforcement can act while the government is shutdown, making it more dangerous than other crises.

Government shutdowns are one of the more serious insults a nation can suffer. Although most are short in duration, there is the possibility that it extends until new elections are held several years later. If the shutdown occurs immediately following an election, this could be a period of two-years or more. There is the expectation that the politicians will price the likelihood of winning subsequent elections into their determination to keep the government shutdown. The longer a government remains shut down by a party, the more likely they are to lose the next election. However, if the party has already determined to use this opportunity to organize a rebellion, they will care less about losing the next election cycle and the two-year delay between elections presents the best opportunity to mobilize the states in open revolt. State controlled national guard armies and local police forces may be enough to overwhelm a federal government is denied appropriations and borrowing authority. War efforts costs substantial amounts of money and the states have an advantage if the government remains shutdown for one or two years before the next elections. After the states start diverting federal revenues collected by firms residing in their territories, the federal government will never fully recover, even after new elections.

No political party threatens debt defaults and government shutdowns unless they are comfortable with the worst-case outcomes resulting from those policies. The body politic should view these policies with suspicion every time they come up in discussion. They are telling of the incentives behind the threats: political parties worrying about demographic shifts will view debt defaults as a means to preserve sovereignty over themselves. This is especially true if they expect to have majority power in the states most likely to declare independence. If the party will predictably lose majority-demographic status in the larger nation, they will naturally emphasize state electoral outcomes and state rights over unity and voting rights

The secessionist party will want to maximize their probability of success. Not explaining their real intentions will help accomplish this goal. Older democratic systems are far more susceptible to crises of confidence or process, despite the public being completely unaware of the risks. It is the job of the majority party to explain the incentives and the consequences of a default prior to the crises so that the voter's price in these outcomes into elections prior to the event. It is not enough to attribute the threats of debt default or government shutdown to entropy or disorder. Political parties are made up of millions of persons and are fully capable of predicting or appreciating the consequences of their actions. Intent can't be obfuscated by mob rule and anarchy if preceded by very deliberate public policy preference. Otherwise, only history can distill the facts and circumstances leading to a default or dissolution. It is written by the political party and society that wins presenting the opportunity for a cover-up.

Most democracies don't have 100% of the public voting in 100% of the elections. Most democracies see only 70% voter participation, where a small minority of 35% can dictates public policy for the other 65%. In secession movements, a minority of voters could decide the future for a majority of persons during a single referendum or vote. This is also the strongest argument against secession movements. Even if a secession movement gains 51% majority, it would irreparably harm the other 49% who did not agree to the terms of separation. This makes most secession movement illegitimate from the very start. It is untenable that a small minority is able to force other residents to surrender their citizenship when citizenship is associated with economic benefits, civil rights, and voting rights. Not only will the minorities face almost certain incarceration risks and worse economic outcomes but there will be no expectations of improving conditions through due process. Without recourse, the minority populations are more likely to resist and protest.

The party seeking secession may be looking forward at a future where immigration and demographics will render them the minority party in national elections and subject to the executive and legislative authority of an emergent demographic group. A secession will allow the party to preserve their national identity and political hegemony. It is the best method an empowered minority has access to maintain power when they cut off support from the national parties preserving laws from passing to protecting their civil rights, voting rights, and economic rights. The demographic majority can reduce the other political party to a permanent minority or worse, suppress their vote by incarceration and other anti-democratic policies. By separating themselves from a larger union, they can acquire more certain electoral outcomes and policy outcomes.

Debt default threats and government shutdown give the political caste and opportunity to dictate terms of secession during a crisis and create economic conditions that maximize chances of success. If the terms of the dissolution were spelled out in more certain outcomes, it would change the preference of both the voters and of the political caste. The economic consequences of a secession should be known before the public votes for that outcome in a referendum. Voters aren't likely to vote for dissolution, if their state budgets would take on a 20% deficit and where their economy loses an average of 3% in economic stimulus every year. An involuntary dissolution might result in trade barriers, tariffs, or economic sanctions that will certainly result in further disruptions to supply chains and new accounting and tax regimes.

An informed public would vote in their best interests and likely stand against a dissolution or secession. If they didn't, they will be less surprised when they lose their job, their home, or their voting rights after supporting the secessionist movement. At least they won't be able to blame the other states and other political parties for their own shortsightedness or terrible judgement. To make matters even worse, those residents forced into this precarious situation involuntarily will start protesting and maybe rioting. This invites the specter of demographic violence against minorities when the governments use institutional power to put down any dissent and restore order to a failing state. The state will be in economic free fall with dissenters everywhere looking to organize and protest the circumstances.

This is why it is incredibly important to identify these shifts in preferences or allegiances early. If this attitude can be diagnosed early, the threats and the consequences of debt defaults can be debated by voters, pundits, and elected officials. The people can price in the expectation of dissolution into electoral output. More importantly, if the public are more aware of the circumstances and consequences before an event, they will make better choices during the crisis. A larger portion of the population will continue to support the political union. The viability of the secessionist cause will decrease, as the number of states supporting the measures sinks. Information asymmetries benefit those seeking to forcibly secede while full disclosure benefits those states and citizens preferring to maintain the union.

One of the better indicators of the likelihood of an event are budget negotiations repeatedly timed to come immediately after elections. This is purposefully engineered to shut down the government for the maximum amount of time if the party does not like the outcome of the last election. This includes off year, mid-term, and presidential election years. In an environment where one party repeatedly threatens default or shutdown, the other party must reciprocate and time budget negotiations for elections where they stand to lose the most. Authoritarianism is often lurking in the looming shadow of reoccurring public finance crises, and minority parties must consider the threat of anti-democratic policies following an illegitimate election.

Parties must recognize the circumstances that make ordinary budget negotiations dangerous. Wealth inequality and demographic shifts can turn predictable arguments into constitutional crises and disasters. Silence is one of the best indicators of risk. When one party makes several obvious and aggressive moves during budget negotiations and the other party does not reciprocate, it is an indicator of weakness. The other party clearly recognizes the threat and are unable to predict or acquire adequate solutions. Their silence is a last-ditch effort to avoid a conflict they don't have a chance in winning.

Silence is the expression of dread. Dread causes hesitation and hesitation leads to poor outcomes. Only an informed electorate can pass the laws it needs to avoid a default or protect voting rights and civil rights. Only an informed electorate can price the risk into elections and avoid candidates who may harm them. Only an active electorate can discourage their political caste from participating in this dangerous behavior or supporting despots. The threat of election loss will make these representatives less likely to exploit budget processes or threaten default. An informed electorate will have the opportunity to look for any and all recourse to mitigate the risk. Democracies most important assets are due process and elections. These properties are the safest and most effective way to negotiate the circumstances contributing to a secession or war.

Outcomes can be improved by clearly describing the deleterious behavior as dangerous and malicious. The electorate will select better candidates in the primaries, vote for better candidates in the general elections, and rebuke politicians for pursuing threats and shutdowns. More importantly, the public will be more prepared for crises that require quick decisions. If silence is replaced with informed consent, the public would not be as susceptible to the public policies and posturing that make crises more likely. Silence only emboldens those who would take advantage of an uninformed public. Silence is an accomplice to those seeking to benefit themselves and preserve political power where they would ordinarily lose it.

An informed electorate provides one other significant benefit. The victors write history but it is far harder to cover up when the public and the media have formed strong opinions and gathered facts the corroborate alternative conclusions. The best defense against coercion, corruption, and complicity by a political caste is the development of relevant facts and strong histories that contradict any lies or mischaracterization of events after the crisis. Silence allows the party in power to dictate how perceptions leading up to the crisis are framed and how the media and academics describe the event afterward. Strong social and political pressures will force the voters to comport their expectations and memories to the new reality. Prosecution and economic ruin will scare away dissent as public opinion regresses to the new mean.

Where individuals do not have the authority or capacity to resist an illegitimate government, the political representatives in the legislature must commit to the use of institutional protests. A prolonged government shutdown may be the only recourse an opposition party has to prevent an authoritarian from consolidating power, ending civil liberties, and disrupting self-rule. Institutional protests are inherently lawful and the most effective strategy for coercing peaceful regime change. If a candidate refuses to vacate office after losing an election, the opposition party is expected to shut down the government until valid elections can be held. If the prior administration still refuses to leave office, the opposition party may consider a debt default and call up the state national guards to protect their protesting populations.

These may seem like drastic moves but if the opposition party does not act immediately by shutting down the government and calling up the national guard, they risk legitimizing the authoritarian regime. If the opposition party hesitates, they may see other anti-democratic policies enacted and the less likely future elections will cure the rot of despotism. Court rulings may be disregarded, laws may remain unenforced, and election winners may not be seated. The longer the opposition party waits to respond, the worse their chances of overcoming authoritarianism and preserving democracy. The more patient they are, the fewer allies they will have in the military and civil service, to rely on when the people rise up against the authoritarian regime. The states that do protest at a later date, risk being occupied and losing their voting rights entirely. If they don't all act as one in the first moments of the crisis, they can expect to be inevitably converted to despotism one by one.

Any effort on part of the executive to circumvent the authority of the legislature must be viewed as authoritarian and anti-democratic. It must be resisted by the entire legislature and all of the regional executives. Most legislatures have the unchallenged right to shut down the government with no recourse through the courts or executive branch. This is the power of an institutional protest. This is the ultimate check on an executive who doesn't respect the law or election cycle. It is a peaceful way to prematurely end the regime of an authoritarians or illegitimate president. It is also easily resolved. If the next election is determined to be valid, or all parties vacate the office if expected, budget negotiations may resume and the regular course of business can be pursued.

2 INPUT EQUALS OUTPUT

Politics is tribal. During crises we rely on family histories, networks or friends and coworkers, and we fear reprisals from employers or local politicians. In this environment it rarely matters who causes a shutdown or is in control when emergency powers are evoked, the nation will break down into sectarian motivations and allegiances. The risk of loss is so great that prior relationships are less valuable than a guarantee of safety in an unsafe environment. Most times, blame is for the historians to record and history is written from the perspective of the winning tribe or party. This usually benefits the majority demographic group, which are also more likely to favor government shutdowns and threats of default. They are typically the land owners, the firm owners, and are more likely to occupy the executive branch with a majority of the electorate. This is one reason why demographic violence is so frequent. It is incredibly effective, with most of the arithmetic favoring them. A superiority in numbers is a useful tool when attrition rates can change the electorate in their favor.

One of the leading indicators of demographic instability is wealth inequality. Wealth smooths over many of the obstacles to political power a waning demographic group fear. It allows them to retain power for much longer if they relied exclusively on fair and open elections. Corruption quickly follows wealth inequality and this will result in weakened law enforcement and oversight. When corruption through deregulated campaign finance and partisan redistricting fails, the outgoing demographic majority will pursue voter suppression, mass incarceration, and other anti-democratic policies to preserve power. The use of institutional abuses predisposes the majority-demographic group to the use of more extreme violence like pogroms and war.

Austerity measures will exacerbate wealth inequality by eroding the culture supporting progressive estates taxes and income taxes. Without progressive estates taxes, wealth accumulates in a small number of well capitalized corporations. These firms monopolize the securities markets and dominate commerce. These owners can entrench themselves in the political process through campaign finance and the promise of future employment and wealth. The concentration of political power makes it harder to pass more egalitarian and sounder tax policies with economic reforms. This is when authoritarians will seek to exploit the weakened political system and pass anti-democratic policies to consolidate and preserve political power.

The majority-demographic group will often horde the wealth of a nation through exploitative economic policies. They maintain a near complete control over the largest companies in the country, preserving a monopoly on the labor and capital. For this reason, the demographic majority will advocate for policies like weak labor laws, low taxes, and poorly regulatory environments. They will relentlessly pursue austerity measures that keep the government under-capitalized and under-utilized. They will refuse to raise taxes to correct the wealth inequality and keep the government buried under deficits and debt. The margin for error increases as the number of options available to the government diminish during a crisis. When conditions deteriorate, the threat of aristocracy or despotism looms over the formerly democratic nation.

No party makes threats of default lightly. They are aware of the consequences. The very presence of this rhetoric is a threat of civil society and democracy. A debt default is part of a long-term strategy of a demographic-majority to keep and preserve power despite their status being challenged by the high birth rate or immigration rate of a minority population. It is the best indicator that the demographic-majority will try to secede or usurp power while they still have dominant demographic, economic, and political positions. Once the rhetoric of debt defaults and shutdowns are accepted by the public it is near impossible to root it out without reforms that require the demographic majority to agree to them.

No short-term outcomes will satisfy the waning majority-demographic group in the long term while their political power diminishes and the options, they have to retain power dwindle. Although the minority demographic groups can accept austerity and budget cuts in the near term, there will be other periods in which the deficit grows and debt accumulates. Unless the rhetoric is soundly defeated and put permanently to rest, the majority-demographic group will have other opportunities to organize a rebellion around a debt default or government shutdown. Most demographic shifts last several decades, eroding the ability to predict or prevent them. The minority party politicians will forget the past and unlearn everything taught to previous generations. This will cause them to hesitate or retreat when discipline and courage are needed the most. This is one more reason why history has the tendency to repeat itself so often.

It is possible a political party develops blindness in regards to possible outcomes. Political parties may not consider the consequences of an event or probability of it occurring if they don't have a recent experience to reference. The public is notorious for under-estimating the likelihood of something happening if it hasn't happened yet during their lifetimes. Generations that may have faced similar circumstances start to die off and the nation loses its community resistance. More likely, the terrible consequences produce stress that disincentivize individuals to discuss it with immediately family, relatives, friends, and coworkers. If poor outcomes are predictable and unavoidable, the opposition party will likely resort to denying the likelihood of an event in a last-ditch effort to reduce the risk of the other political party acting on the opportunity.

If a culture of debt defaults threats and government shutdowns persists for more than just a few years, the odds of an event increase as parties become less tolerant and more brazen in their negotiations. Political parties are people and when outcomes don't match their expectations they will get upset and react rashly. When the parties are fixated on debt default threats and government shutdowns, it creates an incredibly dangerous environment where conflict is only one vote or election away. The parties may become more homogenous making the likelihood of a mistake more likely. If they all come to the wrong conclusion, there is no one to contradict or challenge them. More importantly, the economic or demographic circumstances may change resulting in more incentives or opportunities to launch a successful secession or usurpation. Each year is a new opportunity for disaster, with the number and dispositions of representatives changing.

There will be little recourse for an opposition party that does not defend the nation against threats of default or budget shutdowns. They can't price the consequences of an event into prior elections, and are not likely to successfully defend the nation during an event. The opposition party will be forced to accept the outcomes of an event they barely participated in. Worse, they will only have themselves to blame for not adequately characterizing the consequences and giving themselves an opportunity to pass the laws needed to avoid a catastrophe.

After a default, unemployment will skyrocket, and the labor force participation rate plummet. A large portion of disaffected persons will have too much free time to dwell on the causes of the debt default. They will swell with anger and blame immigrants, minorities, and women. They will be corralled by propaganda and demagogues into protecting and preserving the party that caused the default and economic recession. The demographic-majority will accept a leader that resembles them in religion, skin color, and persuasion. They will permit more unscrupulous behaviors if they believe it will help them preserve their political power and position as the owners class.

If the party causing the default has control over the presidency, they will put down the protests and riots that result from the damaged economy. Demographic majorities may also resort to violence to protect their monopoly on wealth and political power. Pogroms are common and they can devastate communities through death or loss of property. A pervasive environment of violence and disdain will permeate all aspects of society. The more the military and police are used to put down social movements, the more the people will grow to resist. Wide scale conflict is also a risk. Eventually, the president will seek permanent interventions and war power. This opens the door to despotism.

If 70% of the nation is one demographic group and 30% represents minorities, and if they inflict an equal number of casualties during war, the magnitude of loss is nearly twice as severe for the minority groups. This makes demographic violence a highly effective means of controlling the electorate for the majority demographic group. There is even more risk in civilian deaths, where indiscriminate bombing or extrajudicial killings exacerbate the losses to minority groups in territories controlled by the offending party. Democracies will predictably form political parties that separate into more homogenous and heterogenous groups, and this could disguise the demographic-based motivations in partisan conflict over deficits and electoral outcomes.

Demographic groups losing majority status will prefer policies that increase the level of entropy and disorder in the system. If there is a failure, they are far more likely to end up in a superior position. The majority demographic group is able to absorb more losses with little to no electoral impact. Minority groups often suffer twice the electoral impact of a majority demographic group making it far more profitable for a demographic group to rely on violence. Majority demographic groups also monopolize the wealth and resources of a nation making them far more likely to prosecute a successful war for usurpation or secession.

The majority-demographic party need not actually default to win. The party can use a filibuster or strategies to obstruct the legislature while repeatedly underfunding the federal government to preserve the wealth inequality and susceptibility to default threats. By preserving these conditions, they can ensure poor people have no recourse to challenge firms that exploit them or states that oppress them. By preserving these conditions, the majority demographic continues to divert incomes and wealth to their families rather than minority households. The federal government is perpetually at risk for a shutdown or default, allowing the majority-demographic group to prevent a peaceful transfer of political power. If a democratic nation can't effectively regulate itself or tax itself, it is equivalent to despotism. Instead of political despotism, the nation succumbs to industrial despotism. Large firms and the wealth. The threat of political despotism is merely delayed, until it is challenged giving the majority-demographic group an opportunity to install an authoritarian. thy fill the void left empty by the filibuster and legislative obstruction.

Opposition parties can identify these intentions years in advance. Arguments for default and threats of government shutdown are vocal and must be repeated yearly. The opposition party can easily protect itself with public policy and debate. They must examine the prospect of default and secession and explain the consequences to the public. If they respond quickly enough, debate is their most effective tool. If the consequences are deleterious, the public will reject the prospect and support the opposition party. Nothing is guaranteed but it does improve the likelihood of preserving the union and discouraging support for default. This strategy increases support for raising taxes to reduce the deficit. The levers of control that make a default plausible must be eliminated.

Don't underestimate the power of majority demographic party to preserve support by constituents in the period leading up to an event and just after it. There are many examples of majority demographic groups supporting candidates despite their pursuit of anti-democratic polices and aggregated economic exploitation. They continue to support partisan redistricting polices, voter suppression policies, and campaign finance laws that maximize the likelihood of their remaining in power after declining into minority party status. This primes the majority- demographic group for authoritarianism by coercing them into public commitments of polices that oppress and exploit minorities. It sets expectations that if the minority groups will resist, they will be met with violence as their protests are forcibly put down. Their support of these policies before conflict will balance with their continued support after conflict.

If the minority party starts to win majorities, or pass progressive taxes and anti-corruption policies, the majority-demographic group may act on their threats. If the event includes a debt default or prolonged government shutdown, the ensuing crisis afterward will convince them to stay the course and remain in support. They will start making all of the decisions in the basis of religion, race, and money. One of the more terrifying realities of a demographic shift, is that almost all of the electoral outcomes support the majority demographic group. On face value, they will win most elections: gubernatorial, senatorial, and presidential elections all use state-wide elections to determine the winners and in majoritarian elections. A demographic majority with a 51% margin will still win 100% of the elections in hyper partisan electoral environments.

The potential for a debt default and secession is found within the error term and the majority demographic group can excuse it by negligence or ignorance. If they are unaware of the consequences of their actions, they can't be held accountable by voters beforehand. If the attitude and agenda can't be cured through debate and due process, there may be too-few minorities remaining after a conflict to influence elections afterward or hold the majority demographic group accountable for their deleterious actions. With no accountability before an event, and likely no accountability after an event, there are very few disincentives to discourage the majority demographic group from pursuing dangerous and destructive path.

A premediated debt default would cause a terrible economic crisis shortly after it is announced. The insult could destroy stock market, bond markets, and credit markets. It even may cause hyperinflation. In addition to expenditures being twice that of revenues after a debt default and secession, money would devalue when borrowing is impossible and the government would have to rely on printing money. The government, will be forced into more budget austerity with huge cuts to welfare and other forms of economic stimulus. These conditions will paralyze corporate firms hiring and buying decisions.

The insult to the economy will cause profit margins to fall and joblessness to rise precipitously. If the public was not already susceptible to white supremacy, fascism, or aristocracy in its prior environment, they will soon be openly debating the topics. Violence offline follows long periods of economic strife and it is always accompanied by a rise in extremism and other dangerous ideologies. People look for certainty during crises and authoritarianism provides those outcomes. If the majority demographic can control more of the variables into economy and politics, they will make more concessions on civil liberties and economic output.

Debt defaults and government shutdowns are only risks to democracies. Despotic nations aren't threatened by discontented minority parties. Elected officials don't negotiate budgets or raise taxes. There is no chance of user error or opportunity for rebellion. The authoritarian controls all aspects of government; thus, their biggest risk is in economic collapse and civil unrest. Democracies introduce user error into the budgetary process and rely on tradition rather than rules to protect themselves. Despots don't respect rules or tradition and can easily circumvent internal budgetary processes. This makes democracies more susceptible to regime change and internal conflict. Nearly 45% of the world qualifies as democracy but only 12% are considered high-quality democracies[9]. Almost 38% are despotic or authoritarian and immune to debt defaults. This leaves nearly half of the world's nations exposed to the risk. Low-quality democracies suffer from weak institutions and corruption. They may experience unchecked wealth inequality and suffer violence when demographic shifts occur.

Rebellion is a dangerous prospect for democracies. They carry far more risk than most suspect. They are rarely

---

[9] Democracy Index 2018: Me too?, page 2, The Economist Intelligence Unit, retrieved from www.eiu.com

successful and the consequences are almost always ruinous economy. Any attempt at rebellion is more likely to result in another authoritarian assuming control or the nation rather than a minority party successfully challenging a majority party pursuing ant-democratic policies. Democracies defending themselves against the creep of authoritarianism and corruption are much better off patiently seeking reform rather than launching into default and regime change. However, institutional protests may be the only way to dislodge an authoritarian from office. Coercing regime change peaceably through government shutdowns is a lawful and effective way to protect voting rights and civil rights.

Most rebellions will occur when a party or region seeks recourse through a secession. If they purse a policy of debt defaults and government shutdowns, they will have to broadcast their intent years in advance as they communicate their intent to colleagues and voters. It will remain innuendo until after the event occurs. The silence and secrecy maximize support for the debt default and shutdown policies. A much smaller portion of the population would support a debt default or shutdown if they thought it would result in a secession. A far larger portion of the population will support a secession after the default has occurred. The parties and the citizens will be blaming each other and looking for scapegoats. Tempers will flare and the viability of the nation will wane. A government is essentially a financial organization and when it ceases to be able to pay it obligations, it will cease to have the support of the people. When the people expect the nation to fail, they will look for leadership on the state or local levels.

A debt default is the most devastating way to announce independence but it may not be the most likely. Government shutdowns over budgets are far more likely to result in conditions that result in conflict. Budgets generally have to be passed every year giving ample opportunity to opposition parties and majority parties to use them as leverage in an event. Most governments can't function without a passed budget. Tax revenues continue to be collected, but the government has no authority to issue payments. A prolonged government shutdown effectively ends the tenure of the body. Most shutdowns are only a few days in length but they can last several months or years. If a party was committed to prematurely ending a federal government, they could shut it down until new elections are held several years later.

If a government continues to draw money from the treasury and pay its employees, it is an act of rebellion. It can be criticized as authoritarian and may be viewed as the first step towards despotism. In most democracies, the power over the purse is found in the legislature and any act circumventing the institutional protest is inherently undemocratic. Without a budget, a majority of the decisions will be made on the state or regional level. This is extremely dangerous as there is no guarantee of consensus or cooperation. The lack of national leadership imparts the marginal positions held by governors more authority and legitimacy, regardless of the consequences. Outcomes matter and a prolonged budget shutdown can shift the power downward to regional governments in the vacuum of a shuttered national government. This will destabilize even those nations with long histories of solidarity and unity.

Shutting down the government is the best strategy to sow dissent and create the dangerous conditions where a majority of citizens support emergency measures to suppress minorities actively resisting the regime. A shutdown may also be the pretense for a power grab. The executive may invoke emergency powers during a shutdown despite being the cause of the shutdown. It is a high probability play for an executive to grab power and avoid an election loss or arrest. This is similar to how the Reichstag fire was used to demand emergency powers to prevent other democratic institutions from failing.

Emergency powers represents one of the biggest risks to the democratic process because a large portion of the population will consent without any significant thought to the consequences. They may be described as necessary and temporary, but when they are combined with government shutdowns to the discretionary sectors of the government, they will likely result in permanent and substantial reductions in government services or protections. The suspension of government services will likely provoke protests and riots, resulting in the delay or end to democratic elections. All citizens must be wary of emergency powers following unresolved budget disagreements where large portions of the government are considered wasteful, unnecessary, and are ultimately shutdown.

The very presence of government shutdowns and threats of default are enough to verify suspicions that a party is considering secession or usurpation. Rational actors won't threaten a democratic government with harm, unless they benefit from disrupting elections and due process. The risks and consequences of a default or prolonged shutdown are simply too great. Any party repeatedly making threats has already considered the consequences, making the acts premeditated. The possibility of violence against the electorate should not be viewed as a byproduct of their negligence, but more of an ambition.

3 RECIPROCITY AND RETRIBUTION

Game theory is the complex mathematics behind relationships and decisions. Strategies are tested against each other through simulations or experiments with different strategies employed to maximize point gains. One variation in experimental game theory assigns different point values to the players depending on their use of an aggressive strategy or a cooperative strategy. If one player uses an aggressive strategy when the other player uses a cooperative strategy, the aggressive player wins the most points possible for a given game while the cooperative player wins zero. If both players pursue a cooperative strategy that each win a moderate number of points. If both players pursue an aggressive strategy neither wins any points. Each player participates in a number of separate games and tallies their points at the end. The results often depend on which are the dominant strategies used during the competition.

If there are a large number of aggressive players, the total number of points scored by all players is higher but there are significantly fewer winners. Most points are concentrated in a few players and the cooperative players have much smaller totals. If the majority of players employ cooperative strategies, then the total number of points won is lower but there are a larger number of winners. The aggressive players will have the least points. When scientists studied optimal strategies pursued by A.I., it demonstrated that the most successful strategy was reciprocity. The A.I. will always start off as cooperative but whenever there is aggression it will reciprocate. This strategy is called Tit for Tat and it maximized the points earned when interacting with both the cooperative and aggressive strategies.

Political markets are similar to game theory experiments. When political parties are more cooperative, they pass more economic reforms, more financial revaluations, and there are less threats of catastrophic interventions. More of the players in the economy and society have higher standards of living and society as a whole benefit. When one party pursues more aggressive, they can maximize returns for a smaller group in the economy, usually a racial group or the owners' class, and there are a smaller number of winners. The more competitive economic environment changes the individual strategies for voters, and they may use more aggressive strategies in the aggregate. This will make create wealth inequality and may result in less accurate electoral systems. The environment will be less equitable systems, reinforcing winner take all attitudes where the more aggressive parties win more often.

Results from game theory experiments will help political parties assess their current actions in regards to the average output across a number of different solutions. They can predict how effective their current strategy is compared to alternative strategies. Often, one strategy produces great results under optimal conditions but produces terrible results under worst-case or ordinary conditions. An average is taken, to accommodate for all of the known unknowns, unknown unknowns, and known knowns. The variables include economic conditions, electoral output, probability of anti-democratic polices being enforced, and then of course the likelihood of events like compromised elections, debt defaults, and permanent government shutdowns. Democracy with competitive elections make electoral output less predictable which in turn impacts which interventions are available for the parties to force a regime change, rebel, or resist an authoritarian. A strong position in one election cycle does not guarantee a strong position after the next election cycle. This is the wager majority and minority parties make. It is a riskier during periods of wealth inequality and demographic shifts.

Political parties must assess these situations with Nash equilibrium. They must look at the average outcomes and outlier outcomes, with worst case scenarios weighted appropriately. Often, a worst-case scenario will force a reaction by the opposition party, despite the low likelihood of permanent damage done to the democratic institutions. The risk of inaction far exceeds the risk of over-stepping in a protest. If the protest is lawful but unnecessary, there will be no other complications than a loss of elections or prestige. if the opposition party fails to act when an authoritarian first consolidates power, they may never get another chance as governors are replaced, legislators are arrested, and due process ceases to function.

Politics is not always a winner takes all game. One party may not be able to win but they could still lose in different degrees. They could lose their civil rights, economic rights, and voting rights. A union of 50 states could lose 20 or 30. There are a number of low quality but much more likely outcomes when evaluated in terms of more competitive political markets. Often a loss for one party is a gain for another and the worst outcome for one is usually the best outcome for the other. The greater the point differential the less likely that result will be acquired in an informed environment. These simulations are just estimations. An incredible amount of effort and courage are needed to acquire even average outcomes. If one party is more aggressive when the other party hesitates, it changes the weighted average in favor of the party demonstrating more capacity or interest in winning.

A single game takes all outcomes into consideration and assigns a value to each permutation. The strategy that acquires the highest average outcome over a series of games is the most appropriate strategy to pursue, even if the most likely outcome is loss. For national parties, losses may include the secession of states or the genocide of residents. The two outcomes are not exclusive. If some states secede, there will no opportunity for the other states to intervene and prevent losses of political rights or murders occurring in those break-away regions. It's even more complicated than it appears. The act of forcibly preventing states from seceding, to avoid possible future genocide, actually creates the opportunity for those states to make the demographic changes necessary to preserve majority power in a democracy. Wars can cause population collapse through causalities to enlisted and civilian deaths. A 10% reduction in population could preserve the majority-demographics political power for decades. These scenarios are often no-win situations, where leaders have to weigh two unacceptable outcomes against each other and select the one that benefits more over citizens, looking at both short term and long-term goals.

Don't underestimate the fact, that population is an interval level variable that can be altered with incarceration and murder. Interventions can change the democratic equation for entire nations or just a handful of its states. This is another no-win situation, where the only acceptable product is a non-event. The problem with this outcome is war is often not reciprocal. If one side is nearly certain to lose, the other side is guaranteed to win. Clearly, they side expected to win is more likely to force an event even when the other party does not consent. The minority party should not exclusively pursue optimized outcomes, or they risk putting themselves in an inferior position for most of the possible outcomes. If conflict is still the most likely outcome, a strategy that seeks only the optimized outcome will earn the worst returns.

The preferred strategies of A.I. in these experiments justify reciprocal debt default and shutdown threats, timed around elections as means to develop culture of support. If only one party makes the threats and the other party only uses it in emergencies, the more patient party runs the risk of not being supported. The more aggressive party, using the threats will win more elections, more public policy arguments, and more judicial appointments. They will also have the support of a larger portion of the public if they actually act on that threat. If the opposition party rarely reciprocates, and the language and arguments are not explicitly spelled out, the run the very real risk of being criminalized or losing the subsequent election. The party that works on the language of rebellion, develops a culture where it is expected and supported, will have advantages in war and suffer no consequences in short term electoral outcomes.

The preferred strategies of A.I. also take into account the propensity for retribution. Strategies that learn to retaliate against aggression must also be quick to forgive and forget those transgressions. The best strategies will reciprocate aggression only when aggression is present and then retreat back to cooperation as quickly as possible. This minimize the losses when facing more aggressive rivals while maximizing the points gains in more cooperative environments. Don't forget, rivals are learning and adapting. If they are taught, they can't win with aggression, they will accept cooperative environments. Political parties must retaliate when faced with aggression but cooperate when the opportunity arises. Cooperation is easier after a few election cycles, where incumbents lose and new politicians are elected.

This flexibility in the electoral process is also a source of extreme risk. In an environment where one party repeatedly threatens debt defaults or shutdowns, the rapid change in newly elected politicians also signals risk. The party making the threats may have less intent to act on them in the short term, the economic conditions and political conditions could significantly change resulting in a much greater future risk. The future is discounted by uncertainty that can't be predicted. The same attribute that makes political parties more likely to forgive and forget, also maximized the risk of catastrophe as politicians inculcate to the same risky behavior in dramatically different environments. Periods of demographic shift and wealth inequality qualify as conditions which could provoke debt defaults and government shutdowns even when the threat was previously present but not acted on.

Not all political parties optimize their strategies like Artificial Intelligence in Machiavelli styled experiments. Political parties may try to optimize results by suppressing information and moderating their rhetoric despite an escalation by the other party. This is a terrible strategy and will likely result in the worst outcomes. When the voters can't price in the information, elections are less competitive and the more moderate party can find themselves out of office and in the minority. Now, a more extreme and fundamentalist party occupies the presidency, with majorities in the legislature, and the opposition party in the minority and unable to defend itself. Suppressing information and moderating the rhetoric optimizes the outcomes for the other party. Game theory suggest that optimal results are acquired by reciprocating attitude and actions when developing strategies to maximize points, and this includes timing government shutdowns after elections in anticipation of preventing authoritarianism.

A party that is too conciliatory and cooperative, loses the majority at times when faced with more aggressive opponents, unless they have a clear structural majority. If they are in the minority, typical of most demographic shifts, they won't be able to depend on the numerical superiority of a more cooperative environment. The current majority-demographic group will win more elections and have more opportunities to achieve outcomes in their benefit. Even if elections are split between the two parties, this means the more aggressive party will win half posing an imminent risk. During the cycles where they win the Presidency, there will be an increased risk of authoritarianism, and during the cycles they win a simple majority in one of the legislatures, there is an increased risk of default, shut down, and secession. The minority-demographic groups suffer these risks in most electoral outcomes. Overly-cooperative parties reduce the odds they are able to defend themselves while in an inferior executive position, while not improving their ability to defend against a threat while they are in a superior position. Retaliation increases the odds of conflict but reduces the odds of a complete loss. Leaving it up chance is a terrible strategy to prevent authoritarianism and protect minority populations from murder and incarceration.

Game theory demonstrates that more aggressive individuals and parties do better in more aggressive environments. These environments can be predicted by the popularity of austerity measures, rapid debt accumulation, mass incarceration, voter suppression, deregulated campaign finance, and the lack of effective labor laws and progressive taxes. These economies and justice systems are harsher and suggest the cooperative parties will lose more often. Parties that favor despots and authoritarians thrive in more competitive environments. There is less trust in the media, elections, and democratic institutions. There is more reliance on family and closed social networks with voters aligning on racial terms even when not expressly stated. It is in this context, where threats of debt default and government shutdowns can cause a premature end to the game, with all of the points already allocated to the more aggressive players. The parties can easily predict a redistribution of the points if more cooperative parties are given an opportunity to pass progressive taxes and raise wages. An end to the game will prevent this possibility and this may be incentive enough for political parties in decline.

Political parties must be willing to accept suboptimal outcomes to avoid the worst-case outcomes. This takes courage. Political parties won't want to acknowledge the real risks out of fear it will contribute to the possibility of an event. When these likelihoods remain undisclosed, it increases the risk of over-committing to strategies that result in poor outcomes. This includes the worst-case scenarios from surrender to collaboration. However, suboptimal outcomes are much more likely once the parties become active in their own defense. Parties may position themselves for the irrational expectation of optimal outcomes prior to an event and change preferences after the event. Passing priority to the more aggressive party does increase the risk of having an event and decrease the quality of outcomes associated with that event, but it also it maximizes the opportunity for peaceful dissolutions or other nonviolent remedies outside of surrender or collaboration.

Seeking the optimal outcome rather than the most likely outcome increases the risk of despotism in another way. Optimized strategies will be conflict adverse, overly patient, and too complacent when faced with legislative obstruction. The lack of high-quality laws is equivalent to political despotism where the public may continue to elect representatives but they are unable to regulate or tax themselves. The optimized strategy will discount most behaviors or tactics that cause conflict. Any conflict could result in scenarios with unacceptable outcomes. Obviously, the issue is that most other outcomes are excluded as possibilities and the party finds itself pursuing the least likely set of outcomes.

The more complacent political party will moderate their own behavior, trying to earn these unlikely outcomes, and lose support from the moderates, putting the party in an inferior position when the environment becomes harsher and more competitive. They will be viewed as the weaker party and a larger number of residents will support the other more aggressive party because it makes it far more likely they survive a conflict or earn economic benefits associated with affiliation. In an environment of wealth inequality and political corruption, the waning demographic-majority could continue to win enough elections to continue obstructing legislation and threating default or secession to preserve a superior position.

Often parties will pursue the optimized strategy out of desperation, when all of the other strategy result in unacceptable outcomes. If conflict results in genocide or ethnic cleansing, a significant portion of the minority party will accept any terms offered by the majority-demographic group. The owners class is the primary beneficiary during this period. In a poor regulatory and low tax environment, they can continue to abuse labor and resources maximizing profits and personal wealth. When the minority party seeks optimized outcomes by avoiding conflict, it is rewarded and reinforced by campaign contributions and support in the business community. This contributes to the miasma of corruption by making future regulation or taxes less likely. Not only will they lose a majority of the elections but more of their members will be resistant to change. The owners class acquires a low-quality democracy, with virtually no regulation or taxation, without actually declaring support for despotism, or imposing it through debt defaults and government shutdowns.

There are good reasons for a political party to reciprocate the threat of default and government shutdowns. Their presence is an indicator that the same party will pursue anti-democratic polices while in office to remain in office. If the opposition party is unwilling to stand up for themselves against the threats of shutdown, they will hesitate when elections are interfered with, patiently wait out periods of voter suppression, and accept environments of abject corruption. The biggest risk is that they will join the establishment and put down public dissent as the nation slides into authoritarianism. Within just a few years, an authoritarian can assume power and consolidate power. Unless the opposition party is willing to reciprocate when the threat first becomes apparent, there may very little they can do after the fact when civil liberties are weaker and voting rights already compromised.

If the opposition party runs away from their obligations to their constituents, they will lose elections and they will be in a far weaker position. They may never recover enough and gain a majority in the legislature, making it impossible to threaten institutional protests in the future. This is why reciprocity is so critical. It primes the electorate for conflict by providing them context. It gives them the language and the legal arguments to defend themselves. More importantly it keeps them engaged. A better educated electorate is a more responsible electorate and they will feel empowered to intervene through elections and public policy. If the defects in the economy and political process can be cured, conflict and authoritarianism can be avoided. If the opposition party does not explicitly stand up against the slow decline of the democratic process with debate and policy, they will be observers to history, rather than the principals.

It is all about tolerance for risk, and if the leadership of the opposition party does not recognize the risk of an authoritarian regime, they will not resist it. It is a complicated decision, they may overemphasize the risk of property loss, incarceration, or death. Threats of violence are very persuasive strategies to get an opposition party to comply to the new regime. The politicians may under-emphasize the risk after pricing in expectations of collusion or cooperation. There are fewer personal consequences if they don't resist the new authoritarian regime. These are inputs into the decisions each individual politician makes alone in the absence of oversight and accountability. The disposition of the party will reinforce those conclusions: if nobody says anything or does anything, others will look around and model their behavior off of this outcome. The fear is contagious.

THE FERRY: RESISTANCE AND REBELLION

Silence and inaction are easier to reconcile with negligence and doubt. It is more excusable, especially there is no accountability after the loss of civil liberties and media eliminates possibility of criticism. And dissent When the opposition party fails to reciprocate threats of default, it is vectorized information demonstrating the tendency for the party to cooperate with the new authoritarian regime. The direction and speed of the nation's decline will be directly proportional to the ability and interest of the opposition party to protect civil liberties and voting rights. If the opposition party chooses to protect their own profits and preserve their own lives over the safety of their constituents, the rate of decline will accelerate. The opposition party will be under incredible stress to intervene but it is easier to hesitate and patient wait for the situation to resolve itself. Their inaction has consequences.

History does not reflect kindly on those parties and officials that cooperate with authoritarians, but these alternative histories are only found in democratic societies that don't censure dissent or history. These facts will only live outside of the nation with little impact on the new regime and the culture that revolves around it. Those politicians that barter away the civil liberties and voting rights of their constituents will otherwise live long and prosperous lives, filled with abundance and mirth, as long as they keep quiet and support the establishment. Outcomes are often obfuscated by the lack of conflict and the deteriorating conditions in a democracy and may not be expressed for decades. The quality of democratic entitlements may erode in one generation and then be implicitly accepted by the next generation. If they don't protest loudly at the start of decline, it is unlikely they protest later when the odds of successfully defending themselves are lower.

A lack of legislative production should be associated with political despotism when both result in the same product. There is a reason why the two are nearly equivalent. Most low-quality democracies often fall into despotism when challenged and this is an acceptable outcome for a waning demographic group seeking to maintain majority political power despite the change in demographics. All democratic nations suffer the risk of a slow decline into corruption and despotism if the majority demographic group is unchecked by the emergent demographic group. This is especially true for older presidential democracies.

Non-democratic nations aren't susceptible to opposition parties gaining majorities in the legislature and forcing a default or government shutdown. Autocratic counties are susceptible to popular revolts or elite regime change, but they always operate in secrecy with few resources and scant chances to succeed. Opposition parties can't act overtly and petition the business community and public for support. There is also no due process to protect citizens from abuse during investigations. With no legal protections, they will have to cooperate more often to avoid the worse sanctions. With no rights, their personal property and data is more accessible for investigations. This makes non democratic nations more durable than democratic nations.

This is an attractive outcome for businesses that like to control labor inputs and limit compensation to non-management employees. Non democratic nations are less likely to pass intrusive regulations which would otherwise lower profits and disrupt production efficiencies. Corporations often have revenues larger than small companies and highly expert labor forces. Most corporations are not democratic. They are more like little feudal fiefdoms, where the executives and board members have tremendous social and political powers. Principals expect their orders to be carried out quickly and accurately. They aren't often challenged by other employees or regulators. This lack of democratic process and accountability makes them more susceptible to support authoritarian regimes. Democracy is viewed as a threat that could lead to unprofitability and bankruptcy. Democracy is an obstacle to their own rule and decision-making process. If they can subvert the regulatory and oversight process, they will.

If the corporate community inculcate into a culture where they can easily interfere in the legislative process, and expect to defeat industrial regulation and taxes, it sets them up for more disappointment if laws are suddenly passed that disrupt their authority and profits. They will have less faith in democracy itself and soon start organizing resistance to the legislative and electoral processes. Disappointment breeds discontent and they will actively pursue austerity policies than can destabilize the democracy. They will support candidates that are easily corruptible and share profit incentives. They will have lawyers on retainer and teams of lobbyists to interfere in the legislative process. More importantly, they will support parties threatening default and government shutdowns. If the democratic government is forcibly shutdown for an extended period of time, the corporations become the largest, most capitalized, and most capable organizations in the nation. Any previous inhibitions will be lost, and they can organize with impunity. They stand to gain the most in the vacuum of power, and will easily be able to choose the next form of government.

4 BOUNDARIES OF LOYALTY

Nations are defined more by their government type than territorial boundaries. A nation that regulates itself and taxes itself is under a democratic process is more ordered state than a totalitarian regime. Its elections reflect the interests of its citizens. Its public policy is responsive and adaptive to their concerns. Democracy is more than a process; it defines the character of the nation. The United States is in a remarkable position of only ever existing as a democracy. Prior to its incorporation of a nation, it was a group of colonies with limited rights and no sovereignty. As a nation, the United States has not had known any other government type. It has always been a democracy and hopefully will always be. Few states share this distinction. In the new environments of debt default and government shutdowns, where secession is likely, political parties must not risk or sacrifice democracy to protect their territorial boundaries. A democracy ceases to be the same nation if it yields to authoritarianism. However, the same nation may add states or subtract states without making a material change to the substance of its character or identity.

The loss of democracy is far more serious than the loss of territory. Not only could it be permanent, but any effort to resolve the situation is likely to result in loss of states, regardless of the effort. Authoritarianism only delays the risk. Eventually the people will rise to overthrow the illegitimate government, and when that day comes, there will likely permanent changes to the territorial boundaries of the nation. This delay comes at a steep cost, with loss of civil liberties and voting rights, and the inability to lodge an institutional protest. States must immediately organize resistance to authoritarianism even if it risks splitting the nation in two. The chances of recovering the states and restoring their rights is higher if a large number of states retain their autonomy and preserve democracy after the conflict. They can act from the outside, using trade incentives, aid, and international pressure to lobby for the liberation of the occupied and despotic states.

The modern era is more unforgiving than prior periods. The ability for a contemporary government to apply surveillance and disrupt resistance movement is certainly more improved. Other periods allowed the public to meet discretely to plan and organize. Pamphlets and speech were more anonymous. Facial recognition technologies could terrorize a population into non-participation. Poor union membership and labor rights increase the risk for protesters, if they can be fired more easily after being recognized or arrested. Social Media can be a productive piece of resistance movements but it is easily tracked and recorded for use as evidence. It is much easier to vote for candidates who are lawfully entitled to shut down a government and lodge an institutional protest. People are already organized into cities and states and we must leverage that advantage to coerce peaceful regime change and protect our democratic entitlements. It only gets harder after authoritarianism roots itself in the electoral process, due process, and public policy.

Optimizing solutions to protect territorial boundaries and preserve high quality democracy is only possible with informed and engaged electorate. It is the only way a minority party or opposition party can impact the outcome of a crisis while not holding/ the executive office. The circumstances should be priced into all elections prior to an event, with expectations of holding their representatives accountable during future elections. This isn't possible if the public is uninformed or misinformed. The element of surprise and sense of urgency will cause a larger proportion of the public to make worse decisions. They will either be overly risk adverse or they will disregard all of the possible consequence. If all of the possible outcomes are considered prior to an event, the public will moderate their expectations and change their policy preferences. If the politicians then contradict the preference of the people, they are more likely to lose the next election or face incarceration for embarking on a dangerous misadventure like secession.

Full information dissemination improves the outcomes in most scenarios. Optimizing outcomes without an informed electorate is impossible in the most likely outcomes and the worst-case scenarios. Optimized outcomes can't be realized with optimized expectations. They can only be realized with good inputs. Inputs equal output and if there are unrealistic expectations, the preparation and effort will be lacking, producing suboptimal outcomes. This is where tradeoffs are made between preserving democracy and protecting the territoriality integrity. If one expects only average outcomes, then it is very likely that either the quality of democracy is degraded or some of the states are lost to authoritarianism. If the quality of democracy is degraded too much, then all of the states could be lost to authoritarianism and a worst-case scenario is acquired.

Any state in open rebellion benefits from a cause supported by larger sample sizes with more accuracy and certainty, but only those states declaring support for democracy can claim legitimacy. Although the residents seeking secession may have numerical superiority and satisfy thresholds for both accuracy and certainty, they are intended to deny the minority population civil rights and voting rights and this invalidates their claims. Any political act that removes the ability of a future population to invalidate that claim, is invalid itself. A singular act must be able to be cured at a future date, if the sympathies of the same population change their preferences for the previously supported policy position.

A state that secedes but remains democratic, always has the opportunity to support future reunification. A state that successfully secedes, but disenfranchises its population of voting rights, ceases to have legitimate authority to take that action. The minority populations in a democratic state preserve their most important rights and protections, reducing the severity of separation from the larger union. The minority populations in a despotic state suffer the greatest loss in economic rights and civil rights with no guarantee of ever regaining them. Any cities or states seceding from a despotic nation, always have implicit authority and legitimacy if they seek democratic rights during the act for the same reasons. However, legitimacy and authority are not equated with capacity and any adventure may end with a severe reduction in rights or privileges, on a temporary basis for democracies and a more permanent basis for authoritarian regimes.

Sample sizes increase as the state population increases. The larger the populations the more they will consider all perspectives and possible outcomes. This is why individuals can't assume responsibility for the city or state and only the group can assert the right to organize into an institutional protest. The electorate must be educated on the issues, the risks, the benefits, and the probability for success. If there are any informational asymmetries, it could skew the decision and result in poor performance or poor outcomes. When a number of states with populations the size of New Jersey, New York, Illinois, and California all have similar election outcomes on the issues of separation or secession, it reduces the odds of making a mistake in assumptions or evaluations of the risks and consequences. An institutional protest is intended to accommodate the slow deliberative but adversarial process of disentangling democratic states from authoritarian states by way of informed elections and public policy.

The argument that individuals are empowered to openly discuss institutional protests for use in peaceably coercing regime change is based in the fact individuals have no personal capacity to implement the strategy, and if it were acted on by elected officials, it would be with the full authority of the electorate and the upper house of a legislature. There should be no doubt that when the citizenry organizes to protest outcomes of an election deemed illegitimate, they should be fully supported by their representatives with a prolonged government shutdown. Independently, neither individuals nor their legislators have the explicit authority to permanently shut down the government, but when acting together, they hold inalienable rights to protect themselves with an institutional protest. Legislators can act alone, as they have implicit support of the electorate, but it is a weaker position. This is why valid elections are critical. They shutdown will only last as long as they wait until the next election. If the public supports their legislators, they government shutdowns can continue indefinitely until the executive resigns or is replaced during a subsequent election.

Sampling size reduces the likelihood of error. This empowers states to take actions on institutional protests. Although, the probability of error is minimized, the magnitude or severity remains unchanged. An institutional protest may be an inappropriate response but at least the consequences have been considered. At very least there is a discrete number of people accountable to the electoral process who were responsible for the event. It should be noted, institutional protests are only appropriate under certain circumstances. They may always be legal but they are only legitimate when used to intervene in a corrupted or compromised election. They are only appropriate when used to prevent anti-democratic polices from further compromising the electoral process and curtailing civil rights. Most other circumstances can be accommodated by winning elections and passing laws.

All institutional protests are in the eye of the beholder. These decisions and interpretations rely mostly on discretion. The administration will assert the authority to act despite the protest of the legislature, and see any state level indictments as an overt act of rebellion. Most governments act under emergency powers to suppress rebellions and a significant portion of the population will assert the government's right to circumvent the government shutdown. This is especially true when it is expected that future elections will change the disposition of the legislature and end the institutional protest. If the obstruction in appropriations is temporary, there is every expectation the government will be reconstituted, validating their continued operations despite the interim shutdown. It is expected that in highly charged partisan political environments constituents will steadfastly support those organizations and parties they identify more with, regardless of the position or offices occupied.

THE FERRY: RESISTANCE AND REBELLION

Just because an institutional protest is inappropriate doesn't mean it won't be pursued. If these protests are lawful and accessible through due process, there will be political parties and individuals who abuse the procedures. Certain political parties will want to preserve power during demographic shifts. Others will want to preserve power during periods of wealth inequality. There are virtually no other limits on the use of institutional protests outside of intervention by the electorate to remove the advocates from office before the act is performed. As damaging and unpredictable as they are, presidential democracies need the possibility of institutional protests to protect against authoritarians. The people need to be able to discourage the bad behavior. However, all good laws can be abused by bad people and bad parties. It's an exploitation that has occurred throughout all of history and it will continue in the foreseeable future.

Neither the federal government nor the state governments will be acting legally or constitutionally, which reduces all justifications for the behaviors to discretion. If both are in the wrong, citizens are free to choose who to support. it is a wrong decision regardless of the position expressed. This is a fundamental aspect of all crises and conflicts, and which ever group can support their conclusions with revenues and labor will eventually win out. This will pass the priority to states, which collect the taxes and are more proximate in residency. All of the state's revenues collections, personnel management, and appropriations will remain unchallenged placing them in a superior position. The more the electorate relies on discretion the more likely one party deems elections invalid. Once a leader's behavior is determined to be illegitimate and its elections invalid, the nation suffers the greatest risk of permanent separation.

A light source doesn't throw a shadow. Most governments correctly asses the risk in foreign policy but there is a strong unwillingness to consider the threat from the majority-demographic group. This is because they are neighbors, coworkers, family, and friends, at one point or another. However, unless challenged with an institutional protest, they won't interpret their own party's actions as villainous or dangerous without having to resort to violence to protect those outcomes. If the opposition party doesn't resist, the constituents wont object to the majority party's pursuit of anti-democratic policies. Even if violence is used, only a portion of the majority party's constituents will reconsider their part. Many will see the violence as a defense of the nation and their social, political, and economic positions.

The opposition party must quickly evaluate their position and organize an institutional protest to limit the authoritarian's ability to pass laws that may extend their term or install illegitimate legislators and governors. If legislators view the current administration as a threat, they can shut the government down. An institutional protest can last until the next presidential election is held, prematurely ending a president's effective term. It is a risky maneuver and success isn't guaranteed, but if they truly fear an authoritarian pursuing anti-democratic policies, they will be forced to act in this manner. If the opposition party preserves at least one majority in just one of legislative chambers, they can keep the federal government shutdown until the end of the Presidents first full term in office. With borrowing authority and appropriations exhausted in the first few months of the president's first term, the protesting states can wait out the remainder of the president's term without fear of reprisals or other authoritarian interventions.

If the opposition party waits too long, they run the risk of losing a majority in at least one legislative chamber, and losing the authority and capacity to force an institutional protest. The authoritarian could invalidate elections or start arresting members of the activist party. Not only would this neutralize their most vocal opponents but it may subdue the electorate. If the opposition party hesitates, they could lose away their only opportunity they have to prevent a decline of the nation into despotism. The opposition parties should have more confidence during these situations. There is no guarantee that the party shutting down the government loses the next election cycle, which means a federal government could effectively be shut down for an entire presidential term. Four or six years could mean the difference between life and death for the opposition party and their constituents.

THE FERRY: RESISTANCE AND REBELLION

These are new rules. Most rebellions don't occur with institutional support. They occur outside the bounds of the law. They are secretive and illegal. Institutional protests are different. When states are involved, due process is weaponized and supported by aggerates in labor and capital. States are more inhibited and more responsible than individuals. They ae more legitimate actors during rebellions. They act more openly and can be held accountable for their decisions. Institutional protests are far less frequent but will be more effective. Lower order and more spontaneous mob-styled rebellions are typically unlawful and much less effective. Generally, individuals don't have the judgement or the authority to embark in revolt. They are prone to more violence and there are worse outcomes when they are successful. When political parties and states are protesting, the probability of preserving democracy will improving. There are definitely far fewer examples to draw on in history but these acts would set precedent for other rebellions in flawed democracies.

Non-violent protests are more effective than violent ones. One reason, is that they can be planned in advance with little fear of prosecution. If government shutdowns are part of the legal process, it will be necessary to examine the outcomes and plan strategies that will make the institutional protest more effective. The behavior is lawful and incentivized. It is also the purview of the state and not an action any individual can pursue by themselves. This will impart some legitimacy to the protest while supporting it with more resources than any individual can provide. More importantly, the state can act openly in their emergency preparation planning with real applications to plausible situations. Individuals attempting to subvert the government will ordinarily have to act secretly with less information and always fearing prosecution. The openness of the states planning will also work to discourage bad actors within other states or the federal tier, and avoid a situation where an institutional protest may be needed.

The fog of war is not only on the battlefield. Uncertainty follows all who might act to resist authoritarianism. Behaviors that might otherwise not elicit sanctions under a democratic regime may be criminalized under a future regime, adding an air of danger to ordinary conversations or actions. A government doesn't have to take any overt action, they merely have to threaten retaliation for the behavior. This chilling effect will harm the quality of journalism and alter the social networks of citizens. Those people who do not tolerate risk will ostracize those that speak up or demonstrate. People can be fired from their jobs, they can lose their best friends, or be incarcerated for peaceably protesting. When civilians do act out and demonstrate, they will be arrested and serve as reminders of which belief systems will be tolerated by the authorities.

In order for the citizenry to react to authoritarianism before it roots, individuals must accept the possibility of poor outcomes from behaviors that were previously condoned but now are criminalized. This tolerance for risk is not common. Most citizens are risk averse. They have children, careers, and families to protect. They do a simple cost benefit analysis and determine they would survive a totalitarian regime, maybe thrive, so, they don't act. Another group of citizens will recognize the threat and immediately react to the deteriorating conditions They say what needs to be said. These individuals all perform a cost benefit analysis were their voting rights and civil rights are more highly valued than their jobs, friends, and the loss of their freedom. They organize into peaceful protests and demand reform. They mobilize themselves and their communities for more competitive elections. Most individuals don't have the necessary judgement and inhibitions to navigate these situations successfully.

Individuals take on most of the risks when democracy is threatened, but the states are much more effective adversaries of authoritarians. States have the necessary sovereignty to defend their rights and responsibilities. When the states mobilize to protect themselves against authoritarians, they demonstrate leadership. A demonstration of leadership accomplishes two goals. The first, it reduces the stress on individuals to act, eliminating individual acts of violence or terrorism. An increased fear of loss produces an increases risk of bad behavior. Bad behavior is any individual or group pursuing violence towards another group or institution. These acts of terrorism can hamstring a valid institutional protest or popular movement intended to protect against authoritarianism. Terrorism pass priority and authority back to the authoritarian government. A larger portion of the public will fear social groups and states associated with the goals of unlawful terrorist organization.

The second, it implies protection for those citizens organizing protest and speech to defend themselves. When the state makes declarations, it emboldens more of the population to stand with the state, increasing future enlistment, and creating the opportunity for unknown solutions to present themselves. The most effective response is through collective bargaining, and states offer individuals a legal and safer way to protect their economic rights and voting rights. The public will feel more secure with an activist government supporting them. If the terrorists ally themselves with the authoritarian government it passes priority and authority to the democratic government. The state will have more support in passing laws that marginalize and mitigate supporters of the authoritarian regime.

Individuals don't have the judgement necessary to take any other option besides protest or boycott. Individuals don't aren't accountable to the electorate either. This makes them more culpable and they can certainly be arrested. Institutional protests give individuals who would otherwise resist with inappropriate behavior, the outlet to organize and act in a coordinated manner. Institutional protests occur over weeks and months with plenty of opportunity for debate and discussion. This should collar the animal spirit that deforms groups into mob rule. It's safer for the individual because they can avoid arrests and they don't have to commit to individual acts. They can defer to the group and work to peaceably achieve their goals of regime change or reform.

Individuals don't have the judgement to participate in similar acts. They don't have the wisdom and the perspectives an electorate has. The states benefit from the wisdom of a crowd and are superior to an individual's guess or approximation of conditions. An individual, not elected to office, isn't vested with the responsibility to make decisions for an electorate. This makes institutional protests acted on by states and parties far more effective and legitimate than those protests and rebellions initiated by individuals. Individual protests are rarely successful with a high risk of being condemned by the electorate. Individuals have no rights to refuse to pay taxes, or prevent agencies from conducting business, but their elected officials do.

When absolutely necessary, the states must mobilize their militias to ensure the public has the opportunity to publicly protest the loss of voting rights or civil rights. The state police and national guards will protect against abuses by federal laws enforcement or local law enforcement which may be too eager to engage and oppress the public. Calling up the militia is the best protection against an ambitious authoritarian trying to consolidate power after a compromised election. It is a declaration that democracy is non-negotiable and concessions will not be made that result in a deterioration of voting rights or civil rights.

Preventing authoritarianism requires quick action. States have to weigh the fear of authoritarianism versus the loss of political allies in the states supporting the despot. This is the hardest choice to make but it often made by necessity. If the nation succumbs to despotism without an institutional protest by the democrats, then the party won't be in a position to help any of their constituents. They will all share the same fate with little recourse or hope in challenging the authoritarian. However, if a group of breakaway state gain independence and retain the democratic entitlements, they can more effectively defend the civil rights and economic interests of the minority poultice trapped in the authoritarian states. The democratic states can use financial incentives to protect the rights of their political allies. They can use international institutions to lobby and intervene on their behalf. More importantly, the democratic states can martial their capital and martial resources to intervene if necessary. All of these strategies are inaccessible if they remain part of the distressed political union.

Demographic shifts present different political outcomes than ordinary environments. During periods of wealth inequality, homogenous populations will vote for reforms while in heterogenous populations they will vote on issues of racial identity and neglect inequality. Inaction causes the wealth inequality to exacerbate, and the majority demographic will blame minorities and immigrants for the deteriorating conditions. The animus that would normally be resolved by wealth transfers, antitrust regulations, and policies aimed at remediating poverty is transformed into a miasma of mass incarceration targeting minorities and immigrants and industrial deregulation. When a homogenous population is present, the political markets act rationally, but when there are large minority and immigrant populations the majority demographic seeks to preserve the culture and institutions that created the wealth inequality. This erodes the quality of the democratic institutions providing oversight and accountability in elected officials. he wealth inequality and corruption will abrades the confidence and trust citizens have in institutions and the government. This creates an environment where a significantly larger portion of the population will be susceptible to radicalization and authoritarianism.

A nation may overcome an earlier period of wealth inequality by passing labor reforms, progressive taxes, and anti-trust acts but this is no guarantee the nation overcomes another bout of inequality and corruption. A larger portion of the demographic-majority will vote on identity politics and obstruct any attempt to reform the wealth inequality. This increases the systemic risk of authoritarianism, when the poorer segments of the majority demographic group lose confidence in the government as the economic conditions for them deteriorate. They will experience higher rates of unemployment, with lower wages, and less class mobility but have no clear pathway to change the system contributing to their poverty.

They won't identify with the reform party and refuse to support those economic policies that may raise wages, distribute welfare, and grant access to healthcare or education. These voters will be in crisis with no apparent recourse. This may incite them to violence or to organize with separatist or white nationalist groups. The political party favoring the majority demographic group will be pursuing public policy that preserves their political power though policies of partisan redistricting, deregulated campaign finance, and voter suppression. The rapid deterioration of the public sector will reinforce the anti-government or white supremacist tendencies in the population.

Debt default and government shutdowns are an irrational response to debt accumulation. Ulterior motives centered around the loss of political power and majority demographic status, are far more likely to be the source of the incentives for debt defaults and government shutdowns. Spending is a product of the electoral process. In normal environments, parties will be more interested in winning election and making the policy decisions to limit spending and repay debt. When there is an expected loss of majority political power, the party will cease relying on electoral outcomes, and start threatening violence to achieve the same goals. These parties have already assessed the risks of default or secession, and prefer them to losing future elections. The outcomes may even be considered equivalent, which then justifies the support of authoritarians to limit the risks of electoral losses.

The response is irrational because the party claims the only way to protect the nation from excess debts is to use those debts to destroy the nation. The irrationality is a symptom of the intervention advocated for. The parties supporting incremental tax reform and budget cuts as solutions implicitly take into account the long-term outcomes. The parties threatening default only see the short-term welfare of the nation because the intervention sought abruptly terminates the sovereignty of the nation. It factors in the worst possible outcomes in the short term and then punctuates it by the premature end to the nation. It is similar to how the poor outcomes and judgement associated with suicide may artificially create the urgency and poor outcomes used to justify the act.

It's backwards. It's also illusionary. If the party or person automatically rules out suicide, then they focus on long term actions that can improve the expected outcomes. Nations are no different. Parties that aren't ideologically opposed to raising taxes will see it as the natural way to pay off debts. Sovereign debts are also mitigated by inflation and GDP growth making patience of if the best methods to overcome high debt to GDP ratios. If the government maintains a balanced budget for 20-30 years (on average), inflation and

GDP growth will act to devalue the debt on the balance sheet and dissipate the threat. Debt isn't optimal but it does not pose an immediate risk to the sovereignty of the nation.

The motivations for the party making the threats can then be diagnosed as fear of losing political power. An artificial parameter is placed on the expectations of a majority demographic group when that group loses majority status and majority political power. This is the same mechanism suicide presents in individuals. Suicide makes it impossible a person acquires the future outcomes to prove the strategy irrational. The abrupt end forces the individual to emphasis the most immediate history rather than pricing in a future with improved outcomes. The suicidal ideations create urgency when the poor history is punctuated with a premature end, artificially justifying its use. Debt defaults and prolonged government shutdowns simulate suicide for states rather than individuals. The majority-demographic group is basing their expectation of collapse, not on the ability of the government to pay its debts, but on their future support of a government where they are expected to be oppressed minorities. Everybody should beware the consequences of these assumptions.

The waning political party is basing their expectation of loss in sovereignty on their own actions while they have majority power. This is insider information and should be weighted more heavily than the minority party's expectations. The demographic majority party still has the political power to act on their threats while the minority party has few options to defend themselves. The emergent demographic group over-estimates the likelihood of addressing the debt issues, because they under-state the risk the waning demographic party poses. It is wiser to take the parties on their word and predict conflict in the near future. In the same respect the majority-demographic party over-emphasizes the abrupt end to sovereignty, the minority party refuses to accept it as possible. This is also an irrational position based on unreasonable expectations.

When threats of default and government shutdowns are present, it is evidence enough that the waning demographic group has weighed their alternatives and won't rule out a scorched earth approach to maintaining power. It does not matter if the majority of their constituents would support this type of action. This is the other most common estimating error an opposition party makes. Most political decisions are made without the implicit consent of the majority of citizens. The legislators can act on a default or prolonged shutdown unilaterally, without any debate or consideration preceding the event. Republican governments give legislators the authority to act on their own judgement without the need to seek prior approval. This presents another problem. Their constituents are more likely to continue supporting their political party after an event, especially in an adversarial environment with talk of dissolution or secession. Support is likely to increase during a crisis because the risk is greater. Thus, the opposition party cannot count on a rebuke of the party causing the default or shutdown.

A debt default can happen without much of a warning, especially if the opportunity presents itself annually and everybody has inculcated into the culture of regular budget showdowns and possible defaults. The opposition party is fooling itself when they believe that the other party won't act on their threats. They only have two options. They must immediately reciprocate threats and time an event to maximize their chances at preserving the union. Or they must, move their response off the federal balance sheet and develop emergency responses on the state level. State level response will be much more effective, given the propensity for shutdowns to completely disrupt and federal governments ability to intervene in case of secession.

There are other fates worse than an immediate and abrupt challenge to the authority of a democratic government. Perpetuating an environment of default threats and government shutdowns is a win-win situation for the waning demographic-majority group when they can paralyze the regulatory system and public finance system with legislative obstruction and constant threats of default or shutdown. They will preserve a weakened government that can't enforce laws or tax the ever-increasing wealth of federal corporations. They will also preserve the culture of crisis where they can abruptly end the nation with a permanent shutdown or peaceful dissolution after default. In this respect, the reoccurring threat of default or shutdown are hyper-rational from a party that has distinct incentives and expectations from the opposition party.

5 RESISTING AUTHORITARIANISM

Frogs boiling in water often don't respond to the incremental increase in temperature until it is too late. Voters in lower quality or flawed democracies have the same tendencies. Slowly, the older democracies acquire representational deficiencies like partisan redistricting, deregulated campaign finance, Voter ID laws, and other voter suppression tactics. Like frogs, the citizens may not be aware of how dangerous the situation is. They will rely on old data to make decisions and risk assessments. They will overemphasize the monuments and speeches of prior eras, without taking into consideration the new context and conditions. If the parties don't respond with public policy and pressure to reform, the public's expectations will continue to sink. It is when conditions completely deteriorate, the prospect of a secession or dissolution becomes justified.

It is backwards. A lack of education and effort prior to the conflict makes it more likely to occur, rather than less. It is pure superstition to believe the parties can improve the odds of navigating a demographic shift or other obstacles by keeping information and arguments away from the public. Without awareness, there is scant possibility of change. Without change, the nation will falter. When nations falter, they risk authoritarianism or occupation. Adapting to change is a constant. This is true for all biological organisms. Nations and states are no different. They must continue to evolve or face extinction. If we don't change, we won't pass on our principles, innovations, and culture to the next generation.

When an authoritarian threatens due process with anti-democratic policies, it may mobilize the public to protest. Protesters will try and force the president to resign and the larger the number of activists, the more likely this outcome is. Protesters are highly visible agents of change. Protesting is a public demonstration of disapproval and the president's own party may seek to limit their exposure to election losses by coercing a resignation. Protesters tend to be more successful when they acquire at least 3.5% support[10]. It is considered the golden rule for regime change and reform. Protests that exceed this threshold are much more likely to win concessions while protests that miss this threshold have diminished chances for regime change or reform.

All protests falling short of the 3.5% threshold should be supported by government shutdowns. A government shutdown will ratchet up the pressure on the president to reign. Not only will the executive be vilified by public but most of the agencies and departments of the government will be on furlough. This lowers the risks of violence or arrest for protesters and embolden supporters. If the protests don't already exceed 3.5%, a government shutdown will push the number of protesters passed the threshold and win reform or recall[11]. Many protesters may be discouraged by a lack of support by politicians, but when the opposition party shuts the government down, it provides a public declaration of support that should swell numbers, and also inhibit any federal interventions that would otherwise suppress participation. Peaceful resistance must be met with patience or the retaliation efforts could lead to state-level charges and impeachment proceedings. Any use of force by the administration will rally the opposition party to intervene with

---

[10] Darian Woods, "The Magic Number Behind Protests", accessed on 9/10/2019, retrieved from https://www.npr.org/sections/money/2019/06/25/735536434/the-magic-number-behind-protests

[11] Darian Woods, "The Magic Number Behind Protests", accessed on 9/10/2019, retrieved from https://www.npr.org/sections/money/2019/06/25/735536434/the-magic-number-behind-protests

impeachment proceedings or state-level indictments and prosecution.

The power of appropriations is one of the most important responsibilities within the government. It affects almost all public policy and without appropriations authority, the administration would be acting without implicit legitimacy. A government shutdown temporarily disrupts the appropriations authority of the current administration, and unless demands are met, the administration could run out of funding by years end. The political parties can't escape each other when the budget is negotiated every year and funding is explicitly prohibited without an agreement. More importantly, the current administration can't spend money on emergency measures without appropriations; they won't be able to respond to protests movements or other developments, unless money was appropriated before the shutdown. If they do, the current administration will run out of current appropriations faster, forcing them to negotiate sooner with the opposition party shutting down the government.

A government shutdown is a dangerous situation, but ultimately peaceful, and easily reversible when appropriations are later authorized. This sets up incentives for all parties to reach an agreement. If the demands are not met, the opposition party can keep the government shutdown for the two years, or longer, until new elections or developments require other interventions. If the administration acts extra constitutionally or illegally, the opposition party can pursue impeachment, lawful tax holidays, or debt defaults in order to protect their position. Government shutdowns are an overt act that makes other protest acts possible. Without the government shutdown, these other strategies may not be accessible or lawful, reducing their effectiveness.

One of the most important properties of the government shutdown is it gives the political parties the ability to negotiate on concessions and demands in the public's focus. Time stops when the budget doesn't pass and there are no appropriations for the next year. Everybody is watching, similar to the effects of protest movements exceeding 3.5% of the population. It is undeniable in scope and unavoidable to address. Political parties will know their decisions and behaviors will be widely acknowledged by the electorate citizenry, and residents. While the shutdown persists, the government can only provide emergency services so the entire focus is on ending the shutdown. They will be critically aware they are on the clock. The parties will be forced to negotiate and come to terms. If the demands are not met, the opposition party is in the best position possible, while being out of the federal executive office, and possibly controlling only one chamber of the legislature. There may be fewer and fewer opportunities to take a stand, so the opposition party has to weigh the consequences of action versus inaction.

One of the risks of relying on government shutdowns is the timing. Budgets are typically only negotiated once a year, preferably after elections and regime changes. However, events can occur after the budget is agree to, eliminating the best check on authoritarianism or abuses. This could give an illegitimate administration or authoritarian several months to considerate power and disrupt resisting to the regime. Funding levels are fixed at the prior amount agreed to, meaning no new expenditures are authorized. Although not in a great position, the opposition party can still refuse to make subsequent appropriations needed to suppress protestors or states mobilizing their own responses to the current administration. Refusing new emergency appropriations will open up pathways to impeachment, default, and lawful tax holidays, placing emphasis on an oppositions disciplined support for institutional protests. All of these strategies may be necessary to dislodge an authoritarian and resurrect the democratic process within the nation.

Coercing peaceful regime change is the primary goal of a government shutdown. Durable reforms through legislation is the second goal. One party can refuse to pass a budget and this can extend until the next election. There are no law compelling political parties to fund the government. Without a budget, the government can't legally fund law enforcement and military operations. Without passing a debt ceiling motion it will have no authority to borrow. It is within this period a group of states can organize resistance to an authoritarian regime. When large numbers of protesters are present, an institutional protest is reaffirmed by the possibility of maintaining majorities after the next election, despite the prolonged government shutdown.

Protesters represent the raw potential for numerical superiority and the natural authority in a democracy. Democracy is an expression of majority rule and large crowds of protesters represent an applied will. It is impossible to govern when a significant portion of the country or state is protesting. Roads are blocked, public transportation is paralyzed, and fear locks down the economy More importantly, protesters represent a current disposition of voters and future electoral outcomes. The presence of large numbers of dissenting protesters will validate the peaceful and lawful strategies involved in a state-sponsored institutional protest.

Most federal governments give explicit and exclusive power over the budget to the legislature and this makes the government shutdown the most effective institutional protest possible. Any act by the federal government to circumvent the authority of the legislature makes it illegitimate and outside the bounds of the constitution. This also empowers the states to charge offenses related to these illicit acts. One of the first overt acts of rebellion by the states is to enact clear laws on criminal offenses related to agents acting on behalf of entities acting unlawfully. A federal government continuing to operate during a prolonged shutdown will qualify as an unlawful entity and all of their officers and soldiers will be subject to state-level statutes sanctioning the activity of such entities. This will expose the principals ordering interventions to criminal indictment on the state level.

Impeachment proceeds offer an opportunity for regime change if the authoritarian does not resign. An appropriately executed government shutdown will present many opportunities to pursue impeachment if the president continues to deploy federal law enforcement or military despite the loss of appropriations and borrowing authority. The president will likely be provoked into overstepping the bounds when governors call up their national guards or withhold federal revenues through tax-holidays. Any federal can be used as the basis for state-level indictments and impeachment. The use of an institutional protest is a more dangerous version of snap elections for parliaments or recall elections for governors, legislators, and judges. However, it may be the only way the older more vulnerable and less efficient presidential democracies can remove an authoritarian or ineffective president.

It is brutish and less secure, but the methods may be appropriate under certain circumstances. If the opposition party fears an authoritarian consolidation of power, they will have to act fast and coordinate their actions between the federal legislature and states. They may only have one opportunity to intervene and prematurely end the administration until elections are held two years later. The opposition party can't avoid all risk. They have to weigh the risk of shutting down the government for two years or watching as an authoritarian possibly corrupt all future elections.

Winning elections during the next cycle is a necessary component of a balanced equation. Every party shutting down the government, should have the goal of winning subsequent election. They will want as much political power as possible to continue obstructing the federal government. With sound arguments, the party's constituents are likely to continue supporting the party shutting down the government. Even if impeachment proceedings aren't successfully, the prosecution will likely rally supporters to the cause of a continued shutdown. This party will still need to win over moderates and independents over remain in office, but to give up on the fiery-rhetoric of regime change prior to an event is to give up on the expectation of preserving offices during an event.

If the government's borrowing authority and appropriation powers remain intact, there is an express authority to organize and mobilize a response to an insurrection or rebellion. This limits the number of attempts and the severity to only those instances where a majority of legislators from at least one chamber in the legislature support the institutional protest. Authority in democracies always rests on the implicit support of the people and in due process. The states will want keep their representatives at the capitol, responding with oversight hearings and denying a quorum for bills. The biggest risk to an institutional protest is the segregation or invalidation of legislators from the protesting party. If they aren't present, they can't vote to continue obstructing the government and budget. If the protesting party and states withdraw from the union in secession, they won't be able to obstruct the government or suppress the budget. If the states retract their representatives, the other states will have a quorum and can more easily pass a budget and resolutions to put down the rebellion.

Impeachment isn't the only option available. If an administration continues to borrow and make appropriations despite a lawful government shutdown, the opposition party can seek recourse in the court system. They can pursue injunctions and legal remedies preventing the government from continuing to operate. This should be coordinated on both the state level and federal level, to involve as many courts as possible. This is intended to muddy the waters around a protest and give the rebel states enough time to organize their own response to the federal authorities. In most cases, presenting a viable resistance to an authoritarian over-reach will be enough to discourage the bad behavior. If the authoritarian resigns, the states can relent in their protest and re-join the union. If the opposition party fails to coerce a regime change with a government shutdown and impeachment, they can take other more provocative acts to enforce the will of the electorate and the clauses of the constitution.

Tax holidays are the second most effective peaceable protest an institution or state can participate in. It relies on due process, is nonviolent in nature and a well-organized tax holiday can completely destabilize the nation. Once the government is shutdown, the states can make it illegal to remit the corporate income and payroll taxes to the federal government. Once the behavior is criminalized, executives and corporate boards can be held accountable and threatened with long jail sentences for noncompliance. However, incarcerating the owners class is dangerous and the rebel states may want to consider using incentives rather than penalties. More effective tax holidays focus on taxing the funds remitted to the federal government. If a company owes a tax liability to the federal government, the state can levy a prohibitively high tax on that amount to discourage taxpayers from remitting the funds.

They can incentivize the same taxpayers to send those revenues to a state with a tax break. More taxpayer will rather pay the lower rates to the state than the higher rates to federal government. These strategies lack the declaration of making the act of paying federal taxes illegal, but it plays on market conditions with higher participation more likely. States will want to proceed cautiously: the federal government can impose similar taxes on state revenues in retaliation.

The best answer to an authoritarian's use of violence is a coordinated response by governors. Governors have the opportunity to call up the national guard (local militia) to protect protesting civilians. Once the militia are deployed, it will discourage the federal government from suppressing protesters or pursuing other anti-democratic policies. If borrowing authority is exhausted and no new revenues are coming in, the states rallying to the protection of protesters will have a better chance to organize and more adeptly challenge an authoritarian regime.

The state governments will have to act fast and pass laws making it illegal for agents to enforce collection laws for federal tax revenues not remitted back to the government. The states may also want to indemnify the corporations and taxpayer on the possibility of back taxes due after the government is reconstituted. This will lessen the fear of community members suffering harm as the result of the diversion. When the number of voluntary taxpayers increases, the state governments will need rely less on incarceration and other forms of coercion.

Federal representatives involved in a prolonged shutdown should not be involved in any state planning or other activities that could open them up to arrest. They have only two responsibilities; the first is to shut the government down and the second is to avoid arrest to preserve the shutdown. The federal representatives should even stay away from leading the protests directly, instead relying on their public declarations of shutting down the government as a demonstration of support. Representatives can't risk being arrested, reducing their numbers in Congress, when a quorum is still possible.

Likewise, representatives should not have any personal communications or public comments about the actions of state officials. There should be absolutely no coordination; they must have faith that the state level executives and representatives have similar sympathies and are actively planning for contingencies and emergencies, if the shutdown is not lifted, or the authoritarian executive exceeds its authority and deploys law enforcement and military assets, despite appropriations or borrowing authority. The institutional protest is so important to a protest movement or state-level response, the representatives can't risk endangering the prolonged shutdown by directly supporting the protesters or governors.

The federal government will immediately be placed on a clock, with funds quickly diminishing and no borrowing authority to extend time. Not only will they not be able to afford a long war with the rebel states but their economies will be in free fall. Revenues in the loyalist states will decline precipitously and they won't be able to support the federal government. The authoritarian administration won't be able to make up the difference in lost revenues and they will be forced to sue for peace and accept the terms of the protesting states. In the best-case scenario, the institutional protest weakens the position of the autocrat and they coerced into retirement, opening up the possibility the former union is reconstituted and full democracy is achieved.

Rebel states can retaliate against any economic sanctions enacted by the federal government with their own economic sanctions. Any bank incorporated within a rebel state will have to comport to state laws even if they have branches and services in other states. They can certainly use their leverage to counteract the sanctions placed on their leadership by the illegitimate government. Banks will have to abide by all laws passed by the states or risk having their incorporations suspended and assets assumed by the state governments. The states will have an implicit advantage if the federal government is lawfully shut down and unable to enforce its laws. Most corporations will tend to cooperate with the more proximate governments who have immediate authority over their individual branch locations.

THE FERRY: RESISTANCE AND REBELLION

The states should immediately the creation of regional banks that offer deposit insurance and other products normally reserved for central banks. Banks may not have access to these products and services if the central bank is shutdown along with the rest of the federal government. The most important responsibility of this new regional bank is creating new government bonds supporting the protesting states. These bonds will be backed by the government revenues of the rebel states. They are an alternative to the treasury bills offered by the defunct federal government. During the institutional protest, the federal government won't be able to cover debt obligations and this includes the federal treasuries. These regional banks will want to assume a portion of the federal bonds that are placed in default after the government shutdown. This act will restore faith in the credit of the protesting states. The states can choose which creditors are paid and in what order. They may take on a large amount of debt, but they will also have more predictable access to future revenues from borrowing.

Part of every states' emergency preparedness plan will include sections on human resources with positions clearly mapped out, costs assessed, hiring authorities prepared, and financial incentives to attract disaffected or furloughed federal employees. If the federal government is shut down for two years or more, the state governments will want to be able to quickly onboard the staff they need to protect themselves during an event. The states wont only want formerly enlisted soldiers, they will want former analysts, law enforcement agents, tax -collection agents, and a whole host of other support roles. Enlistment for combat roles is often the easiest condition to satisfy with conscription. The more technical and specialized support roles take longer to fill.

Most standing armies are mostly comprised of support roles and this is where state governments can gain the biggest advantage. They only expect to act locally, so they can re-tool police training facilities, easily find barracks and housing, source food, and initial equipment. All of this can be planned out years in advance with emergency preparedness. If threats of default and government shutdown are prevalent, every state government must prepare for situations which include permanent government shutdowns or where the finances of the federal government are devastated by debt defaults and tax holidays. The tests are clearly stated and quick responses must be prepared. That is the role and responsibility of all governments.

The main objective of preparing or passing these laws are too cool the ambitions of an authoritarian. They are intended to discourage bad behavior and increase the penalties for transgressing democratic norms. If the states have a stronger and quicker response to authoritarianism, there will be fewer opportunities for authoritarians. Despots prefer when citizens don't protest and don't organize. If the people don't have high confidence in their ability to protect themselves, they remain silent and attempt to patiently wait out a term. They may even join the party and contribute to their own exploitation and oppression. If the authoritarians have less confidence in their likelihood for success, they will respect democratic institutions more. There estimates are all outcome-based. To discourage bad behavior, there must be consequences. The states offer the best opportunity to defend against an authoritarian and their capacity must be honed with theory and practice. They must have access to the public policy necessary to enforce civil rights and voting rights and protect democracy within their territorial boundaries.

A word of warning. There are no legitimate actors during an institutional protest. Any actions taken by the federal government while shutdown is unconstitutional and illegal. Any actions the states take to resist the federal government may also be illegal. Institutional protests are organizing revolution through due process, and are lawful and peaceful in nature, greatly reducing the risk of incarceration for participants. Although the federal government is shutdown, its laws may still apply. However, the federal government can't enforce the laws without appropriations and budget authority. This will be a lawless environment based on the discretion of elected leaders. There is always the threat of accountability after the prolonged government shutdown ends, but if the institutional protest results in peaceful regime change, there likely won't be any retaliation. It is also possible that the government shutdown is permanent, and there are no consequences for the tax holidays and other peaceful protests coming from the states.

In ordinary times, tax holidays are prohibited and government shutdowns are rarely used. In extraordinary times, when governments act outside the bounds of their own laws, it requires responses that also fall outside of normal expectations. The authority of the states to pursue these interventions rests in the legitimacy of their elections. Local elections are generally perceived as more valid than federal elections. Residents have more tacit control over the electoral process and it is assumed the policies passed more accurately reflect the interests of constituents. This is a significant advantage for the states during a constitutional crisis. When democracy starts to fail, the citizens will rely on local governments for leadership and protection. Most of the public policy responses to resist authoritarianism start and end on the state level.

Rebel states can increase their odds of reasserting democracy by having these laws prepared ahead of the institutional protest. If the statutes are already written, they can be presented and passed by state level legislatures in the first few days of a protest. This will clearly spell of the terms of the institutional protest and make it more effective. States should also have prepared their emergency services for quick deployment, with financing and supply chains squared off before an event. They can prepare all of the documents and polices beforehand and only act on them if the emergency actually occurs. In many cases, states have sovereignty and the certain authority to prepare for emergencies caused by debt defaults and government shutdowns. It would be extremely careless of the states not to prepare in an environment where these insults are ever-present. The better prepared the states are for this possibility, the more these threats will be discouraged.

6 INSTITUTIONAL INEQUALITIES

Taxes are the primary means of contact between the government and its people. Every income earner or property owner must pay taxes when they are due. This is not voluntary and is non-negotiable. Many people see it as coercion and feel as though all of the benefits of government go to other people. Those that pay the taxes rarely rely on welfare services and aren't often the targets of law enforcement. They feel these obligations are unnecessary and an obstacle to their own success and economic security. This promotes anti-government sentiments in the population. When politicians adopt public policy focused on austerity and low taxes, they increase the level of dissent and disdain in the public. When the government ceases to accommodate for the inherent defects of a market economy, it creates opportunities for profiteering and institutional abuses like mass incarceration and disenfranchisement. The public will start to view the government with disdain and contempt. Eventually they will adopt counter-productive or dangerous ideologies. Extremism will proliferate through the countryside and cities, threatening the nation with rebellion or revolution.

The biggest risk to a nation is a direct product of austerity measures. If the political parties continue argue for low taxes or make concessions to reduce taxes, the government will start accumulating large amounts of public debt. The debt servicing costs will crowd out the welfare, military, and law enforcement services provided by the government. Discourse will quickly be subsumed by partisan bickering over tax rates and deficits. The parties will start to rely on threats of debt defaults and government shutdowns to coerce the other party into reforms or concessions. This increases the risk of economic catastrophe from an unintended debt default. It also increases the risk of a prolonged shutdown, resulting in either a peaceful dissolution or a war of secession.

No rational actor sees a debt default as a productive outcome when negotiating for economic benefits. It would devastate the public finance system for the nation resulting in a possible recession or depression. Any engagement increases the risk of default. The very presence of threats for default indicate that the leadership of the offending party has considered secession or dissolution, and these outcomes may be ulterior motives. The public at large may not understand the consequences but the political leaders do. It is the responsibility of the opposition party to explain the dire economic and political consequences of debt defaults.

Once the culture is rooted, it may be impossible to eliminate. Debts do diminish over time through inflation and economic expansion, but these are periods expressed in decades rather than years or terms for elected officials. If the anger of the public is not discharged, it could lead to other partisan conflict over electoral outcomes and immigration. Worse, once the culture of debt defaults and shutdowns is accepted, politicians can resurrect the threats over almost any other issue. This introduces the systemic risk of default and then dissolution.

Although accessible and highly effective, it is fairly unlikely that a majority party will start a civil war by using a default. It is far more effective for them to pass anti-democratic laws eroding the quality of elections and civil liberties. Majoritarian parties can impose restricted electorates and even apartheid conditions when their government remains fully funded with borrowing intact. The majority party could then rely on the federal law enforcement and military to keep order during their transition to authoritarianism. With the façade of legitimacy, they could more easily oppress the populations protesting deteriorating conditions.

An opposition party may consider their own default to stop the progression but authoritarian governments are more likely to disregard an interruption in debt servicing and continue paying the obligations. Authoritarian government are also far less likely to be stopped by filibusters and government shutdowns. If they can still collect on tax revenues, they don't need the consent of the legislature. In fact, every challenge presented by the minority party in these conditions, may help the majority party consolidate power and rally their supporters. These institutional protests are merely punctuation marks with most of the resistance coming from the state or regional governments.

Romantics will assert that minorities and poor will be able to more aggressively and successfully negotiate for civil rights and economic concessions with threats of debt default and government shutdowns within presidential systems. This is faulty conclusion. Debt defaults or government shutdown are violent in nature and minorities and the poor stand to lose more if they destroy the organization protecting them. It is the government which protects free speech, unions, voting rights, minimum wage laws, and provides welfare.

Corporations and wealthy households forcibly deny these rights in order to maximize profits and political power. The risk is too great to threaten dissolution or bankruptcy in order to gain incremental reforms. Despots and authoritarian parties benefit more from a threat of destroying the government by either winning an important concession or disrupting the organization regulating or taxing them. It is clear that presidential systems are more susceptible to defaults and shutdowns, giving important advantages to the authoritarian parties pursuing policies like restrictive electorates, partisan redistricting, voter ID laws, wealth inequality, and austerity measures.

In most circumstances, the authoritarians are trying to preserve their political influence and wealth, thus they will see government as an adversary or rival to their own power. Authoritarians believe they will be better off without government oversight or interventions and more confident they will survive the brutal environment created by economic depression or armed conflict. Authoritarians only respect due process when it benefits them. While democrats constrain themselves to what is legal or moral, authoritarians can consider many more strategies and outcomes. This gives a huge advantage to authoritarians over a longer time line.

This is often the default position of a majority-demographic group, which superficially would have a greater chance to survive or retain majority political powers after a conflict. Minority groups are at severe disadvantages and suffer disproportionately from economic sanctions or martial violence. The authoritarians can change the demographic make-up of the electorate by pursuing more violent policies. The rate of incarceration, death, or disability will be far greater in the minority population producing an incentive for the majority demographic group to initiate violence.

The most authoritarian segment of the population is the owners class. They are the policy drivers of austerity measures, weak regulatory systems, weak democratic institutions, and exploitative labor agreements. They stand to lose the most when progressive taxes are applied to reduce the deficit or when trust busting breaks up their monopolies. Corporate boards and CEOs are also more homogenous in their ideologies and family histories. This makes them more susceptible to sectarian beliefs. They certainly share economic interests with each other and will defend them against perceived political adversaries. Corporate board members and executive officers also expect that their orders are followed. A loss in a predictable electoral outcome may more easily anger the owners and move them to activism. As leaders in their industry or fields, they may be more emboldened to take riskier positions.

THE FERRY: RESISTANCE AND REBELLION

Corporations often rival states and small nations in their accounting balance sheets and access to labor. They may be pivotal allies during a rebellion or occupation. They collect income taxes, sales taxes, and payroll taxes. They can withhold or redirect the revenues to a rebel government. They can do the same with military equipment, food, or other necessary supply chain products during a conflict. Their most important influence may be on voters who could be coerced to support secession or occupation through local, state, and federal elections. They are fulcrums of will that can be easily bent towards an authoritarian goal of preserving political power or wealth. Corporations are autocratic by their very nature and it is assumed a significant number of them would support a challenge to democracy, whether it came from a minority party or a majoritarian party. Above all else, they will seek to preserve the flow of revenues from weak labor laws or poor regulatory systems and profits from low taxes.

The poorer states may resist the movement towards progressive taxes but they are also the biggest recipients. Poorer states generally receive more federal tax subsidies than the wealthier states and this helps accommodate the poverty and build wealth in the states[12]. For example, in the United States nearly 57% of taxes are paid by the Democratic states while federalist subsidies are split evenly between the between the Democratic states and Republican States[13]. Republican States pay only 43% of aggregate taxes but receive nearly 50% of all federal subsidy[14]. If federal taxes represent 20% of GDP, then the Republican States earn approximately 1.4% of GDP in economic stimulus every year while the Democratic states acquire a 1.4% penalty on their product[15]. This artificially stimulates the Republican States economy when their policies may actually impede economic equality in outcomes and GDP growth. Overall GDP growth is typically

---

[12] Department of Treasury, Internal Revenue Service Data Book 2017, retrieved from https://-www.irs.gov/pub/irs-soi/17databk.pdf

[13] Department of Treasury, Internal Revenue Service Data Book 2017, retrieved from https://-www.irs.gov/pub/irs-soi/17databk.pdf

[14] Jonathan Gruber, (2013), "Public Finance and Public Policy", page 14. Worth Publishers, New York, NY.

[15] Multiplying estimate of 20% GDP by 7% for Republican state shortfall of federal tax contributions (set at roughly 50% liability)

just 3% in the United States so a 1.4% boost or penalty actually represents nearly half (50%) the total GDP growth[16]. Public policy experts may make a mistake and label the Democratic state policies as less productive than Republican state policies for GDP growth if they don't use federal subsidies as an instrumental variable to tease out the actual rate of economic growth resulting from local and regional economic policies.

The public finance disposition in the U.S. is even more tenuous when the consequences of a government shutdown or debt default are considered. The 1.4% GDP penalty will be assessed to state and municipal budgets along that axis, with those states onboarding budget shortfalls of 10-20%. In order to compensate for the budget deficits, the Republican States would have to either raise taxes or cut benefits. Raising taxes will hurt economic output, further reducing government tax revenues. It's a Hobson's choice with either strategy producing large groups of dissenting voters and residents. Borrowing may not be an option either, if there was a default on the federal budget or where an economic correction produces a drought in lending capital. It is within this chaotic moment that military and police will be used to brutally suppress minority groups, commit war crimes, impose authoritarian policies. This will be seen as an opportunity for the owners class or oligarchs to secede and regain control over the economy.

Small imbalances in federal subsidies expressed over long periods of time represent a critical flaw in the economy. These excesses often result from the exploitation of structural deficiencies in the legislature. In conventional democracies, the senate is this source of weakness. The United States Senate is the best example of this common representational deficiency. In 1776, the Founding Fathers agreed to the terms of two Senators to every state when there were far fewer states. The difference in population between the most populated states and the least populated states were far smaller in the late 1700s than they are now[17]. There were also far

---

[16] World Bank, GDP Growth (Anual %), Accessed on 7/8/2019, retrieved from https://data.worldbank.org/indicator/NY.GDP.MKTP.KD.ZG?-locations=US

fewer states that qualified as small when compared to the average state[18].

It was during the Civil War and shortly afterward where a larger number of the least populated territories gained statehood. Now, there are 50 states producing a very dangerous imbalance in representation. The less populated states are in the majority with four states (California, Texas, Florida, and New York) hosting nearly a third (30%) of the total population but only 8% of the total representation in the Senate[19]. This was never intended. The states with the least educated, poorest, and fewest residents, now greatly outnumber the more metropolitan and wealthier coastal states. The Founding Fathers would not have set the terms to so heavily favor the least populated states.

As it stands right now, nearly 60% of all Senate seats are in states affiliated with the Republican party[20]. However, only 51% of the population live in these 28 states providing the Republican party a huge representational advantage in the Senate[21]. The Senate is a necessary part of the bicameral legislative process and no laws can pass without its express consent. Even more troubling is the accelerating use of the filibuster. A filibuster requires 60 Senators to support a measure before it can be passed. The concentration of 60% of Senators in one party makes it far less likely that the minority party will ever approach a filibuster proof number of Senators.

---

[17] Thomas Legion, Population of the Original 13 Colonies, accessed on 7/8/2019, retrieved from http://www.thomas-legion.net/population_of_ the_original_-thirteen_colonies_fr-ee_slave_white_and_nonwhite.html

[18] Thomas Legion, Population of the Original 13 Colonies, accessed on 7/8/2019, retrieved from http://www.thomas-legion.net/population_of_ the_original_thirteen_-colonies_fr-ee_slave_white_and_nonwhite.html

[19] U.S. Census, 2018 National and State Population Estimates, accessed on 7/9/2019, retrieved from https://www.censu-s.gov/newsroom/press-kits/2018/pop-estimates-national-state.html

[20] Anecdotal. The estimation of political affiliation isn't based exclusively on Presidential election year results but a combination of off-year, mid-term, and Presidential election years, taking into consideration gubernatorial and state legislatures election. Most states have mixed outcomes over time but they also demonstrated preferences for these parties. Other sections of the book may rely on different allocations of party affiliation.

[21] U.S. Census, 2018 National and State Population Estimates, accessed on 7/9/2019, retrieved from https://www.censu-s.gov/newsroom/press-kits/2018/pop-estimates-national-state.html

These are nearly insurmountable structural disadvantages for any opposition party.

When one political party is so insulated from impeachment it erodes accountability in the institution and party. If a president isn't fearful the opposition party will be able to successfully impeach them and then prosecute them for their crimes, the executive won't moderate their own behaviors. They won't expect other principals in the executive branch moderate their behavior either, and soon the highest offices in the nation will be overrun by agents who are effectively above the law and corrupt. When the legislature does try to provide some oversight, there will be no significant consequences and this weakness will be declared. Once this culture of unaccountability is acknowledged, a culture of lawlessness will follow and the quality of institutions decline and fall into disrepair. The public will cease to trust in them and there will be no expectations of order and fairness.

Although the opposition party will occasionally win majorities in the institution, most of the legislative authority will be vested in the party with the systemic advantage in number of Senators. If one party has a considerable institutional advantage in the Senate, it will attract the attention of firms and corporations as an identifiable weakness to exploit. Corporations and wealthy individuals will concentrate their lobbying efforts on the political party that wins more often in those territories. In the United States, the Republicans have nearly 150% more likely seats than the Democrats and this invites a culture of corruption within the Senate. Corporations will form relationships and networks with the party and candidates from the stronger party. It's a sounder wager and more profitable arrangement.

The political party will reciprocate by favoring business practices and policies preferred by the corporate community. The Senators will use the significant imbalance in Senate representation and filibuster to prevent economic reforms, preserving the profits associated with weak labor laws, overt and rampant discrimination, regressive taxes, and exploitative wage laws. Therefore, it is a safe assumption that democracies relying on senates are more susceptible to corruption and inherently less stable. Unfortunately, this concept of a Senate has proliferated throughout contemporary democracies despite their innate deficiencies. Arbitrary forms of representation are thought of as necessary component of bicameral legislatures.

Arbitrary systems of representation are an inverse of other forms of representation. If it is paired with a demographic chamber, the senate will take on an inverse of demographic representation. If it is paired with a GDP chamber, it will take on the properties of being an inverse of econometric representation. This property runs contrary to the conventional interpretation of democracy. Democracy is premised on majority rule and popular support. The senate is an affront to these principles. Senates are aristocratic in nature. They provide poorer, more rural, and less educated states far more representation than the wealthier and more populated states, far more susceptible to the influence of firm owners and the leisure class.

A state with just 500,000 residents has 78 times as much proportional representation as a state with 39,000,000 residents[22]. It is an absurd belief that elevating the status of a state 78 times smaller than another will produce sound public policy. This is a deficiency that can be easily exploited by foreign powers or domestic usurpers. Corporations are quite possibly the biggest beneficiaries of the senate when they can focus their corruption efforts corrupting on a single institution or party. This risk is much more pronounced in nations with private campaign finance laws and weak electoral oversight.

One of the more important properties of the U.S. Senate has been lost over time. The original U.S. Constitution had governors appointing senators to the Congress. The Founding Fathers wanted other executive branches to have oversight over the federal executive and the ability to intervene if the federal executive ever overstepped their boundaries. The original check on the federal government was the governors' ability to write federal laws, oversee federal agencies, and confirm federal judges and cabinet officials. The governors have access to state militias, local police forces, regional budgets and are the only effective check against an illegitimate

---

[22] U.S. Census, 2018 National and State Population Estimates, retrieved from https://www.censu-s.gov/newsroom/press-kits/2018/pop-estimates-national-state.html

or authoritarian government. Governors can mobilize the resources necessary to check a wayward president while legislators can only debate, or shut down the government.

When the Governors appointed the Senators as their representatives, they would have immediate and implicit access to the classified information legislators normally have access to. Governors would be more aware of all federal domestic surveillance programs. Governors would be aware of which National Guard Armies are sent overseas[23]. Governors would be more aware of foreign threats and responsible for ratifying all treatise. Governors would have more oversight over federal law enforcement and election laws. Governors would have quicker more informed responses to domestic threats and have more capacity to respond to them. More importantly, they could have direct influence over a chamber of legislature that has the authority to implement an institutional protest. This would coordinate the legislature with state level governors, and all of the revenues, military, and police assets they have access to. There is strength in numbers and when a group of governors thought there was enough cause to commit to an institutional protest. They have access to more information than individuals and they have more experience handling critical state security and public safety issues.

The Senate has lost most of its purpose when its representatives became popularly elected rather than appointed by governors. The federal government became insulated from outside control and less accountable to the only other executive officers who had the necessary perspective and experience to evaluate their actions. The composition of

---

[23] In 2005, The Republican administration sent a National Guard rotation to Iraq compromised exclusively of Democratic state enlisted. None of the other governors were aware of this troop deployment and the Democrats in Congress were unable to object or alert the public to the threat due to its classified status. The rotation represented nearly 20% of all Democratic National Guard Armies and should have been made of half Republican and half Democratic units. The Republicans were responding to the possibility of another compromised Presidential election in 2004, following the 2000 election when the Supreme Court intervened in the favor of George W. Bush. The information located in CRS documents was retroactively classified in 2011 and can't be cited.

the Senate changed dramatically shortly thereafter, when the states were expanded from just 13 states to the current number of 50. The entire statehood movement would have been changed if governors had retained the oversight over the federal government. Governors may have resisted the rapid expansion or at lease restricted the number, so that the least populated and poorest states didn't control 60% of the Senate seats. The more populous states would have made sure they retained more political representation in the Senate, if the Senate was more responsible to the governors.

Unfortunately, the North used statehood to coerce support from the territories and win most of the battles but ultimately lost the Civil War when the majority of political power in the U.S. was assumed by a coalition of southern states and former territories. Jim Crow laws were an expression of this future outcome. They resisted integration because they correctly estimated they could in the new representational paradigm. They surrendered their arms only to embrace a Senate remade in their image. This demonstrates an important trend in politics. If the public believes their behavior can earn them more political power, they will accept conditions that earn them less representation up front with the expectation of future improvement. It is the promise of more representation in the future that will shape their public policy and electoral decisions. It will also imbue the voters with patience needed to successfully negotiate for improved civil rights, labor rights, and economic reforms. This may be an immensely powerful tool during nation building.

The only way to circumvent the filibuster is with budget reconciliation. Budget Reconciliation requires bills to associate laws with fiscal policy but permits passage by a simple majority. Parties can start passing progressive taxes and industrial regulation with simple majorities rather than waiting for filibuster proof margins of 60 or more Senators. The Congress can start dealing with wealth inequality, civil rights, environmental protections, and other critical issues every time they hold simple majorities in both chambers. The biggest risk of budget reconciliation, is that it degrades the quality of the political union by requiring all laws to have taxes associated with them. The public may start to resist the fees and tax penalties assessed during simple industrial and environment regulations. The nation will be more of an economic union rather than a political union, with weaker bonds after the imbalance in federalist tax subsidies and Senatorial representation are examined more closely. Obviously, the danger is greatest when threats of debt defaults and government shutdowns are prevalent.

The arbitrary systems of representation found in most senates are dangerous implements during demographic shifts or periods of wealth inequality. Senates are a source of exploitation and instability when they are used to obstruct progressive taxes, economic reforms, and industrial regulations. Despite the terrible outcomes, most contemporary democracies still use senates to offset their demographic chambers. It need not be this way. Tax-based representation is a perfect substitute for a senate. Tax liabilities are correlated to population but not completely derivative of them. Pairing a wealth-based institution with a demographic-based institution, provides a public with an incentive to improve representation with economic growth. It also better satisfies the conditions of democracy with a representational coefficient closer to demographic than any arbitrary system currently allows.

Tax revenues directly support the government and the services it provides. Better services can be provided by more revenues. Higher revenues also produce more representation. This brings an aspect of self-determination to democracy. Those states that want more representation will make more sacrifices for the nation and work harder to increase the economic output of the state. A better funded nation will have stronger militaries, more effective law enforcement, better roads and transportation, and more research subsidies in health and technology. The investments will stimulate GDP growth and create a positive feedback loop to higher tax revenues.

Those states that refrain from over-taxing will increase GDP over the interim period and gain proportionally more political power than the state pursing shorter-term goals for gains in representation at the expense of GDP growth. These tradeoffs will help create the political culture found in the nation, and alter the traditional small state vs. large state or liberal vs. conservative divides. Political parties will have more diverse platforms dependent more on the individual circumstances of the states and the preferences of the politicians. This will promote deal making between the politicians and parties as short-term gains are traded for long term gains. These more complicated political platforms erode party control over individual politicians by reducing the effectiveness of central tenets and agendas. This will make elections more competitive across institutions and parties.

Unlike conventional wealth-based systems of representation, there is no personal benefit to paying higher taxes. Individuals don't gain more access to their politicians, or have more of an effect, than other voters. All of the positive effects of tax-based representation are expressed in aggregate terms, with the benefits for communities organized into districts or states. Wealthier states are more likely to have more districts, but each district will contain a unique electorate. Hopefully, this translates into more competitive elections with equal access among the political parties. Large portions of the electorate will associate taxes with political power and seek to maximize contributions. This will ensure the nation has the funding it needs to deliver on services for the poor and for proper law enforcement. The electorate won't resist tax rate increases when it increases their regions representation in the union or state. This makes it far more likely to avoid debt default and shutdowns in the short term.

Over the long term, tax-based representation will make sure the neediest people receive unemployment income, shelter subsides, and food subsidies enhancing their support for the government during a crisis. Tax-based representation will dramatically cut down on the number of white nationalists, separatist, or extremist sympathizers operating in the territory, prolonging the life of newly incorporated democracies. If the nation is recently formed there will a large number of veterans or radicals in the population already, and poor welfare and slow economies could incite them to disorder more quickly. The dual mandate for order always includes managing both sides of the public safety equation, welfare and enforcement, to ensure a low ratio of dissidents to police officers.

One of the biggest advantages of wealth-based systems of representation is the disposition of representation between the states can be altered by majority control over the legislature and subsequent elections. This decouples political power away from demographics. Demographic shifts result in a very slow and predictable change in political power, which may elicit violence from a political party trying to retain power despite the change in demographics. Tax laws are mutable, and thus may contribute to sounder transitions when one demographic group eclipses another in a short time span. Tax based representation can be paired with demographic representation to avert these crises while continuing to provide universal suffrage and other high-quality democratic entitlements.

Tax-based systems of representation take into consideration raw economic output but its virtues really rest with personal and community responsibility. Those taxpayers making larger commitments to the union will receive more representation. Those regions with more wealth have the capacity to earn more representation but they must agree to those terms. Likewise, regions with less economic output can negotiate for more regressive tax policies. This has a tremendous benefit to make the state more resistant to threats of default and shutdown. When the taxpayers see a direct benefit to paying taxes and it is elevated to a civic responsibility associated with voting, there will be stronger support for fully funding the government. Tax-based representation mitigates the mostly negative relationship citizens have with the nation. They won't see it exclusively as a liability. They won't regard it as a punishment.

Debt default threats and government shutdowns are the single biggest risks to democratic governments as they are the most effective means to disrupt a federal government's ability to put downs an insurrection or secession. If the federal government can't borrow any money to fund a war effort and can't pass a budget to mobilize federal law enforcement and military, it is very likely to result in a successful secession for the breakaway region. There are no other more effective ways to secure independence from a larger nation. However, if a rebel group is less likely to succeed in secession, they are less likely to bear the risks of discovery and face incarceration or execution.

Tax-based systems of representation make these threats of default far less likely and less effective. States that pay more in taxes will earn proportionally more representation and be better able to protect themselves. These states are more likely to raise taxes and reduce the number of opportunities the opposition groups have to threaten default or shutdown the government. In this tax-based system, states are incentivized to pay more taxes when their proportional representation increases to match their contribution. The states paying fewer taxes will be less able to defund the government and create the conditions where excessive deficits start to accumulate. If the confederate states can't effectively pursue austerity measures and threaten default, they won't form the culture around rebellion and revolt. With a diminished chance of success, there will be no popular support for the movement and the nation will less at risk of secession or insurrection.

This is especially true during economic corrections or other crises. In most crises, revenues will flatten while expenses increase to unsustainable levels. This won't be too disruptive to the representational disposition of the nation. Fiscal representation is based on the proportion of taxes paid by the state rather than an aggregate amount. If all tax revenues fall by 10% then the ratios of representatives between states will remain equal. This will make the response more predictable which always helps during crises. Politicians may already be frantic in their expectations of loss of property and prestige, and it would be made far worse if they thought they would immediately lose their political office. Political parties would fear the loss of political power in the event of ordinary economic cycles and the corrections that follow them. It would breed an environment of opportunism and exploitation.

Unfortunately, an uneven distribution of economic pain during recession is common. Revenues may fall by 20% in one state and only 10% in another. This can't be avoided but there are certain inherent advantages to econometric representation based on taxes. As the economic crisis worsens from one year to the next, the populations least affected will win more proportional seats in the institution while the states hurt most will lose seats with lower economic output. Although, this sounds exploitative or unfair, it will give the states with the better economic performance more political power to implement policies intended to accelerate recovery from the crises. Wealthier states have residents with better educational outcomes, better employment outcomes, more expertise, and a generally more comfortable with diversity in heredity, culture, and political ideology. This will allow the nation to overcome any populism that may otherwise result from an extended economic crisis. It is also very likely that the poorer states have worse economic outcomes for longer, giving the wealthier states an even better opportunity to pass the economic reforms and regulations needs to overcome the wealth inequality or poor business practices creating the crisis.

However, this natural advantage may discourage smaller, poorer, and more rural states from joining the political unions based on econometric representation. These states can be reassured that a census held every 10-years to smooth-out the apportionment process and avoid abrupt changes resulting from economic corrections. It is very unlikely an economic correction lasts for more than 4 years[24], allowing for the less economically developed state to recover and retain its proportional representation. If the correction lasts more than 10 years, it justifies a change in the representational disposition of the legislature that will make public policy interventions more likely. A loss in representation does not necessarily translate to a loss in federal subsidies. In fact, a recession may increase the amount of subsides as the political union attempts to compensate for the loss in GDP to limit more wide spread damage to economic production. As the regional GDP decreases, the relative size of the subsidies will increases providing more aid within the current federal framework for aid.

Most corrections will occur earlier or later than a census year and not impact the number of representatives earned by

---

[24] Cameron Kong, (Oct 23, 2018)," Recession is Overdue by 4.5 years. Here is how to prepare". Forbes.com, retrieved from https://www.forbes.com-/sites/-cameron-keng/2018/10/23/recession-is-overdue-by-4-5-years-heres-how-to-prepare/#5-71075324-0d8

each state. Overall, the system will be fair due to the randomized timing, length, and severity of economic corrections, but all states will have an eye to regulate more effectively to avoid situations that may result in representational changes. Elections will price in the expectations of apportionment losses if policies aren't passed to correct the lack of oversight or regulation in an industry susceptible to corrections. This will contribute to a better funded and sounder regulatory environment, making the nation more durable with a more competitive economy.

Ultimately, tax-based representation provides one of the most secure paths towards durable and equitable representation. In the short-term, it over-represents the wealthier states with larger populations and more educated voters. In the long-term, it rewards those states passing sounder public policy that achieve better economic outcomes. Tax-based representation also defends nations against threats of default and government shutdowns by incentivizing higher revenues with better collections compliance. The properties of econometric representation lend itself to high-quality democratic entitlements, preserving universal suffrage and the bicameral process. Tax-based representation has an opportunity to improve nation building efforts by offering an alternative to the Senate that appeals to all of the stakeholders in democracy.

7 ORGANIZATIONAL STRUCTURE

In Ancient Greece, each citizen was granted the right to vote directly on laws and public policy[25]. They took turns working as civil servants and leaders in the government. In Rome, the Senate was appointed from aristocrats and the Assemblies, comprised of elected representatives, were lesser institutions[26]. The Roman Republic introduced representative democracy. In representative democracies, citizens vote for agents to represent them rather than voting directly on issues. The democracy in the United States was a major improvement on the two earlier versions. The United states married a representative chamber with an arbitrary chamber. In arbitrary systems of representation, each state earns the same number of senators regardless of population or wealth. Arbitrary representation takes on the special property of being an inverse to any other representational system used in the government. In all of the different types of democratic government, voting right were exclusionary, usually

----

[25] Robert Longley, July 7th, 2019, Direct Democracy Pros and Cons, retrieved from https://www.th-oughtco.com/what-is-direct-democracy-3322038

[26] N.S. Gill, The Roman Republics Government, March 30th, 2019, retrieved from https://www.th-oughtco.com/the-roman-republics-government-120772

dependent on a mix of wealth requirements, citizenship, and gender.

All of these governments incorporated different aspects of aristocracy, authoritarian, and democracy in order to achieve their goals. This opens the door up for engineering new institutions based on descriptive statistics and econometrics. An institution doesn't have to be perfectly representative in order to preserve legitimacy. A nation could employ a chamber based on per capita tax liabilities, which resembles an arbitrary form of representation, but introduces slightly more variation between the more exceptional states. A nation may also decide to preserve demographic representation while splitting the electorate by tax liabilities. Other nations may elect to create an exclusionary chamber called a net-tax chamber that only admits states with positive contributions to the government revenues. These alternatives to conventional democracy all satisfy the basic requirements for representative democracy.

The first method discussed is a micro-political median partition where individual voters are separated into below median tax liability chamber and above median tax liability chamber. The second method discusses a macro-political median partition where districts or states separated into below median tax liability chambers or above median tax liability chambers. The median partition uses a median value to split a population into two equal parts, inclusive of all voters regardless of their ability to pay taxes or need to pay, providing each vote exactly one vote during each election, protecting its status as a high-quality democracy.

These two methods can utilize either national median or a state median tax liability. A national median tax liability will separate the states into different chambers while the state median tax liability will divide each state into equal parts with equal participation in both the median tax liability chambers. Each of these variations will have distinct properties, legislative outcomes, and political cultures. All of these options are considered class-based systems of representation due to the number of representatives continue to be determined by the size of the population, but each individual, district, or state is assigned to a classed chamber.

THE FERRY: RESISTANCE AND REBELLION

The third method discussed is a straight representational coefficient based on aggregate tax liabilities. This is a wealth-based system that assigns a number of representative districts to the states depending on the proportion of federal taxes paid. A slight variant of this method is the median tax chamber. It uses the median tax liability for the state, multiplied by the population, as the representational coefficient. Both of these version help protect the nation from threats of default and government shutdown by over-representing the states that pay more taxes, reducing the likelihood of states gaining enough support to forward those policies on the national level.

The fourth method is a tiered arbitrary system that only allocates the number of representatives to each state based on a per capita tax liability. Per capita tax liabilities produce a discreet range of representative far smaller than the straight method and is much closer to a conventional senate. The fifth and final method is a net-tax chamber that allocates representatives to only those states which make surplus federal tax contributions. States that receive more federal tax subsidies than they pay in federal taxes don't receive any representation. All of these methods rely on a single chamber and may be used in conjunction with other strategies for producing a bicameral process.

The two main types of taxes used to determine representation are income taxes and real estate taxes. In median partitions based on income taxes, the non-income earners will be included as zero entries and thus make up a moderate part of the below median chamber. In median partitions using real estate taxes, renters and other non-owners are allocated to the below median income chamber. In all instances, all eligible citizens are allocated to one of the two median chambers. Without universal suffrage, majority rule can't be determined, and the democratic system must be considered inferior.

The below median income tax liability chambers will typically be a mix of non-income earners and low-income earners. Non-income earners are a diverse demographic with retired persons, students, disabled, and the unemployed included into the group. The below median real estate tax liability chamber is comprised of non-owners and those with smaller or less expensive homes. In both cases, the below median chamber provides a wealth of different experiences and perspectives for voters and the chambers are coequal and of equivalent status or power of the above median tax liability chambers.

In a conventional median partition, there will be two coequal chambers with an equal number of representatives in each. Tax documents are used to determine which chamber individual voters belong to. Citizens who pay less than the median tax liability earn eligibility in the below median chamber while citizens who pay more than the median tax liability earn eligibility in the above median chamber. Citizens who don't pay taxes or don't submit tax documents are associated with the below median chamber. This ensures that the two electorates are of equal size and preserve the standard for "one person, one vote". Higher quality democracies generally rely on proportional representation and this is perpetuated by determining the number of representatives afforded to each state by the relative sizes of their populations. Both of these properties must be present for a democracy to be considered high quality.

When citizens are separated into separate chambers based upon their personal tax liabilities, it interjects class into political system. Those who pay less taxes generally have lower incomes, making them more dependent on union protections, labor rights, government subsidies, and welfare programs. It also makes them more susceptible to the impact of fiscal policy which may significantly lower their net or disposable incomes. They are the beneficiaries of government planning but also suffer greater hardship. These two contradictory properties make the below median tax chamber more complicated in terms of political agendas and role identity. This will shape the politics of the electorate.

The voters in the above median tax chamber will pay the vast majority of taxes and not receive many benefits. The above median electorate includes most firm owners and professionals or experts. However, this chamber also has a complicated identity. Most firm owners seek weak labor laws and lower taxes but the professionals and experts see the value and benefit in stronger labor protections and higher taxes, creating an adversarial relationship between voters in the same chamber. Hopefully, this chamber will be more likely to make concessions to the below median chamber to preserve the regular course of business.

A micro-political median partition allows for voters to change associations over a life time. Their incomes should increase as they age or meet certain milestones. Students are expected to have low incomes while graduates are expected to earn above average incomes. Working professionals will have much higher incomes than when retired. A voter can expect to vote in both the below median tax chamber and above median tax chamber during their lifetime. This will help randomize political preferences of the voters and the institutions. Not only will they acquire better role identity depending on their current economic condition, but it will make them more amenable to making concessions to those constituents during negotiations on laws coming out of the chamber.

Voter tax liabilities are assessed every year and an average is used to assign them to a particular chamber. Using an average will limit the number of times a voter switches from one chamber to the other making the association more durable. This also limits the more immediate effect tax policy has on the electorate. When changes aren't immediately expressed in the electorate, there are fewer incentives and opportunities to manipulate the tax code to gain or preserve majority control. Unlike other versions of econometric systems of representation, taxpayers can't improve their political power by raising taxes and thus will see less of a benefit in raising taxes. Both median tax chambers have the same number of representatives and an equal number of voters supporting them. The median value always separates a group into two equal parts. Regardless of how much in taxes they pay, the person will have a single vote and their state will receive a number of votes equivalent to population (or some other chosen coefficient).

There may be surprising outcomes when the nation is split by tax liabilities. The states with higher incomes tend to be more liberal while the states with lower income tend to be conservative. Liberals advocate for higher taxes and better welfare, while the conservatives pursue austerity measures and less economic regulations, creating an opportunity for coalition building. The liberals in the above median chamber can reach out to minorities suffering wage discrimination in the below median chamber. The conservatives in the above median chamber will be able to rely on strong support from the more rural, poorer, and less educated districts within the political union. Success is dependent on outreach making elections more competitive in both chambers. This will ensure that due process and debate in the political process remains robust and fertile.

The median partition empowers both classes. The below median chamber has as much influence and political power as the above median chamber. In fact, the median partition forces the two classes to interact and negotiate with each other. The below median chamber can't pass laws without the above median chamber, and vice versa. This means that either class can block laws passed by the other chamber. It forces the two classes to negotiate and agree on economic policy and tax policy.

An extremely important anti-discriminatory property is produced. If a demographic group suffers from predatory policing practices and economic discrimination, their incomes will be lower, their unemployment rates higher, and the aggregate taxes paid will be less. This will concentrate them in the below median chamber where they may consolidate their electoral power and demand better conditions. This may provide a single demographic group, or a plurality of demographic groups, a majority in the chamber. A majority can be used to embargo laws passed by the above median tax chamber until concessions are made on civil liberties, labor rights, and voting rights.

For example, if the two largest minority groups in the country were 16% and 22% of the population and they faced extreme wage discrimination resulting in 80% paying below median taxes, they would acquire majority control over the below median chamber. Together, they represent only 38% of the total population, but when concentrated in the below median chamber, they represent more than 60% of the electorate. They can use this position to demand more civil rights and economic protections. Laws require both chambers to confirm them, and this will force the above median tax chamber to meet the reform demands of the below median tax chamber before other business is conducted

When these demands are finally met and their wages increased, their tax liabilities will increase, and the minority voters will be more evenly distributed between the two chambers. After successful negotiations, the minority coalition would only represent 38% of the below median tax chamber and 38% of the above median tax chamber. Their representation in each chamber would be exactly their proportion of the total population. This adaption eliminates the fear of a constant monopolization of the political process by minorities. A micro-political partition is reactive, making it for better than conventional democracies at overcoming demographic inequities. Other democracies are more at risk from not successfully reforming their economy and preserving a condition of fear that may result in permanent exploitation or discrimination, and possibly even demographic violence.

There are other advantages in this form of econometric representation. Tax-based representation uses a median petition in most circumstances, providing an adversarial relationship between two chambers with proportional representation. This permits a nation to employ a bicameral process without relying on an arbitrary chamber or direct democracy which would introduce representational deficiencies into the legislative process. Proportional Representation is the highest quality form of democracy possible and the bicameral process makes it more deliberative and more secure.

Tax-based representation may include eligibility criteria for representatives in the below median chamber creating a fiduciary duty which can be enforced. When the representatives live in the same communities, use the same businesses, and go to the same schools, they will share more interests with their constituents and suffer many of the same economic pressures. This produces higher quality agency the representatives will be better advocates for their constituents. Nations will pass stronger labor rights, more equitable tax laws, and more effective regulation and oversight. These are the properties that make econometric systems superior to conventional democratic systems.

Representatives can be required to maintain an average tax liability equal to or less than the median tax liability, in order to continue running for office. A running average is used and if the elected official ever exceeds the median liability threshold, they can be barred from seeking re-election. This eligibility constraint will ensure those who represent the below median liability chamber have the same economic interests and experiences as their constituents. The wage paid to representatives can be set at an amount that automatically produces the maximum tax liability or at some other amount below the threshold, but the median tax threshold will apply to the entire household.

A macro-political median partition divides states or districts by above median and below median tax liabilities and allocates them to one of the two adversarial chambers. All states or districts will be ranked from highest liabilities to lowest tax liabilities, and separating them into the two groups by the median value. The use of districts will help diversify the composition of the chambers when each district is evaluated separately, and they are distributed unevenly among the two median chambers. States will be uniformly distributed between the two chambers. State-wide elections allocate all of the seats to the same classed chamber, producing more homogenous chamber dispositions,

With more accuracy in the allocation process, the states will have better role identity as either tax donor states or tax welfare states. The partition into high liability and low liability chambers will serve as a constant reminder of the institutional advantages some states have over others during debt default threats and government shutdown. This may change which platforms, policies, and measures they support. Tax welfare states that repeatedly call for austerity, despite being a primary recipient of federal subsidies, will be called out as hypocritical. Tax donor states may have more implied authority in oversight if they remind the below median chamber of the sacrifices their residents make.

The above median liability chamber will have institutional advantages when threatened with government shutdowns or debt ceiling measures. They depend less on government subsidies and therefore will be hurt less if the threat is acted on. If the threats come out of the below median liability chamber or any principle associated with the chamber, it can be immediately rebuked with a fiery description of the consequences of such an action. If the tax welfare states are more aware if their precarious position, they will seek more peaceful remedies to policy disputes. Hopefully, this will work to quiet dissent and force the parties to seek recourse through less violent policies

Macro-political systems have a lower order of organization. This may be an advantage to the nation. Each state or district has a mix of high income and low-income citizens producing competitive elections regardless of whether a straight value or a per capital value is used for ranking. Electoral outcomes are less predictable with more diverse electorates. This is in direct contrast to the micro-political systems, which rely more heavily on class distinctions and role identity. It should be safer to obfuscate the financial obligations or incentives of citizens by aggregating them into districts or states. In a macro-political partition, candidates can advocate for political policies or economic reforms without assigning blame to another party or institution. This may smooth over the wrinkles that form in class-based systems, and stoke fears of economic embargo or violence

Similar to the micro-political systems, these institutions benefit from the voters changing preferences over the course of a lifetime. Incomes may increase, education can be attained, employment status can change, while others will retire, marry, or become disabled. However, this association with institution will be dependent on where they live. This may imbue some longevity into their political affiliations and loyalties. Each party and institution will have a different culture attracting a different cross section of voters, altering the organizational strategies of the national parties, having a profound impact in leadership membership and policy preferences. More importantly, voters will develop empathy for other socioeconomic classes or demographic groups. Voters in micro-political systems have the tendency to stay in one economic class and form rigid economic beliefs with a more adversarial attitude.

The wealthier areas of the state usually pay more taxes due to progressive nature of tax laws. This will result in a much more disparate outcome in representational ratios between districts. Dividing the state into equally populous districts randomizes the distribution of representation among areas of different economic output, tending to over-represent the less population dense and poorer areas of the state. However, in states with roughly equivalent economic output the areas with larger populations tend to have higher economic output and will thus receive more representation in a tax-based system. A significant difference in representational ratios between districts in the same state will be more controversial than the slight over-representation of poorer states. When districts are determined by population rather than tax liabilities, the public will view them as more legitimate and fairer despite the wealthier states paying a disproportionate amount of the taxes.

The over-representation of wealthier states will improve the odds of the nation preserving democracy over a longer period. Nations with higher per capita incomes have been demonstrated to have more longevity than nations with lower per capita incomes[27]. As a nation increases its per capita income, it can expect to preserve the quality of democratic entitlements. By over-representing the states with higher GDP and per capita incomes, the state may be more likely to acquire faster GDP growth rates in the lower performing states. This will improve confidence in the democratic process and reinforce public policies that promote wage growth and labor rights. In time, the economic disparity between the states will even out with the help of redistributionist federal subsidies, and the representational ratios between the states will gain parity.

The most straight forward method is using aggregate tax liabilities to determine the number of representatives. Each state is allocated a proportional number of representatives

---

[27] Adam Przeworski, "Minimalist Conception of Democracy: A Defense." *Democracy's Value,* edited by Shapiro, I. and Hacker-Cordon, C. (Cambridge: Cambridge University Press, 1999), pg. 16

equal to the gross amount of federal income taxes remitted or real estate taxes collected. States that collect more taxes receive more representation than states that collect fewer taxes. Tax-based systems are more productive than other forms of wealth -based representation because the number of representatives are directly correlated to the taxes remitted to the federal government. This property has several advantages over conventional democracies with demographic or arbitrary forms of representation.

The states that receive the most representation in the federal system, provide most of its revenues. Role identity will help insulate the nation from threats of default and government shutdowns. The representatives that typically favor austerity measures and deregulation come from poorer states. They will have fewer seats. When they are in the minority there will be fewer opportunities for them to hold the nation hostage during budget negotiations and debt ceiling measures. The proportion of representatives from the wealthier states will increase, creating more opportunities to pass laws that benefit the nation and economy.

Governments that use real estate taxes as the representational coefficient will bolster state and municipal governments. State and local governments are more likely to pass higher property taxes to increase their representation, allowing them to subsidize higher quality education, emergency services, more infrastructure projects, local development projects, and stronger national guard armies. This is regardless of a party's electoral success on the federal level. However, austerity parties typically support states' rights and decentralized systems of control. They perform better on the state and local level, and when real estate taxes are used as the representational coefficient, it creates stronger states. Using real estate taxes is a concession to parties that might otherwise lose their ability to threaten of government shutdowns and debt defaults to forward their agenda on the federal level.

Governments using income taxes for a representational coefficient will benefit parties focused on deploying the federal government to check wealth inequality, protect civil rights, and maintain a strong foreign policy. Federal governments rarely use property taxes as revenue with most of the funding coming from progressive income taxes, payroll taxes, and corporate taxes. States that remit more income taxes typically vote for parties that advocate for expanding voting rolls, improving labor rights, curtailing wealth inequality, and limiting monopoly and corruption. When these states receive more proportional representation in the union, they will be able to pass economic reforms more easily and suffer fewer electoral consequences afterward.

In conventional democracies, there are significant political and social pressures favoring lower taxes and this can have a deleterious effect on a nation. The social welfare net is weaker, wealth inequality grows unchecked, deficits and debt accumulate to dangerous levels in nations that prioritize tax cuts. This erodes the public's confidence in the government and exposes it to insults over budget negotiations. Although, these tendencies will still be present in a tax-based system, the structural incentives towards higher taxes will balance them out. The states that pay fewer taxes and receive less representation may continue to prefer policies that promote lower taxes, but they will rarely be in a position to weaken the state to the point of breaking it.

The biggest risk in tax-based representation is the over burden of taxes. However, there is a natural check on this outcome too. Whenever taxes are in excess, a majority of stakeholders will rally behind tax cuts or other economic reforms to ameliorate the condition. Taxes may be adjusted to meet the expectations of constituents and stakeholders. States that pay more taxes are likely to continue paying more taxes even in lower tax environments, creating the opportunity for negotiation on the tax rates. More progressive tax rates will permit the higher GDP states to pay more taxes and receive more representation while allowing states which favor lower taxes to continue paying fewer taxes. This political tradeoff will smooth the average electoral output and legislative production of the nation, especially when the higher revenues support the projects and agenda goals of most parties.

The tiered arbitrary method uses per capita tax liabilities to determine the number of representatives allocated to each state. Unlike the senate, with a fixed and unmoving number of senators for each state, a chamber based on per capita income allows for states to increase their representational ratios through immigration or economic performance. Nation-building efforts often require concessions to states with smaller population or less economic activity, and the tiered arbitrary system is a lot fairer than a traditional arbitrary system. It is simply a better concession than a conventional arbitrary system due to the larger range of representational outcomes. States with larger populations or more economic activity do retain more representation but it is at a far smaller ratio than proportional systems. This will entice the less endowed states to participate without creating an environment where the smaller states can completely dominate the larger states in a bicameral legislature. It over-represents the smaller states by a smaller margin than most other arbitrary systems.

States that use public policy to increase tax revenues while their populations remain the same, will inevitably acquire more senators. States losing population to immigration despite maintaining the same economic output, will also see the number or representatives increase. States may pursue economic reforms that promote higher minimum wages and union protections as a means to increase tax liabilities and the number of representations apportioned to them. The incentives are there but moving the average takes considerable effort. It will be a very competitive market with all of the states trying to acquire a superior number of representatives. More representatives often result in more federalist tax subsidies, more jobs, and more investments into the state. However, they will all strive for these outcomes creating a moving average reducing the effectiveness of their efforts.

Arbitrary systems, like the U.S. Senate, contribute to majoritarian political parties and status as an illiberal democracy. Most senates use state-wide elections and this empowers the demographic majority by dramatically under-representing minorities. In state wide elections, the demographic majority will dictate the outcomes of most of the elections resulting in far fewer minority seats, resulting in public policy that promotes mass incarceration, voter suppression, deregulated campaign finance, and rampant wealth inequality. Tiered Arbitrary systems are more compatible with district elections when the state is divided into a larger number of representational territories. It is more likely that a concentrated minority population gain majority control over one of these regions. Tiered arbitrary systems don't eliminate the threat of majoritarian representation if state wide elections are used, but it does make the institution more compatible with district-wide elections. A typical senate with two senators split the state into regions where minorities are less likely to gain a majority in elections, where as a state with 4 or 5 territories are more likely to have minority-majority territories.

The last method described is the net-tax chamber. This institution only provides representation to the states with surplus federal tax contributions. These chambers will typically have terms that coincide with the executive office or another legislative office, with a determination for eligibility made the year preceding elections. All of the federal tax subsidies paid to a state are tallied and deducted from its total federal tax contributions. Every state with a positive number of gains eligibility, with the number of representatives determined by tallying the total amount of surplus federal tax contributions and dividing the chambers total number of seats into this value. Each state receives a number of representatives equal to the number of times their tax contributions can be divided by this figure. Every term, each states' eligibility is determined with the number of seats may change, imparting a measure of uncertainty into the legislative branch.

The net-tax chamber will usually be used as a triangulation chamber with authority only to confirm the laws written in other institutions. The net-tax chamber can confirm laws coming from any other institution, allowing the representatives to negotiate and make their own compromises. In many bicameral legislatures, the quality of laws suffers under filibusters or split party control. A triangulation chamber increases the frequency and improve the quality of laws passed when a split congress is excluded as a possible outcome.

The net-tax chamber can be organized around state-wide jurisdictions or districts depending on the framers of the institution. State-wide jurisdictions promote more homogenous electoral outcomes while districts provide more diversity. Districts will increase the odds of opposition parties earning representation in the chamber and ensuring that states not represented in the chamber have some allies within the chamber. States typically have homogenous outcomes for state-wide elections and more densely populated and wealthier states will monopolize the institution.

The net-tax chamber will optimize public finance by placing voluntary constraints on spending. Not all states will seek to maximize their representation but many will, making it more likely that the nation only spends on necessary programs and services to keep their budgets streamlined. The nation will run more efficiently with lower expenses and higher revenues. States will look forward to the next apportionment and adjust their spending to acquire representation, making the chamber more competitive.

The states who tailor their spending and services to receive less aid in order to maximize representation will deny their states the economic stimulus that will otherwise grow their economy. Over the long term, their economies will stagnate and suffer from lower growth rates, resulting in the likelihood they lose their surplus contributions and representation in the net-tax chamber. States which accept aid and welfare at the expense of representation will be a much better future economic position. States with stronger economic performances have sounder electorates and make better fiscal decisions. More economic stimulus will create conditions where future federal tax surpluses are more likely with fewer consequences to limiting or rejecting aid.

The net-tax chamber promotes sound fiscal policy in another respect. All debt servicing and debt repayment removes money from the federal system without allocating it to any of the participating states. This increases the likelihood states acquire positive balances as they make contribution but receive a smaller portion. Federal government will be less likely to accumulate risky amounts of debt when there are so many benefits to repayment. When excess debt is acquired after economic corrections or wars, the representational benefits to states will make it more likely it is repaid faster.

The net-tax chamber is an institution that decouples the economic benefit from representation improving the quality of decisions made. Most econometric systems favor the states with the highest tax liabilities, allowing them to repatriate the dollars in the form of subsidies and welfare programs. In a net-tax chamber, representatives will not divert funds from the federal government to their states for fear of losing their office in a subsequent reapportionment. This will allow them to perform more accurate cost benefit analysis on government programs and services. However, this may also result in states depreciating the living conditions of the lowest income earners and welfare recipients for personal gain and prestige.

The biggest risk from a net-tax chamber is the perpetual under representation of poorer states. This may breed resentment over extended periods, increasing the possibility of rebellion or secession. At the very least, it would increase the amount of dissatisfaction with the federal government and reduce trust in its institutions. This could develop into a robust anti-government culture contributing to political ideologies favoring austerity, under-taxed, and deregulated economies. These types of cultures undermine democracy in the wealthier states and put the whole union at risk of worse economic outcomes for poorer residents and diminished civil rights or voting rights.

Tax-based representation should be considered strictly superior to GDP or class-based representation due to its ability to protect against shutdowns and its ability to compensate for discrimination in the electorate. Tax-based representation is generally correlated to population size giving it the legitimacy it needs to justify support of the public and classification as high-quality democracy. This is the promise of econometric representation and tax-based coefficients will deliver. Over-representing the wealthier states will encourage sounder fiscal policy and economic reforms that benefit people over firms and wealthy households. The combination makes Tax-based representation one of the more equitable and secure methods for distributing democratic entitlements.

The anti-discrimination properties make it far less likely that a demographic shift results in demographic violence. It empowers minorities with greater representation in the lower chamber when wage discrimination is present. They will be able to act on oversight and regulatory powers to protect their civil rights and voting rights when a coalition of minorities only need to exceed 26% of the population in order to acquire a majority position in the below median chamber. Minorities can rely on collective bargaining and institutional protests or powers to protect their interests and when the wage discrimination ends, so does the over-representation in the below median chamber.

These anti-discrimination properties make it ideal for nation building. If large minorities are present in the occupied nation, they are more likely to support a government which increases their odds of preventing discriminatory practices and other forms of abuse and neglect. This promise could end secession movements, rebellions, or any other insurgency that threatens fledgling democracies. The benefits to the demographic majority group can't be understated either. They get implicit political power and assume the majority of economic or financial benefits of maintaining a stable and growing economy. Econometric systems of representation increase the benefits to more of the stakeholders in an occupation government and promoting participation and patience in the newly incorporated state.

During periods of demographic shift, minority parties should already have enough political power in the lower chamber to protect their civil rights and voting rights. The presence of debate and oversight will cool tempers in an environment where violence is possible and avoid most of worst conflicts. This is not true of demographic systems where majority parties can more easily abuse minorities by denying them due process and access to military or law enforcement assets to protect themselves. Many offices in a democracy are majoritarian with state wide elections posing a significant risk of homogenous outcomes for majority demographic groups and a lack of recourse or protections for minorities.

In econometric systems different ethnicities and classes can negotiate in discrete terms of accounting gains or losses. The interval variable is income or tax liabilities, which tentatively avoids purely racial affiliations. There will be better outcomes for minorities in the econometric systems than the demographic systems. Econometric systems of representation can alter their political dispositions through public policy which is significantly safer than pegging it exclusively to birth rates and incarceration rates. This lever could divert enough momentum away from a fearful and angry majority demographic group that may be more susceptible to bouts of violence.

The language of political barter is different between demographic and econometric systems. In demographic systems, mass incarceration and murder remove the threat of loss of majority political power. The interval variable is number of persons, categorized by race. This places emphasis on racial properties of voters rather than econometrics or class. When negotiating, the classes can seek specific financial remedies in tax-based systems of representation. Accounting terms are measurable and performance can be tested in discrete terms. This allows concessions to be evaluated with more accuracy where the benefits clearly stated. Framing concessions and compromises differently will have a significant impact on the severity of conflicts. This is not possible in demographic systems where the only metrics are persons asserting voting rights, and this is the both the object and obstacle depending on perspective.

Econometric representation is intended to interject tension into the deliberation and representational process with the express intent of forcing the classes to moderate their views and come to more equitable compromises. However, this increased tension comes with the risk of increased violence. The larger number of class-based conflicts increases the odds of significant loss for one of the classes and the class may retaliate with political violence or martial violence. This potential for violence increases if there are large minority groups present in the below median chamber and they exert majority control over the chamber to embargo laws and disrupt the ordinary business of the state.

Demographic-based systems have a much slower rate of conflict but they are usually much more severe. Demographic changes are also far more predictable producing the opportunity for the current demographic majority party to pursue laws that exploit and marginalize the emergent demographic group. This is how resentment builds and how bad behavior is justified. The primary way demographic groups retain majority political power is incarcerating or murdering the minority demographic groups. In this dystopian nightmare, a majority-demographic group could use pogroms and violence to preserve majority political power and still qualify as a high-quality democracy predicated on majority rule and universal suffrage

The larger number of less intense political conflicts in econometric systems of representation will reduce the odds of a more severe violent conflict. With the increased number of conflicts comes the opportunity develop more coping mechanism and strategies for managing the stress of losing political conflicts. By ensuring a large number of less intense conflicts, it actually may make more severe and violent conflicts less likely. This may not necessarily be true for demographic systems which won't interpret winning in losing as temporary adjustments to household or firm balance sheets, but rather a winner takes all contest based on histories of abuse or fear of retaliation from abuse. The cost of losing a short-term political contest in an econometric system can be evaluated more discretely in accounted terms while losses in a demographic shift may be interpreted as more permanent and be more emotional.

8 LIABILITY SIMULATIONS

The United States is the first contemporary democracy to experience a demographic shift that will transfer implicit political power from a waning demographic majority to a new emergent demographic majority. This is precedent. This is history and all warning lights are flashing. The current demographic majority is pursuing voter suppression, partisan redistricting, and policies that make the United States more susceptible to corruption and electoral interference. They are fixated on debt default threats and government shutdowns as strategies to secure and preserve their political power. Citizens should be more concerned that our civil society and political process breaks down during a crisis.

Older democracies like the United States are far more susceptible to public finance crises than newer classes of democratic governance. There are more ways for a budget negotiation to fail in the United States. There is a presidential veto, a filibuster in the Senate, and a split Congress. There are also annual debt ceiling measures that retroactively raise the nation's borrowing authority after the country has already authorized the spending in the budget. Most years require a separate budget to be passed, and each negotiation presents an opportunity to shut down the government. Due process is not in the peoples' favor. Elections are held every two years in the House of Representatives, and if a government shutdown occurs in the first few months of an election, the shutdown could remain in place for nearly two years until the next elections are held.

A secessionist movement would have nearly two years to organize itself into a new state, with a fully funded military, and its own set of local elections to validate the effort. In the United States, nearly 50% of its front-line combat troops come from the state National Guard Armies. These units are more easily supported by local communities even if cut off from the support structure of the larger standing army. Local police forces have numbers that rival the standing army, with many of their recruits having veteran status and access to surplus weapon systems. The seceding states would have the means and opportunity to defend themselves against loyalist attempting to preserve the union.

A few months into the prolonged government shutdown, the federal government would lose all borrowing authority, and without a passed budget it would have no appropriations authority. The hamstrung federal government could not sustain the military and the secessionist states could easily declare independence, asserting state sovereignty. Before any conflict occurs, a large portion of the armed forces would stop receiving pay and this would cause them to defect back to the states. Without continued funding, the law enforcement agencies that typically suppress rebellions, will be rendered inert and unable to investigate and enforce laws. The likelihood of the loyalists preserving the union would fall precipitously, to the point of no return, even after new elections are held two years later.

Not all government shutdowns start on the premise of independence, but they all invite the possibility of ending with rebellion. The longer a government shutdown persists, the more likely a party is to commit to secession. It introduces a moral hazard where the party shutting down the government is more likely to lose the next election, making them more likely to attempt to secede to protect themselves. Three months into a prolonged government shutdown, the party will realize the consequences and fully commit to the bid for independence. The parties regularly threatening default and shutdown have already considered the consequences or secession and are more comfortable with the outcome. It is impossible to reconcile the strategy with an ignorance to the consequences of acting on the threats of a permanent shutdown. if the demands are not met, a permanent shutdown is a likely outcome, and should be expected in more competitive political markets.

It is also an incorrect assumption that the party threatening a prolonged government shutdown will automatically lose the next election cycle. In the United States, nearly 50% of the public refuses to vote and there is no guarantee a prolonged government shutdown coerces them to vote during the next election year. One must also consider the negative impact partisan redistricting and deregulated campaign finance has on the accuracy of future elections. Lastly, one must consider the fact that the majoritarian party has nearly a 20-seat advantage in Senate, with most seats being found within safe jurisdictions for them. There is no guarantee that after a two-year government shutdown, the majoritarian party loses enough seats in the House or Senate to end the shutdown. A shutdown could easily extend beyond two years, to four or more. It is a profound political gamble to assume the same public that elected these officials in the first place, would then sanction them and remove them from office after the political event.

There is other evidence to suggest an electorate would not punish a party for shutting down the government for a prolonged period of time. The number of debt default threats and government shutdowns has increases tremendously since the 1970s, and both parties remain competitive. There has been a government shutdown or debt ceiling embargo most years since 2011 and the Republicans won a majority of state legislatures, governors offices, Senate and House elections despite for being responsible for threats of default and government shutdowns[28][29]. It culminated in winning the Presidency in 2016[30] with a Republican majority in both chambers of Congress. If the electorate sanctioned debt default threats and government shutdowns, the electoral outcomes would have been dramatically different from 2012 to 2016.

If the consequences of debt defaults and government shutdowns are not expressed in electoral output unless acted on, then they may never be priced into elections. It is intuitive to assert that an electorate will respond to a debt default or permanent shutdown by voting against the offending party, but either one of these events could prevent future elections from occurring. This eliminates the chief disincentive to default or permanent shutdown. In many circumstances, it may be an incentive to default or shutdown. If the offending party expects to lose the next cycle and is suspicious of their likelihood of winning future elections, they may commit to this course of action without fearing the consequences.

When the electoral consequences are not expressed in elections prior to implementation, there is virtually no recourse for opposition parties and administrations. The Congress has exclusive authority to pass appropriations and budgets. The courts can't intervene. The executive branch can't act in any way or it will be construed as

---

[28] "America's Choice 2012 Election Center", Nov 2014, CNN Politics, retrieved from http://www.cnn.com/election/2012-/results/race/governor/,

[29] "Election Central", updated 12/23/2014, Politico, retrieved from https://www-w.politico.com/2014-election/results/map/governor#.XSyJkPZFz85

[30] "Election 2016", Nov 2016, CNN politics, retrieved from https://www.c-nn.com/election/2016/results

illegitimate or authoritarian. The powers are clearly dictated in the Constitution and the only check is state sovereignty. Federalism gives the states priority to respond in these situations, presenting more risk of dissolution or secession. Whenever there is the threat of default or prolonged government shutdown, most of the solutions are on the state level. It has always been a state issue and will always be a state issue, making these environments especially dangerous. There is no way to successfully predict how a large number of states will respond to a crisis. Each one will pursue its interests, to maximize its own electoral security and financial benefits, often to the exclusion of the union.

There should be no doubt that debt default threats and government shutdowns are the most effective way to successfully secede. Institutional protests be the most significant political export from the United States in recent decades. Populism and authoritarianism are on the rise in Europe and South America, and these strategies can quickly proliferate. All that is needed now is a concrete example for the fascists to model their behavior on. The number of debt default threats and government shutdowns is increasing, along with their severity. It is a reasonable assumption that with an increased number of attempts comes an increased likelihood of an event. Every year brings a slightly different group of politicians, under different economic and political constraints, that will produce a different result. Eventually there will be a reference point to mark the decline of liberal democracies in the world.

The culture of debt defaults and government shutdown are a reoccurring and persistent threat. Any opposition party can impose a blockade on budget negotiation creating an opportunity for a successful secession. It only takes a split legislature for an opposition party to refuse to pass a budget and these embargoes can last up to two years, maybe more if they win the next cycle of elections. If there is a budget negotiation ever year, there is an almost inexhaustible number if opportunities for an opposition party to secede from the union. Holding all other variables constant, when the dominant political party threatens debt defaults and government shutdowns on an annual basis, there is a strong likelihood of an event. It must be considered a leading indicator that conflict is looming on the horizon. They have already contemplated the consequences of an event and prefer it to other outcomes.

The odds of a conflict are increased during periods of wealth inequality and demographic shift, and the United States is currently experiencing both. Nations undergoing demographic shifts are at more risk of violence or authoritarian policies. The current majority-demographic group expects to lose majority political power to an emergent demographic group, and they are responding by monopolizing both wealth and power. The demographic shift is the precipitating cause to the worst wealth inequality in the United States since the 1920s[31]. This condition is due specifically to the abuse of filibuster procedures.

The filibuster has prevented Congress from passing progressive taxes, higher minimum wage laws, and stronger union protections that would have prevented the current wealth inequality. The legislative obstruction has caused significant annual deficits with debt quickly accumulating. This debt is being used as an excuse to embargo budgets and force government shutdowns. The number of filibusters and government shutdowns has skyrocketed since the passage of the Civil Rights Act and Voter Rights Acts. Since these two laws passed there have been more than 787 cloture votes, representing an increase of 2000% from a period of time only half as long, 1919-1969 versus 1970-2009[32]. During the last 50 years, wealth inequality has increased to its worst levels since the Gilded Age (1920s). In 1979, the United States scored a 34.6 on the Gini Index and now it is estimated to be 41, a marked increase in wealth inequality and inability to improve economic mobility [33]. There have been 21 shutdowns of varying length occurring since the 1970s, and none prior[34].

Neither filibusters nor government shutdowns were used in great numbers prior to the civil rights movement laws. Now filibusters and government shutdowns are nearly constant fixtures in political discourse. This presents strong evidence that demographic shift is the source for the debt default and government instability. There is no easy remedy. The nation can't escape this persistent threat simply by enacting progressive taxes to avoid large deficits and correct the wealth inequality. Any political success by the emergent demographic group will be viewed as a threat, provoking a response by the waning party to protect their power. At some future point, the political party expecting to lose power will assess their odds at continuing to win majorities and make the fateful decision to declaring independence wand secede.

---

[31] Alexander Eichler and Michael McAuliff, Dec 6th 2017, "Income Inequality Reached Gilded Age Levels, Congressional Report Finds", HuffPost, retrieved from https://www.huffpost.com/entry/income-inequality_n_1032632

[32] Jason Chafetz, May 2011, "The Unconstitutionality or the Filibuster". Connecticut Law Review, Vol 43, No. 4, retrieved on 2.24.2018 from https://papers.ssrn-.com/sol3/papers.cfm?-abstract_id=1730782

[33] World Bank, "GINI Index (World Bank Estimate)", retrieved from https://-data.worldbank.org/indicator/SI.POV.GINI

[34] Tom Murse, May 25th, 2019, "All 21 government shutdowns in U.S. history", retrieved from https://www.thought-co.com/government-shutdown-history-3368274

This section examines the United States under the prism of micro-political and macro-political representation in its entirety. How would representation change in the nation, if it retained all its states and if those states based their representation on federal taxes? This is intended to offer a proof on the assumption, tax-based representation provides a strong check against parties threatening debt defaults and government shutdowns. The states that pay the most taxes also receive the most representation, making these insults less frequent and less severe. Subsequent simulations, separate the states into two equal population groups, with Democratic states in one group and Republican States in the other. The prism of micro-political representation is interposed on these nations as well, allowing one to peer into how they might be organized after a peaceful dissolution or successful secession. The states have a fairly predictable political disposition and all of the relevant demographic data and econometric data is available.

None of these models are expected to be completely predictive, given how a debt default or dissolution might negatively impact current GDP and tax revenues, or how future state legislature and governor elections might change the territorial boundaries of newly incorporated states after a secession. These events don't have to actually happen for the simulation retain their value. The axes of evaluation can be interposed on other unions or nations covering almost any scenario. The roles and positions of the states are fungible and can easily apply to other circumstances, places, and persons.

The first simulation demonstrates how tax-based representation could protect the nation from threats of debt default and government shutdowns. The representational coefficients used are aggregate tax liabilities which distribute a discrete number of seats to each state. The first property to notice is that the Democratic states would gain a total of 246 seats of 435[35]. The Republican states would have to settle for 189 seats of 435[36]. These aren't fixed outcomes and competitive elections will produce results that are much closer, but the Democratic states will have a decided advantage. The Democratic states will have access to nearly 57% of all seats which is nearly equivalent to the advantage in seats the Republicans have in the U.S. Senate[37]. Despite the Republicans having a significant structural advantage in the Senate, the Democrats are still competitive enough to win majorities.

It is expected that with 57% of the seats in the chamber, the Democrats would be more successful in passing progressive taxes and avoiding the circumstances where threats of default or government

---

[35] Table 1: Tax-based Coefficients (Democrats)
[36] Table 1: Tax-based Coefficients (Democrats)
[37] Table 1: Tax-based Coefficients (Democrats)

shutdowns are more justified. With higher revenues, deficits will be proportionally smaller, and they can't be used to justify the threats. Austerity policies are popular in Republican electorates, but with only 43% of the seats, they won't gain traction in the institutions and the threats won't be plausible. Progressive taxes will limit the number of opportunities that can be exploited by the opposition party, making the nation more secure and less susceptible to a premature end from insults to its public finance system.

There are other noticeable changes in representation that occur with a tax-based representational coefficient. Texas has nearly 9% of the total seats which is less than double that of New Jersey at 5%[38]. With demographic-based representational coefficient, Texas would have more than three-times the number of representatives as New jersey[39]. California has only 13% of the total number of representatives and only slightly more than twice that of New jersey[40]. California would normally have close to six-times as many representatives[41]. More telling is the comparison of New Jersey with Florida with nearly equal tax-based representation despite demographic-based representation favoring Florida by a margin of 3:1[42]. The states with higher standards of living and GDP pay disproportionately more taxes, and therefore earn significantly more representation. New York, California, Texas, and Florida have large populations, but lower per capita incomes, resulting in a moderate number of representatives compared to the less populated and denser states, with higher median wages, like New Jersey, Massachusetts, and Ohio.

If the reoccurring threats of debt default and government shutdowns resulted in a permanent dissolution of the Union, the disposition of representation would change within the two independent nations. In the union created by the Democratic states, California with 22%, and New York with 15%, represent 37% of all seats in the econometric chamber and 46% of the population[43]. Illinois and New Jersey earn representation at a combined 17% despite a population of only 13% the total for the new nation[44]. In the Republican confederacy, Texas and Florida acquire 32% of the total seats which nearly match the proportion of population[45]. Ohio gains the largest proportion of representation, with close to 10% of the seats and only 7% of the total

---

[38] Table 1: Tax-based Coefficients (Democrats)
[39] Table 1: Tax-based Coefficients (Democrats)
[40] Table 1: Tax-based Coefficients (Democrats)
[41] Table 1: Tax-based Coefficients (Democrats)
[42] Table 1: Tax-based Coefficients (Democrats)
[43] Table 1: Tax-based Coefficients (Democrats)
[44] Table 1: Tax-based Coefficients (Democrats)
[45] Table 2: Tax-based Coefficients (Republicans)

population[46]. The Republican states will have lower per capita incomes and distribute their representation much more evenly. The Democratic states have a few high GDP and low population states, which makes them the biggest beneficiaries of tax-based representation.

Straight tax-based representation is often included in a bicameral legislature which predisposes the use of demographic representative coefficients or arbitrary representation. The more rural and poorer states would ordinarily object to a tax-based system of representation, but marrying it to a senate may offset the individual benefits of both chambers. It is a perfect compromise, where the poorer and more rural states occupy 60% of the senate seats while the urban and wealthier states enjoy a 57% advantage in the tax-based chamber. Elections will remain competitive enough, where both parties can gain control of either chamber in any given year, but where neither party has a permanent and systemic advantage in either chamber. During nation building efforts, administrators can approach stakeholders and offer each an opportunity they otherwise wouldn't have. Nation building requires tradeoffs, and tax-based representation provides a new tool to negotiate with. This is more important for those nations with large disparities between the population of states and diverse ethnicities and religions.

Tax-based representation is a critical advantage for rebels trying to organize a democratic state. Tax-based representation favors more populous and wealthier states, eliciting more support from the more developed parts of the country. It will attract supporters with more capital, firms with access to labor, and a diverse cross section of the public. Other econometric systems have properties that can protect the civil liberties and economic interests of minorities, making them a natural ally and reliable partner. Local and state governments, along with firms are expert at assembling tax data and economic data, which will aid credibility and support for a movement towards democracy. If these organizations mobilize, it greatly improves the chances for success. With more resources, a rebellion will have better outcomes. These expectations will increase the frequency of attempts. History reflects outcomes more than intentions, and econometric representation is specifically engineered to improve performance during these trials

Insurrection isn't the only path to democracy. Wars occur and occupying nations will often impose democracy on the temporarily subdued nation. The occupying nation may make recommendations to the newly incorporated democracy, but it will ultimately be the citizens of the new state that choose their own system of representation. Having

---

[46] Table 2: Tax-based Coefficients (Republicans)

a number of options available will improve outcomes by permitting the citizens to create a democracy that more resembles their own culture. Econometric representation provides the leadership of the occupied nation another means to organize their state into a productive democracy. They may fear the arbitrary representation of a senate in a state with sectarian rifts. They may doubt the sturdiness of demographic-representation in an environment of populism. Tax-based systems of representation offer the new nation more solutions to overcome their history of authoritarianism or aristocracy. Let them choose for themselves and let this experiment in democracy test new strategies in representation and due process.

These organizational strategies will make the democratization process more effective at all stages of consideration and implementation. Control over these concepts will permit an occupying nation an opportunity to seek out elites and organizations that will benefit from the structure. The beneficiaries of econometric representation are generally found in the wealthier and more populated states and any war or reconstruction effort will need their cooperation to be successful. At the very least, these states will offer weaker resistance to the occupation after the war is fought and lost. All firms and natural persons respond to incentives, and wealth-based representation plays on these instincts.

Democracies with higher per capita incomes typically preserve their democratic entitlements for longer periods than poorer nations[47]. Like other econometric systems of representation, tax-based systems can improve the lifespan of fledgling democracies by over-representing states with better economic outcomes. In tax-based systems, the states with higher per capita incomes receive more representatives than the states with lower per capita incomes, possibly resulting in better entitlement outcomes. When the nations per capita income is adjusted in proportion to the disposition of representation, they will have outcomes associated with wealthier states. The less developed states will have fewer representatives than the more developed states, allowing voters with better economic outcomes more of an opportunity to shape policy and laws.

Fledgling democracies also benefit from tax-based representation by providing more stability through higher tax revenues and an inherent resistance to debt defaults and government shutdowns. Recently incorporated nations are more susceptible to threats of default if there is a persistent war effort or unstable economy. Citizens have less trust in

---

[47] Adam Przeworski, "Minimalist Conception of Democracy: A Defense." *Democracy's Value,* edited by Shapiro, I. and Hacker-Cordon, C. (Cambridge: Cambridge University Press, 1999), pg. 16

due process and the candidates running for office. There are far more ways a new democracy can fail and minimizing the threat of default or budgetary conflicts will bring more certainty to the democratization process. A risk of failure is always present. When the loss of capital and labor isn't justified by a successful conversion it could discourage other democratization efforts.

Tax-based representation may increase the frequency and quality of outcomes for attempts to install democracy in previously authoritarian nations. If the high cost of war and occupation can be better justified with a higher probability of conversion to democracy, then more nations may pursue democratization efforts as a means to make their environment more secure. These two properties are synergistic. Over-representing states with higher per capita incomes creates a tendency to preserve democracy longer, while the culture of tax-based political systems will make them more resistant to premature ends due to debt defaults and government shutdowns. Improving longevity increase the success rates for revolutions and occupations resulting in national building efforts

Nation building efforts utilizing tax-based representation may contribute to sounder growth for the newly incorporated states. Fiscal policy is a major input to economic output; tax subsidies can accelerate consumption and increase profits, while high rates can limit them. Whole industries can be promoted by subsidies while others choked off from sustaining revenues. Associating political representation with fiscal policy will change the equation when it comes to economic management. More districts and states will support higher corporate taxes and progressive income taxes to produce more aggregate revenues and representation. This is very different from the current culture, where individuals try to suppress most tax liabilities for themselves and the companies they work for. The majority of persons will see a major advantage is forcing firms and wealthy households to pay higher taxes, allowing the government to take on more obligations for general welfare and law enforcement while protecting the free market economy.

With more of the most critical aspects of civil society adequately paid for the nation can stand apart from the private economy. With stronger law enforcement the nation can quash corruption and fraud. Regulators can focus on trustbusting and break up monopolies and oligopolies. When the public has free and unfettered access to healthcare, education, and other services that are easily exploited for profit, corporations can focus on more competitive and less sensitive components of the economy. The public will offer fewer complaints about the quality of economy, making them far less susceptible to extreme ideologies like communism, socialism, or totalitarian capitalism. They will also have more confidence in the judgement of their elected officials and government. The electorate will be more moderate with sounder expectations. Fiscal representation will deliver a more capable and sounder form of democracy that will promote equitable public policy and more stable electoral system.

Other nations may prefer tax-based representation that continues to use demographics for the representational coefficient. A macro-political median partition can be easily applied to the United State in another set of simulations. Each state is allocated to one of the two bicameral chambers, with eligibility determined by the gross taxes remitted to the federal government. States are ordered by revenues, from lowest to highest, and then split into two equally sized groups. Half of the states are sent to the below median chamber and the other half are admitted to the above median chamber. This process groups states into discrete chambers, allowing some of the larger states to monopolize the seats of a chamber. There are significant implications when a coalition of just 26% of the states will acquire more than 51% of the seats in one chamber, giving them tremendously more bargaining power.

In the U.S. model, California already controls more than 24% of the seats allowing them to easily cement majority control with another partner[48]. Even in competitive elections where an opposition party wins a third or half of the state's elections, it puts the CA delegation in a superior position to negotiate back to a majority. The Democratic states already control nearly 63% of all seats in the above median chamber giving them a clear advantage[49]. This position is significantly more important than the reciprocal advantage the Republicans earn in the above median chamber. The Republican states may control 63% of the seats but it is distributed over a much larger number of states[50].

With competitive elections, the opposition parties have an even greater chance of winning. There is a greater likelihood that deals can be struck and compromises made to get more bills to the floor for a vote. The smaller number of states with more homogenous electoral outcomes is a stronger position for the Democrats in the above median chamber. This arrangement will pull the legislature to the left, with more opportunities to pass progressive taxes, stronger regulations, and more civil rights and labor protections.

Although demographic representational coefficients are the highest standard for democratic representation, arbitrary systems like

---

[48] Table 3: Above Median Chamber (by Population)
[49] Table 3: Above Median Chamber (by Population)
[50] Table 4: Below Median Chamber (Democratic, by Population)

the U.S. Senate, are not only acceptable but preferable. It is thought the demographic chambers are more susceptible to populism and other animal spirits. A bicameral process that includes a senate, with longer terms and a non-proportional allocation of seats between states will be more insulated from circumstances radical movements calling for massive redistributions of wealth or political power. However, arbitrary systems can be improved by econometrics. A per capita income or per capita tax liability will achieve many of the benefits of an arbitrary system, with an added measure of variance.

Per capita values result in a range of outcomes constrained between roughly 1% and 5%[51]. Most states will acquire just 2% or 4% of the total number of representatives due to averaging out the representational coefficient[52]. In this respect, it is similar to the Senate. Each state receives a number of representatives roughly equal to each other. For example, California receives only 2% and New York receives only 3% of the total number of representatives despite being responsible for a combined 19% of the overall population[53]. New jersey acquires 4% of the total number of representatives and Delaware 5%, despite the two states only accounting for just 2% of the overall population[54]. Those states that pay more into the federal system, earn more seats in the same tiered system. The amount paid in must be significantly larger than the other states to get even a small number of more seats.

Representational coefficients based on per capita values break up the monopoly larger states might have due to population and aggregate revenues. It is the average contribution each one of their residents makes that determines their representational power. States are incentivized to generate larger incomes and pass more tax revenues along to the federal government. This benefit both the federal government and the states that pass sounder business laws. Even when states gain a disproportionate amount of political power, the amount is often more reasonable under a per capita system. In this example, Delaware is by far the most influential state but it only acquires 5% of the total vote[55]. In conventional demographic systems, states like California have more than 13%. These are the same benefits a Senate typically provides but this version of arbitrary representation has more variability.

---

[51] Table 6: Per Capita Tax Liabilities (Democratic)
[52] Table 6: Per Capita Tax Liabilities (Democratic)
[53] Table 6: Per Capita Tax Liabilities (Democratic)
[54] Table 6: Per Capita Tax Liabilities (Democratic)
[55] Table 6: Per Capita Tax Liabilities (Democratic)

When the nation is separated into two individual nations, the per capita representational coefficients have a similar effect. The range for the Democratic bloc is much larger with several results of 1% near the low end and several results above 7%[56]. Most of the states acquire an average of 3-4% so a result of 7% is only double that of the most likely outcome[57]. Only Delaware with 9% of the representation is a significant outlier at almost 3x the average outcomes[58]. For states that object to the tyranny of a majority presented by conventional democracy, or a tyranny of the wealthy presented by most econometric democracy, the arbitrary representational coefficient, adjusted for per capita values and larger ranges, is a perfect compromise. It offers more variance than a typical arbitrary system, yet breaks up the monopoly of demographic or econometric democracy.

The Republican bloc has much more even outcomes. Their range is between 1 and 4 with most being either 3% or 4%[59]. This is a much more equitable distribution if one is trying to imitate the function of a conventional Senate. The Republicans have been the overwhelming beneficiaries of the Senate in the U.S. system, it would be interesting to see if the most populous and wealthiest states in a new Republican confederacy, the same concession to a much larger group of more rural and poorer states. If this chamber is paired with a demographic chamber, then it may be a more acceptable outcome. From the onset, the two most populous and wealthiest states in the new union will have demographic trends that will predictably move the states to majority minority where African Americans, Hispanics, Asians, and Jews have majority political power. This will complicate a decision where the Republicans chose secession over participating in a larger democracy with the same demographic trends and electoral outcomes. Maybe, the question is not what type of democracy the Republicans will accept, but rather will they continue to prefer it over authoritarianism and industrial despotism.

The next method for tax-based representation is the best for cure for older presidential democracies like the United States. Presidential democracies beset by filibusters and vetoes can overcome these hurdles by installing a net-tax chamber as a triangulation chamber. The net-tax chamber only admits those states that make surplus contributions to federal tax systems. It rewards the sacrifice made by their taxpayers with exclusive access to a third legislative chamber. When authorized, this chamber can write laws and ratify laws coming from either of the

---

[56] Table 6: Per Capita Tax Liabilities (Democratic)
[57] Table 6: Per Capita Tax Liabilities (Democratic)
[58] Table 6: Per Capita Tax Liabilities (Democratic)
[59] Table 7: Per Capita Tax Liabilities (Republican)

two other legislative chambers. It will also have oversight responsibility for the central bank, department of treasury, and similar agencies.

One party will always have majorities in at least two of the chambers allowing them to pass laws. This will accelerate the bicameral process and improve quality of legislation. The president retains veto powers limiting the legislator's authority, but this will only curtail half of the opportunities presented. It is in this respect the United States can overcome its history of legislative obstruction to pass progressive taxes and end the threat of default and government shutdowns.

There are two primary ways to organize a net-tax chamber. The first is using population for the representational coefficient after federalist tax dollars are used to determine eligibility. The second method uses the surplus federal tax contributions as a representational coefficient after eligibility is determined. Using an econometric representational coefficient allows state to determine its own political power through sounder fiscal policy and economic decisions. However, using demographic-based representational coefficient comports to a higher standard of entitlement and is more predictable from year to year if the same fiscal policy and regulatory regime persists from year to year.

The demographic coefficients produce fairly conventional results with California, New York, and Texas accounting for nearly 47% of all seats in the chamber[60]. The other 17 participating states range from just 1% to nearly 7%, but they account for only 53% of the seats[61]. The Democratic states hold 302 of the 435 seats, giving them a clear majority with slightly more than 69% of all seats in the chamber[62]. The Republicans have just 133 seats for a total of 31%, but half of them come from Texas with 67 seats or 15% of the total[63].

The Republican states have even less representation in a net-tax chamber governed by econometric coefficients. Texas and Ohio have the largest share at 8% and 9% respectively, but the remaining 6 have less than 2% each, for a total proportion of just 21% of the chamber[64]. The Democrats control 79% of all seats with New York commanding 15% and New Jersey 14%. California falls to just 12% of the seats and Minnesota has an equal amount. Illinois has more than 10%, Massachusetts has almost 7%, Connecticut has nearly 4%, and

---

[60] Table 10: Net Chamber Eligibility (Democrats)
[61] Table 10: Net Chamber Eligibility (Democrats)
[62] Table 10: Net Chamber Eligibility (Democrats)
[63] Table 11: Net Chamber Eligibility (Republicans)
[64] Table 11: Net Chamber Eligibility (Republicans)

Delaware occupies nearly 3% of seats[65]. The other states have only a negligible number of seats, but at least 1 per state[66].

Net-tax chambers do exclude a number of states from participation. However, when demographic coefficients are used, the chamber resembles the current Senatorial disposition. The nation continues to vest vests authority in the Senate despite 60% of the states predictably voting Republicans[67]. This is not substantially different from a chamber where 69% predictably vote Democratic[68]. There is also one very significant difference between the Senate and a net-tax chamber. States only slowly change their political preferences, while participation in the net-tax chamber can change every term. The states can determine for themselves if they want to participate next term by refusing federalist tax subsidies and by maximize federal tax revenues.

Democracy is often viewed with suspicion by minorities as it is believed that minorities are swept under the torrents of majority political will. This is the fear of a tyranny by the majority. Contemporary democracies do little to assuage this fear as most continue to rely on state-wide elections for presidents, governors, and senators. District-wide elections are often restricted to just a single chamber if the federal legislative branch. In state-wide elections even large minorities are denied representatives that resemble them in policy and ideology. It's a winner take all system and large minority groups consistently lose by large margins.

Even when the state is split 45% minority and 55% majority, a demographic majority will have monopolistic control over all electoral outcomes. If there are just two state-wide legislative offices, there is a strong possibility that they will both be occupied by the same party. A smaller number of representatives accommodates less diversity in political ideology and economic interests. If the majority voting block consistently votes in a homogenous manner, there is virtually no opportunity for the minority party to win office. District-wide elections avoids this by giving groups of concentrated minorities an opportunity to elect representatives that align more with their interests. A larger number of representatives also allows for more perspectives and positions to be held by the politicians. When divided by districts, it is more likely that the elections will be split by party, making the overall electoral system far more competitive.

When a senate is paired with a demographic chamber in a bicameral process, it more or less puts the entire legislative chamber

---

[65] Table 10: Net Chamber Eligibility (Democrats)
[66] Table 10: Net Chamber Eligibility (Democrats)
[67] Anecdotal
[68] Table 10: Net Chamber Eligibility (Democrats)

under the explicit control of the demographic majority. This pairing undermines the district-wide representation provided to minorities in the demographic chamber, by subjugating it to the consent of the demographic majority in the senate. The demographic chamber can't pass laws on its own and must defer to the senate for confirmation. When a senate relies on state wide elections, its officers can disregard the rights and interests of most minority groups, presenting an obstacle to the minority groups gaining any civil rights protections or protecting their economic interests. If the senate employs a filibuster, overcoming it may be near impossible resulting, in a low legislative production rate and laws exclusively benefiting firm owners, the wealthy, and demographic majority.

The micropolitical median partition limits the number of state-wide elections resulting in more electoral equity being distributed to minority groups. The median partition also continues to rely on a bicameral process making it more secure than a unicameral chamber. The two chambers will often have adversarial electoral outcomes, setting them up to check each other with oversight. Each chamber will have their own culture and electorate making it very likely different parties are in office. The two chambers will have to learn to compromise on bills in the regular course of business.

The bicameral process typically entails strong partisan identities within the two median chambers, with electorates split between above median taxpayers and below median taxpayers. This role identity will help establish boundaries and moderate expectations between the two chambers and establish a competitive or adversarial relationship. This is intended to improve the quality of debate and laws coming out of the bicameral process. State-Wide elections will still dictate Governors and Presidents but at least more of the legislative authority will be vested in districts.

A micropolitical median partition based on tax liabilities also provides anti-discrimination properties. Tax liabilities are a proxy for incomes, and if there is wage discrimination or employment discrimination, it will concentrate minorities in the below median chamber. When this happens, it makes it more likely the minority group can protect their economic interests and civil rights and reverse the negative effects of discrimination. When a demographic group is concentrated in one of the two median chambers, it can effectively double their representational power. If minority groups capture just 26% of the below median income chamber, they can embargo or boycott laws coming from the above medina chamber until they earn concession on civil liberties and economic rights.

If a nation like the United States had demographics of 13% African American, 18% Hispanic, 1% Native Americans, and 2% mixed race, and if wage discrimination lowers their household incomes to 80% of the median wage is located in the below median chamber, this coalition will command a 26% share in the electorate, granting them a 51% share in the below median chamber, and majority control over the legislative process[69]. In the United States. African Americans have approximately $39,000 average income with Hispanics earning close to $47,000[70]. The median wage for the overall population was $59,000[71] where the median income for non-Hispanic whites is more than $65,000[72]. The fastest growing demographic group found is Asian Americans, currently 5% with an average wage over $81,000[73]. It is estimable that a combination of the income properties and growth rates will produce a majority in the below median chamber, for non-white citizens within just a few years

When the coalition of minority groups effectively defends their economic interests, their wages will increase and distribute the populations more evenly across all communities, reducing the concentration of minority voters in the below median chamber. As a consequence of their success, the minority groups will lose their representational advantage. There will be less distinction between the policy preferences and economic outcomes, reducing the danger of a demographic majority's interests deviating from those of minorities. The tyranny of a demographic-majority will only persist for as long as economic opportunity and wages are fairly distributed to all demographic groups in the democracy.

During a demographic shift, the median partition will deliver a disproportionate amount of political power to the growing minority groups if discrimination is present, allowing them to protect their economic interests and civil rights a representational advantage in the below median chamber. As wages fall and wealth inequality increases, a larger portion of minorities will be concentrated in the below median chamber when they need it most. With quick legislative action, they can ameliorate the discrimination and stabilize the nation with

---

[69] U.S. Census, Quick Facts United States, retrieved from, https://www.census.gov/quickfacts-/fact/table/US/PST045218

[70] Heather Long, Washington Post, Sept 15th, 2017, retrieved from https://www.latimes.com/-business/la-fi-african-american-income-20170915-story.html

[71] Heather Long, Washington Post, Sept 15th, 2017, retrieved from https://www.latimes.com/-business/la-fi-african-american-income-20170915-story.html

[72] Heather Long, Washington Post, Sept 15th, 2017, retrieved from https://www.latimes.com/-business/la-fi-african-american-income-20170915-story.html

[73] Heather Long, Washington Post, Sept 15th, 2017, retrieved from https://www.latimes.com/-business/la-fi-african-american-income-20170915-story.html

progressive taxes, stronger labor rights, and higher wages. If legislative obstruction is unable to be overcome, then the minority populations can respond with rhetoric and debate that focuses on the voter suppression, wage exploitation, and the risk of authoritarianism. Public acceptance of the current conditions will provoke state governments and cities to develop policy responses to the threat of conflict. It will help the electorate, civil service, and political caste to mobilize in defense of the union and minority populations.

Analysts can examine all scenarios where civil society breaks down or where the federal government fails. They can look at the ramifications to the local economy. They can look to see how the loss of federal tax subsidies or the repatriation of those dollars might affect them. State governments can prepare laws that promote tax holidays and divert revenues away from the federal government or offending states. More importantly, the governors can start preparing their national guard Armies and coordinate with city and state police forces for an emergency response. The governors can start looking at ways to enlist large numbers of new soldiers, train them, and quickly equip them. Analysts will pour over supply chains, and look for weakness in their own organization and the other states. All of this can occur under the guise of emergency preparedness, and none of it has to be implemented unless there is conflict.

The best way to avoid conflict is to discourage it with an organized response. When legislators are more aware of the circumstances, they can prepare the public for a quick response, and ensure that state and local politicians have policies they can quickly deploy in an emergency. The risk of loss is not enough to discourage bad action. Only an organized response will reduce the likelihood of successful secession or usurpation by increasing the sanctions on individuals and organizations participating in the behavior. Due process must be protected and a fully aware electorate is more likely to price in the consequences of a conflict into subsequent elections. The more prepared the states are for an event, the less likely the event will be successful, and the less likely it will be attempted.

In an environment of debt defaults and government shutdowns, the most appropriate responses will come on the state level. If the states can organize an effective response to these threats, it will reduce the likelihood of an event. The higher the costs, the more likely the majority demographic group will retreat out of fear of economic loss or population loss. Democracies with state sovereignty and federalist systems have a better chance of imposing worse sanctions on majoritarian parties that may want to usurp power or secede.

There is another significant advantage to promoting a state-centric response. Their response will be more diverse there is a better chance to diffuse the situation or provoke a more moderate outcome. They can defer to the leadership of regional executives and rely on their ability to prepare emergency responses. The federal government may have more expertise and resources, but it may not be available after poor electoral outcomes for minority parties, or after debt defaults and prolonged government shutdowns. The states will have to determine their own security and chances for preserving both their voting rights and traditional territorial boundaries, which may be at risk.

Developing public policy and rhetoric is a huge advantage for those intending to preserve the union during a crisis. The opposition party can't openly dissent or prepare prior to the crises whereas loyalists can prepare contingency plans and openly advocate support for the nation. More importantly, they can expect their civil servants and public to support their policies. They can debate the benefits publicly and expect better electoral outcomes. If the culture can be changes prior to an event, the challenge can be avoided. Avoiding a conflict produces the best outcomes for the nation and its citizens.

The second biggest advantage is public finance. When there are imbalances in representation there are known weaknesses in public finance. In the United States, the Democratic states pay almost 57% of the taxes and only receive 50% of federalist tax dollars[74]. During an emergency, the Democratic states will have significant surpluses in revenues while the Republican States suffer large deficits. Reminding the opposition party of their dependence on federal tax subsidies will discourage many of their supporters and prevent them from acting on their threats of secession.

These arguments can be used prior to a dissolution or conflict to convince more red state governors or voters to preserve the union and refrain from debt defaults or government shutdowns. If the Republican States examine their finances prior to an event, provoked by Democratic state public policy and emergency preparation, many more will fear the shortfall in revenues and opt to stay in the Union. The Republican States only pay 43% of federal tax revenues but receive 50% of all federal subsidies, resulting in a loss of 20%, of revenues prior to assuming the liabilities of a dissolved federal military and other discretionary departments[75]. The shortfalls will need to be made up with taxes equivalent to twice that of current federal rates, before pricing in emergency police or armed forces costs. A dissolution or

---

[74] Table 8: Payments and Revenues 2015 (Democrats)
[75] Table 9: Payments and Revenues 2015 (Republicans)

default will disrupt the market economy putting even downward pressure on tax revenues.

If undeterred, the Republicans are likely to successful secede regardless of which party is in office. Democrats have much more to lose from conflict than to gain from peaceful separation. A default will erode many of the advantages of peaceful dissolution without the antecedent of war necessarily occurring. This outcome results in the worst outcomes. It disrupts the Democrat's ability to discourage state-sanctioned violence with economic sanctions and trade treaties. Most of the repatriated dollars will be used to steady the consequences of default to the financial system.

Peaceful dissolution gives the Democratic states opportunity to leverage their massive economic advantage when Republican states are in state of emergency due to public finance crises. Democrats can use repatriated dollars to support aggressive immigration policies to relocate vulnerable populations from risky area of country to more secure and less populated regions within their territorial boundaries. Democrats can also use economic sanctions to coerce performance from Republican States to ensure former citizens are secure from loss of property or violence. The alternative to peaceful dissolution is economic ruin, resulting in permanent loss of GDP and tax revenue for all states.

The threat of demographic violence in the Republican states is high and there are no guarantees of protecting it, even with economic sanctions or a threat of military intervention. The Republican states will be suffering under public finance crises, with populations protesting and likely rioting. It won't take much for them to forcibly oppress minority populations and deploy force to validate their decisions. Republicans will be seeking to alter the demographics of voter dispositions so that they can maintain political dominance in a democracy. After the split, they will rely on incarceration or manslaughter to achieve these goals.

The Republicans are on the clock. Demographic-violence is often timed to occur just prior to the emergent demographic group gaining numerical superiority in late adolescent and young adult populations. War efforts require significant numbers of physically fit recruits, and demographic shifts result in a severe dilapidation in expectations for performance. For example, if half of all children in the nation are ethnicities other than the majority-demographic group, then despite maintaining a superior position in voters and wealth, they may have trouble recruiting an army from younger generations. This sunset clause creates urgency in the majority-demographic group evidenced by their irrational support for debt default threats and government shutdowns.

The threat pf authoritarianism can persist for years after the demographic-majority group becomes outnumbered by the new emergent demographic groups. Even a small number of ideologues supported by the aristocracy poses a risk. Most wars of rebellion or usurpation are fought by small margins of ideologues. A demographic group of 30-40% overall population will still occupy the highest echelons of the military, political offices, and industry. They could easily leverage and support a fighting force of just 1-2% of the total population.

The United States has already entered this phase of the demographic shift. This is the most dangerous period, where Caucasians are still more than 60% of the population, but represent less than 50% of all children[76], when threats of debt default are frequent, and government shutdowns have lasted for longer than 1 month[77]. The United States has the worst wealth inequality in 100 years[78] and an extremely low legislative production rate compared to prior years[79]. There are no examples of contemporary democracies successful navigating a demographic shift where one majority group peaceably transfers political power to a plurality of other ethnicities. If one looks at number of obstacles currently facing the United States, no one should be 100% certain that both voting rights and current territorial boundaries are preserved.

---

[76] Jens Manuel Krogstad (July 31, 2019). "A view of the nation's future through kindergarten demographics". Retrieved from https://www.-pewresearch.org/fact-tank/2019/07/31/-kindergarten-demographics-in-us/?fbclid=IwAR2KUcxTv4aV7-EZH2kX-SpvEaiYmmGvCfEa-6TjdGwvqzaf4AFaqKqvHNhy4

[77] Mihir Zaveri, Guilbert Gates, and Karen Zraick (January 25 2019). "The Government Shutdown Was the Longest Ever. Here's the History", retrieved from https://www.nytimes.com/interactive/2019/01/09/us/politics/longest-government-shutdown.html

[78] Drew Desilver (December 5 2013). "U.S. income inequality, on rise for decades, is now highest since 1928", retrieved from https://www.pewresearch.org/fact-tank/2013/12/05/u-s-income-inequality-on-rise-for-decades-is-now-highest-since-1928/

[79]" Statistics and Historical Comparison". Gov Track., retrieved on https://w-ww.govtrack.us/congress/-bills/statistics

9 FISCAL MEDIAN PARTITIONS

If the authoritarian has already consolidated power and imposed constraints on elections and civil rights, the opposition party and minority groups will pursue insurrection rather than a lawful and peaceful institutional protest. Open revolt can still be aided by institutional protests like debt defaults and government shutdowns, but the rebellious states will need to incorporate other strategies and support an entirely new government. Tax-based representation can be a selling point for the revolutionaries. It provides several advantages to a newly imported state. They are more durable than conventional democracies, they posit stronger minority rights, and imparts more role identity in the electorate with improved agency for representatives.

New states are more unstable and tax-based systems of representation make it more likely the nation survives into middle income and mature democracy. Tax-based representation accomplishes this by providing minority groups more representation with median partitions. More minority representation will attract a larger cross section of supporters among the disenfranchised or oppressed residents. This can be a critical component of coalition building between demographic groups and opposition parties. It is a known property of many econometric systems of representation that minorities have an exceptional opportunity to gain majority power over the below median chamber if they are routinely discriminated against. However, most political parties are built from many different ethnicities and this only improves the likelihood of a more diverse political party acquiring a majority in the below median chamber. Many below median wage earners from within the majority demographic group will also identify as party members allied with the minority group discriminated against.

For example, if 80% of a discriminated minority group equaling 25% of the population is found within the below median chamber, it requires support from less than 10% of the demographic majority group to overcome the 25% threshold for majority control of the below median chamber. Even in highly sectarian environments, where one political party is homogenous in ethnicity, the opportunity is present for a coalition of minorities and their allies to secure majority power in the below median chamber. This is the value imposed by the median partition. The representational power for minorities effectively doubles when discriminated against in wages and employment. The more discrimination there is in the economy, the smaller the margin of support they need from the other demographic groups to acquire enough political power to protect their civil liberties and economic rights.

This is an important property for econometric systems. When less discrimination is present, minorities can expect better economic outcomes with higher wages and higher employment. As a result, a smaller number of minorities will be in the below median chamber and a larger number of voters in the majority demographic group will ally with them. The inverse is true when discrimination exists. A larger proportion will be found in the below median chamber, greatly improving their representational power, thus making them less reliant on a majority demographic group for support. This representational system is far more adaptive and reactive to adverse conditions for minorities than conventional democracies.

If these properties can be advertised, a larger proportion of minority groups will support an opposition party resisting an authoritarian regime. It will be more likely that a rebel group form a coalition large enough to dislodge the authoritarians from power. Even when there is significant discrimination present in the economy, a larger proportion of the demographic group outside the power dynamic of the entrenched authoritarian will be willing to provide enhanced civil rights and voting rights to minorities in exchange for a successful regime change. All parties face tradeoffs when negotiating constitutions and government architecture. The median partition is one of the more predictable concessions a majority demographic group can make to minorities in a sectarian society.

High-quality democracy is predicated on demographic representational coefficients. Micropolitical median partitions satisfy this condition in both chambers of a bicameral process. States can expect to win a number of representatives proportional to population in any political union forged through negotiated reforms or revolution. This imparts majority rule with the natural checks and balances of a bicameral process. Each of the two median chambers are comprised of exactly half the electorate which is easily recognizable as equitable.

The below median liability group is generally underserved in most conventional democracies. However, in a micropolitical median partition, it maintains exactly half of the legislative authority and half of the electoral power to elect executives. This is a marked improvement over conventional democracies that over-represent the above median income populations. The segregation of below median liability voters into a separate but equal chamber will engender more role identity in the public policy discussed within the chamber.

Capitalism is predicated on individuals pursuing their own interests, creating markets where competition creates the tendency for more accurate pricing in labor and commodities. One of the more important components of Capitalism is the division of labor where more specialized expertise creates values for the organization or corporation selling the commodity. With a division of labor, workers can produce more commodities, faster with higher quality, creating more value for their collectivized labor. Each individual could only produce a smaller number of less sophisticated products for a much smaller net profit.

This is the underlying principle of econometric representation. When the electorate is divided, they can specialize their labor and gain expertise in the public policy that maximizes their individual returns. The role identity will allow them to pursue their own interests more effectively. Their representatives will have similar balance sheets and pursue the same policies. The political parties will have to adapt their policies to achieve success in both chambers and this will moderate their over-arching ideologies and agendas. The public policy product of the below median chamber will have more value for the electorate and produce higher wages and more profits for the below median voters.

The value of collective bargaining can't be understated. Most of the electorate in the below median chamber are employees of firms rather than the principals. They will rely on the bargaining force of the bicameral process to acquire concessions from the owners class and investor classes. In this respect, the median partition is much more effective than collective bargaining on the individual firm level. Firms can isolate union members or employees more easily when the employees aren't organized into a below median chamber. The electorate can make broad sweeping reforms that reach out to underserved segments of the economy. They can more easily pass regulations than negotiate individual labor contracts. However, most will have access to both. A below median chamber will likely advocate for strong union protections first, and then pursue public policy outcomes.

The differences between micropolitical and macropolitical median partitions are significant but they are both a major improvement over conventional bicameral systems. Most bicameral systems today involve a senate which is one of the lowest quality institutions found acceptable in contemporary democracy. All arbitrary forms of representation take on an inverse property to the chamber they are set in opposition with. A senate takes on anti-demographic properties when married to a demographic chamber. If the proportional representation provided by a demographic chamber is considered the highest standard for democracy then the senate is the lowest by comparison. Worse, one can only expect average output when a high-quality institutions performance is averaged with a lower quality institutions performance.

It doesn't make any sense to over-represent more rural and poorer districts. There are more worthy beneficiaries for over-representation. First, minorities discriminated against will receive a boost in representational power until policies can be enacted that eliminate the gap in wages and employment. Second, minorities don't benefit, then none will benefit. Senates don't empower or protect minorities, they elevate poorer, less educated, and less populated states above more urban and diverse states. Accepting arbitrary forms of representation may invite threats from aristocracy and despotism. As soon as a lower quality form of democracy is accepted, it may depreciate into non-democratic forms of democracy.

Senates are only acceptable in the absence of adequate alternatives. All median partitions provide a bicameral process using two chambers that can accept demographic representational coefficients. This allows the performance of one high quality institution to be averaged with the performance of another high-quality institution. Bicameral legislatures impose checks and balances on each of the two individual chambers and the other branches. This is a critical component of successful democracies. The median partition captures these properties while maintaining a higher quality output from the two median chambers. The other properties of role identity and eligibility criteria only make the median partition an even more equitable substitute for senates.

The first example of a micropolitical median partition is the **Unitary Presidential Micro Liability Partition**. It uses a median partition based on individual tax liabilities split by a national median. Otherwise, it is a conventional presidential republic with bicameral legislative process. The demographic representational coefficients in both chambers ensures proportional representation between the states and chambers. This is necessary to perpetuate the highest standard for democratic entitlements. This configuration uses districts to limit majoritarian elections to the executive office. This improves access for minority populations to the anti-discrimination properties of the median partition.

Unitary Presidential Micro Liability Partition

Primary Traits:

- Unitary president

- Median liability partition with national median

- Micropolitical partition

- Demographic representational coefficient

- Eligibility constraints on below median income representatives

Advantages:

- The median partition splits above median from below median populations resulting a higher order electorate with better role identity. When the electorates are divided by median income, they will focus more on the policies that directly benefit them and view politics through the prism of their class.

- The median partition is based on household tax liabilities. It uses a national median liability value to split each state into two parts. The above median and below median are of equal sizes on the national aggregate but are different sizes within the individual states. The representational ratios produced by the uneven division of an electorate will still be in a range far lower than the difference in representational ratios between states using a conventional senate. The different sized electorates will contribute to a more partisan identity for states, One of the two electorates will have numerical superiority in gubernatorial elections and demonstrate a preference in presidential elections. This adds flavor to the political identity of the state or nation and may have benefits in coalition formation.

- One of the more important properties of a micropolitical partition is its anti-discriminatory properties. If discrimination is present, the minority group suffering income discrimination will be over-represented in the below median chamber until the abuses is corrected. This will make it more likely the nation acquires stronger civil liberties, labor rights, and voting rights. Minorities will be able to protect themselves with due process, debate, and passing reforms making it safer and more equitable than other flawed or lower quality democracies.

- The anti-discriminatory properties of a micropolitical partition are changed by using the national median liability. If discrimination is present in poorer states, a larger number of the affected minorities will be concentrated within the below median chamber. This will be a significant benefit to minorities across the whole nation. However, minorities in wealthier states may have higher wages, and despite suffering similar rates of discrimination, may earn smaller concentrations in the below median chamber.

- The eligibility threshold for the below median chamber is tethered to the median liability for all tax payers in nation. This improves agency between the legislator and their constituents when their financial interests are aligned. In order for a legislator to acquire financial security they will have to write laws that benefit the other median voters. This will result in higher-quality legislation for below median income earners. Using the national median imbues some flexibility into the representational system. In states with lower standards of living, the elected officials have slightly higher incomes attracting better educated and candidates with stronger employment histories. In states with higher standards of living, the representatives will have lower incomes and the more competitive environment will incentivize them to pursue more aggressive interventions and policies. Each state has both a below median and above median chamber, so representations will have room for advancement within the legislature.

- Eligibility is determined by term. If the term of the office is 6 years then eligibility is determined by an average of 6 years tax returns. If the average exceeds the median value for the nation, the representative must vacate their office at the end of their term. Once disqualified, the representative must wait for one full term to test eligibility again. A voter is assigned to the below median electorate if their tax liabilities are below the national median and reassigned to the above median electorate when it exceeds the median. This will effectively align interests between the constituents and their representatives resulting in more role identity and the passage of higher quality laws.

- The number of representatives apportioned to each state are proportional to their populations. The above median and below median chambers get an equal number of representatives despite any differences in electorate sizes due to the imposition of the national median. Each representative faces a district-wide election with all voters from either the below median or above median electorate participating.

Disadvantages:

- Class-based rhetoric might provoke more institutional protests. Hopefully this results in more economic reforms passing but it could also result in more incidents like government shutdowns and debt defaults or wars.

- Each chamber will split their members into 3 groups, with elections held every 2 years for each group. This will present an opportunity for a party to organize an institutional protest but it will be more limited than chambers where all members are elected in a 2-year cycle.

- The president maintains veto powers reducing the raw propensity legislatures have to pass laws. This results in higher quality laws but each bill must be viewed through the prism of class and the intervention by the President will have political consequences. The median voter will dictate most electoral outcomes producing a gradient towards Presidents who support more equitable public policies.

Executive;

- **2.i (Unitary Presidential),** 5.a (National), 6.a.iii (6 year terms), b.ii (2 terms maximum), c.i (lifetime maximum, d.ii (sum of elected), 7.a.i (publicly funded), **b.ii.xxxx (One citizen = One** vote), c.x (direct elections), 8.a.v.b (Citizen), bi.ii (to vote and hold office) c.i (exclusive), 10.b (voluntary voting), 14.1.a.2.a (Macropolitical vote, Veto)

Legislative:

- 1.i.xx.z (Bicameral legislature, 1st House), ii.x (Representative), iii.1.2.a.3.5.7.a.b.i (Laws, Oversight over Unitary, Ratification, Appropriations, and Appointments), iv.1.b.2.d (Independent, proportional, one for one, rotating), 5.a (National), 6.a.iii (6 year terms), b.i iv (unlimited terms), c.i (lifetime maximum, d.ii (sum of elected), **e.1.i.2.iv.3.ii. (liability eligibility determined by median value, full terms, averaged values), f.iii.z (Wage set by median value of income for eligible voters),** 7.a.i (publicly funded), b.i.x (Presidential), b.ii.xxxx (One citizen = One vote), c.x (direct elections), **8.a.iv.b.i.b.ii.z.d.zz.a. (tax liabilities, below median, individual), ,zzz.i.zzzzz.iv (national median, eligibility by term),** v.b (Citizen), b.i.ii (to vote and hold office), c.i (exclusive), 10.b (voluntary), 12.b (districts), **13.a.i (Representative of Population, by jurisdiction)**

- 1.i.xx.zz (Bicameral legislature, 2nd Chamber), ii.x (Representative), iii.1.2.a.5.10.13.a.ii.b.i.c.i (Laws, Oversight over Unitary, Appropriations, Taxes, and Amendments), iv.1.b.2.d (Independent, proportional, one for one, rotating), 5.a (National), 6.a.iii (6 year terms), b.i iv (unlimited terms), c.i (lifetime maximum, d.ii (sum of elected), **e.1.i.2.iv.3.ii (income eligibility by term), f.i (Wage set chamber),** 7.a.i (publicly funded), b.i.x (Presidential), b.ii.xxxx (One citizen = One vote), c.x (direct elections), **8.a.iv.b.i.b.ii.z.e.zz.a. (Income, above median, individual), zzz.i.zzzzz.iv (national median, eligibility by term),** v.b (Citizen), b.i.ii (to vote and hold office), 10.b (voluntary), 12.b (districts), **13.a.i (Representative of Population, by jurisdiction)**

Judicial:

- 3.A.i (Judicial, Hierarchical), b.i. (Judicial powers), c.ii.x.2 **(appointed by the President),** 5.a.(National), 6.a.iv (Unlimited), b.iv (unlimited), c.iii (Unlimited), d.ii (sum of elected), 8.a.v.b, b.ii (citizen to hold office)

The six-year terms in the legislature will impart representatives with the necessary experience to perform their public policy roles. They will be less responsive to short-term political incentives that make other systems more susceptible to populism. However, this may distance them from the interests of their constituencies. Fortunately, the Unitary Presidential Micro Partition includes an eligibility constraint for the below median chamber which will lock in the interests of representatives with their constituents. Below median representatives will continue to respond to their electorates needs despite the long term between elections.

The six-year term makes institutional protests more effective along only one axis. When the political parties are insulated from elections, they may have more confidence of preserving their seats despite an institutional protest. This may increase the frequency and severity of protests even when many of the underlying causes such as wealth inequality, poverty, and corruption have been removed. Demographic pressures will still be present and a host of external drivers could provoke conflict between the dominant political parties. Institutional protests could last much longer than two years under certain conditions posing a significant risk of loss of security when the federal militaries, law enforcement, and regulators are forcibly shutdown.

The **Bipartite Presidential Liability Partition** uses two adversarial Presidential Offices as a check against majoritarian elections on the federal level. Having two executives elected in different years helps limit the risk of a single party acquiring all of the executive functions at a single time. Midterm elections during a four-year presidential term have demonstrated to often favor the opposition party[80]. This helps counteract the inherent defects of majoritarian elections when the party winning the executive office is more than likely to lose the subsequent election for the Attorney General. Majoritarian elections overwhelming favor the majority demographic group and by splitting the executive powers into two equal offices, it reduces the odds a party occupies both.

---

[80] Tom Murse, Aug 30 2019, "Why the Presidents Party Loses Seats in the Midterm Elections", access 9/21/2019, retrieved from https://www.thoughtco.com/historical-midterm-election-results-4087704

The other major change is the use of state median liabilities to partition the public into the below median and above median chambers. This ensures that each state, regardless of its population, is equally represented in both chambers, in proportion to the overall population in the union. A state will have as many below median representatives and above median representatives with two equally sized electorates. This change will make the executive elections more competitive when all parties must sharpen their rhetoric to attract support within the two median chambers. The need for one party to negotiate public policy within both chambers will moderate their belief systems. They must advocate for contradictory ideas equal when seeking majorities in the two adversarial chambers or winning state and federal executive offices.

Bipartite Presidential Liability Partition

Primary Traits:

- Bipartite president split between president and AG/Treasurer

- Median income partition with state median

- Micropolitical partition

- Demographic representational coefficient

- Eligibility constraints on below median income representatives

Advantages:

- The median partition splits above median from below median populations resulting two nearly homogenous populations based on class. They will be able to identify role models more accurately and policies that support their specific economic interests. Tax-laws are more easily manipulated than incomes, resulting in more control features over the electorate and eligibility criteria.

- Not all incomes are equivalent. Fiscal policy could be used to send one type of income earner to the below median liability chamber while other types are elevated to the above median liability chamber. If one type of income is more prevalent in one demographic group and not another, it may be a form of discrimination to target those groups. However, if it can be diagnosed, it can also be treated.

- The median partition is based on household liabilities. It uses a state median income value to split each state into two parts. The method will produce two equally sized electorates in each state resulting in equivalent representational ratios. No class has a numerical advantage in gubernatorial elections or presidential elections. The parity may contribute to a culture of concessions and compromises accelerating the rate of passed laws and improving their quality.

- The liability threshold for the below median chamber is dependent on the household median liability for all tax payers in state. The below median representatives will share more economic concerns with the below median electorate producing a strong check on the owners and investors classes. Most contemporary legislators naturally align themselves with the owners class and elites of the nation resulting in a reduced number of economic reforms benefiting the lower class and middle class. When eligibility criteria for holding office is established, it strengthens the connection between elected officials and their electorate, result in lower wealth inequality and a more equitable distribution of public goods within the economy

- Term lengths and limits are important but role identity is more important. When the electorate has access to education, healthcare, and higher incomes they will exhibit sounder judgement. This will change the expected electoral outcomes and shape the culture of the country. People tend to base their political expectations on the laws passed rather than anything else. Obstructed legislative environments produce different cultures than efficient ones. Histories of successful reform will build trust in the government while the lack of reform will produce contempt and mistrust of the government.

- The anti-discriminatory properties of a micropolitical median partition are preserved by state-based medians. Liabilities in each state are compared to the median liability of each state to determine which chamber voters participate it. This is a more accurate evaluation and will produce the intended anti-discriminatory effects when wage or income discrimination is present.

- The bipartite presidential office introduces a significant advantage over unitary executives if used in conjunction with a median partition. When the two bipartite presidents are in agreement, they can confirm laws passed by a single chamber. This improves the rate and quality of laws passed. Even a small increase in the number of laws passed could have a tremendously positive impact on lifestyle quality for residents. This is true for both contemporary legislatures and median partitions but class-based systems may benefit more due to the role identity and improved agency in the below median chamber.

- Splitting the presidential office into two parts allows opposition parties more opportunity to gain office when in the minority of one or both legislative chambers. This is a significant check on power for a political system that is premised on class tensions. More revolving pieces will result in more successful elections for all parties and classes.

- The bipartite presidential offices are not constrained by the median partition and the nation votes as a whole for each candidate. This bypasses any class tensions when voting for the two executive offices.

- The salaries of the above median representatives is not determined by the median household income for the jurisdiction. Therefore, the above median income chamber will have much higher salaries. This will create an incentive for below median representatives to relocate to the above median chamber to improve their economic outcomes. If more below median representatives leave office for highly paid jobs, it frees up more seats making the chamber more responsive to current political demands. This may make the nation more susceptible to populism but this will already be priced into the class-based system of represtenation.

Disadvantages:

- Both chambers in the median partition have 2-year terms where all representatives are chosen each election cycle. The elections are staged so an entire chamber is elected every year. When one chamber is elected, the other chamber has their safe year. This improves accountability in the chambers by making them more responsive to the electorate. On the flip side, it does make the nation more susceptible to populism and institutional protests. With access to new elections and new majorities every year, a minority party will see opportunity in shutting down the government for an entire year. This could help mitigate the risk of authoritarianism, but if the nation is suffering from populist attacks on the median and democratic institutions, the more frequent elections could increase the risk.

- Splitting the Executive branch into two offices increases the odds of conflict between the political parties. A single executive may discourage dissent in a winner take all system while a bipartite executive gives a minority party recourse with an institutional protest supported by militias or militaries. The President may control the army, air force, and intelligence agencies but the Attorney General can marshal the federal law enforcement agencies, coordinate with the state national guard armies, and organize the local militia groups (police departments). Both executives have the capacity to defend their constituents and possession of the offices will rotate between the political parties. This is an exceptional check on the potential loss of democracy by usurpation but it also increases the odds of conflict.

Executive;

- 2.ii.x.c. (**Executive Presidential**), 5.a (National), 6.a.i (6 year terms), b.ii (1 terms maximum), c.i (lifetime maximum), d.ii (sum of elected), **7.a.i, b.i., ii.xxxx, c.x (publicly funded, presidential, one person = one vote, direct elections)**, b.i.ii (eligibility for voting and holding office), 10.b (voluntary voting), 14.1.a.2.a.b (Macropolitical vote, Veto and Confirmation)

- 2.ii.x.cc.ccc (**Executive Attorney General and Treasury**), 5.a (National), 6.a.i (6 year terms), b.ii (2 terms maximum), c.i (lifetime maximum), d.ii (sum of elected), **7.a.i, b.i., ii.xxxx, c.x (publicly funded, presidential, one person = one vote, direct elections)**, 8.a.v.b (Citizen), b.i.ii (eligibility for voting and holding office), 10.b (voluntary voting), 14.1.a.2.a.b (Macropolitical vote, Veto and Confirmation)

Legislative

- 1.i.xx.z (Bicameral legislature, 1st House), ii.x (Representative), iii.1.2.a.3.5.7.a.b.i (Laws, Oversight over Unitary, Ratification, Appropriations, and Appointments), iv.1.b.2.d (Independent, proportional, one for one, rotating), 5.a (National), **6.a.i (2 year terms),** b.i iv (unlimited terms), c.i (lifetime maximum, d.ii (sum of elected), **e.1.i.2.iv.3.ii. (eligibility determined by median value, full terms, averaged values), f.iii.z (Wage set by median value of income earners),** 7.a.i (publicly funded), b.i.x (Presidential), b.ii.xxxx (One citizen = One vote), c.x (direct elections), **8.a.iv.b.i.b.ii.z.d.zz.a. (Income, below median, individual), zzz.ii.zzzzz.iv (state median, eligibility by term),** v.b (Citizen), b.i.ii (to vote and hold office), c.i (exclusive), 10.b (voluntary), 12.a (Jurisdictions), **13.a.i (Representative of Population, by jurisdiction)**

- 1.i.xx.zz (Bicameral legislature, 2nd Chamber), ii.x (Representative), iii.1.2.a.5.10.13.a.ii.b.i.c.i (Laws, Oversight over Unitary, Appropriations, Taxes, and Amendments), iv.1.b.2.d (Independent, proportional, one for one, rotating), 5.a (National), 6.a.i (2 year terms), b.i iv (unlimited terms), c.i (lifetime maximum, d.ii (sum of elected), **e.1.i.2.iv.3.ii. (income eligibility determined by median value, full terms, averaged values), f.i (Wage set chamber),** 7.a.i (publicly funded), b.i.x (Presidential), b.ii.xxxx (One citizen = One vote), c.x (direct elections), **8.a.iv.b.i.b.ii.z.e.zz.a. (Liability, above median, individual), zzz.ii.zzzzz.iv (state median, eligibility by term),** v.b (Citizen), b.i.ii (to vote and hold office), 10.b (voluntary), 12.a (Jurisdictions), **13.a.i (Representative of Population, by jurisdiction)**

Judicial:

- 3.A.i (Judicial, Hierarchical), b.i.a (Judicial powers only, general), c.ii.x.2 **(appointed by the President),** 5.a.(National), 6.a.iv (Unlimited), b.iv (unlimited), c.iii (Unlimited), d.ii (sum of elected), 8.a.v.b, b.ii (citizen to hold office)

The two-year terms in the median partition of the Bipartite Presidential Micro Liability Partition are a big departure from the six-year terms in the Unitary Presidential Micro Liability Partition. Both chambers will be tethered to the short-term interests of the constituencies. The below median chamber will want wage inflation and benefits while the above median chamber will chase shareholder returns and lower taxes. The parties will have to remain competitive in both chambers which requires lots of negotiated concessions. The more responsive party will win more often. The party that passes more laws will be able to reference more policy wins and win re-election.

Macropolitical median partitions are much different than micropolitical median partitions. Instead, the individual voters being allocated to one of the two class-based chambers, entire districts are allotted. Districts may have individualized properties, but by their very nature, they are an aggregate of many different and divergent interests. This softens the hard delineation between chambers found in the micropolitical chamber. Every candidate will have to navigate the intersection of an electorate with more diverse interests and experiences. The two median chambers will be separate but their electorates and representatives will be more similar. A below median district will still have wealthy communities and a healthy cross-section of demographics. The above median district will continue to have blue collar and rural communities within its borders. The concentrations may differ from one district to the next, but the opportunity will always be present in both chambers.

The first example of a macropolitical system is the **Unitary Presidential Macro National Partition**. It marries a macropolitical median partition with a conventional unitary executive and bicameral process with demographic representational coefficients. This system is the best approximation for interposing a median partition on a conventional democracy like the United States. It captures the most important traits of many contemporary presidential democracies and simply adds the properties of a macropolitical median partition.

The partition uses a national median to separate the two electorates. Two median chambers which will see larger concentrations of districts from the same states. A national median will allocate all districts from a state that fall below the line to one chamber and all districts that rise above it in another. Entire regions may fall into one of the two median chambers imposing a distinct identity within the legislature.

State often have limited sovereignty and when entire states and regions are allocated to one of the two chambers, it makes the prospect of institutional protests more dangerous. Not only do the state's share more interests with the other states within the chamber, but states are already organized and ready to mobilize for conflict. The states from the above median chamber may have more capacity to win conflicts but the states from the below median have less to lose and therefore are more likely to start wars. There are a large number of benefits to organizing a macropolitical median partition but conflict mitigation is not one of them.

Unitary Presidential Macro National Partition

Primary Traits:

- Unitary executive

- Median income partition with national median

- Macropolitical partition

- Demographic representational coefficients

Advantages:

- This configuration is the most conventional of all macropolitical partition systems. It maintains two demographic based chambers and a unitary executive. This avoids the representational deficiencies typically found in bicameral legislatures with senates while preserving the checks on each branch. The macropolitical median partition layers class on top of this foundation making the political machinery more effective at preserving high living standards for the lower and middle classes.

- The legislative production rate is nearly equivalent to conventional presidential systems with a bicameral process and a Presidential Veto. This will temper law production by forcing the two median chambers to negotiate and compromise on laws. There is no filibuster unless one of the chambers creates a rule imposing a filibuster, but like all institutions, rule changes can occur with a simple majority making the filibuster voluntary in nature.

- The two median income chambers use demographic representational coefficients satisfying a major requirement for high-quality democracy. Universal Suffrage and majority consensus are critical components of all democracies and demographic coefficients are the primary delivery mechanisms for these entitlements.

- There are no eligibility constraints imposed on the below median income chamber. Each of the districts or jurisdictions contain a broad cross section of income brackets within the electorate. It would be inappropriate to align the elected official with a specific class within the electorate.

- The macropolitical median partition uses demographic representation coefficients to determine the number of districts in each state. Each state is evaluated individually and then allocated to either the below median or above median chamber. The national median liability threshold produces two equally sized groups of districts split between the two chambers.

- The total number of districts will be arbitrarily set at an even number so each chamber has the same number of representatives. The individual chambers will have an odd number of seats so there is always a clear majority for a political party or coalition.

- Districts within a single state will have more similar tax liabilities as other districts within the same state. This will concentrate a state's legislative seats in one of the two chambers imparting a distinct political identity aligned with one of the two classes. This will also be a leading indicator of an advantage in the governor's elections and presidential elections.

- Unlike the micropolitical partitions, each district includes a cross section of voters regardless of class. It is possible to have voters with below median liabilities voting for a candidate in the above median liability chamber. The district may have a distinct class-footprint but the electorate will continue to be diverse.

- There are weaker anti-discrimination protections for minorities in macropolitical partitions but districts tend to provide higher- quality representation. Districts are much more democratic than state-wide elections which allow majority demographic groups to dominate a larger number of the elected offices.

- The two chambers have confirmation powers over the executive appointments in the unitary executive and judicial branch. One chamber is allocated confirmation powers over the judicial nominations and the other chamber is tasked with confirmation over the executive branch. The chambers rotate responsibility for the institutions after every census, regardless of which parties have majorities at any given point. The two-year terms for both chambers allow for the powers to be swapped every 6th term.

Disadvantages:

- The two-year terms for all offices make the nation more susceptible to populism. Elections will be governed more by short term political goals and environmental factors. Unlike many conventional democracies, there will be no foil to the two-year term with a 6-year term. Instead, the nation will rely on better judgment imposed by the below median and above median partition. Hopefully, the issues that motivate the below median chamber electorate will pit off the above median chamber electorate.

- By allocating all of the high tax liability states to one chamber, it sets a clear advantage for a party during institutional protests. A party will develop the culture and attitude that goes along with paying for the majority of government expenditures. They will take the lead during budget negotiations and leverage the sacrifices they make towards the federal government.

Executive;

- **2.i (Unitary Executive),** 5.a (National), 6.a.iii (6 year terms), b.i (1 terms maximum), c.i (lifetime maximum, d.ii (sum of elected), 7.a.i (publicly funded), **b.ii.xxxx (One citizen = One** vote), c.x (direct elections), 8.a.v.b (Citizen), bi.ii (to vote and hold office) c.i (exclusive), 10.b (voluntary voting), 14.1.a.2.a (Macropolitical vote, Veto)

Legislative

- 1.i.xxx.z (Multi-cameral legislature, 1st House), ii.x (Representative), iii.1.2.a.3.5.7.a.10 (Laws, Oversight over Unitary, Appropriations, Appointments, Taxes), iv.1.b.2.d (Independent, proportional, one for one, rotating), 5.a (National), 6.a.iii (6 year terms), b.i iv (unlimited terms), c.i (lifetime maximum, d.ii (sum of elected), **e.1.i.2.iv.3.ii. (eligibility determined by median value, full terms, averaged values), 6.f.i (Wage set by chamber)**, 7.a.i (publicly funded), b.i.x (Presidential), b.ii.xxxx (One citizen = One vote), c.x (direct elections), **8.a.iv.b.i.b.ii.z.d.zz.b. (Liability, below median, aggregate), zzz.i.zzzzz.iv (national median, eligibility by term)**, v.b (Citizen), b.i.ii (to vote and hold office), c.i (exclusive), 10.b (voluntary), 12.b (Districts), **13.a.i (Representative of Population)**

- 1.i.xxx.zz (Multi-cameral legislature, 2nd Chamber), ii.x (Representative), iii.1.2.a.3.7.b.i.13.a.ii.b.i.c.i (Laws, Oversight over Unitary, Ratification, Appointments, and Amendments), iv.1.b.2.d (Independent, proportional, one for one, rotating), 5.a (National), 6.a.iii (6 year terms), b.i iv (unlimited terms), c.i (lifetime maximum, d.ii (sum of elected), **e.1.i.2.iv.3.ii. (eligibility determined by median value, full terms, averaged values), f.i (Wage set chamber)**, 7.a.i (publicly funded), b.i.x (Presidential), b.ii.xxxx (One citizen = One vote), c.x (direct elections), **8.a.iv.b.i.a.ii.z.e.zz.b. (Liabilities, above median, aggregate), zzz.i.zzzzz.iv (national median, eligibility by term)**, v.b (Citizen), b.i.ii (to vote and hold office), 10.b (voluntary), 12.b (Districts), **13.a.i (Representative of Population)**

Judicial:

- 3.A.i (Judicial, Hierarchical), b.i.a (Judicial powers only, general), c.ii.x.2 **(appointed by the Prime Minister)**, 5.a.(National), 6.a.iv (Unlimited), b.iv (unlimited), c.iii (Unlimited), d.ii (sum of elected), 8.a.v.b, b.ii (citizen to hold office)

This configuration can be converted into a more conventional system by employing a state median in the partition. A state median would allocate the same number of districts to the below median chamber as the above median chamber when there is an even number of districts. It would diversify the chambers and make them resemble traditional demographic chambers. Class tensions still exist but the states are more evenly distributed among the two chambers with the two chambers having a high variance in incomes from participating states.

The **Unitary Presidential Macro State Partition** is identical to the Unitary Presidential Macro National Partition except for the very obvious change in how the median value is calculated. Both maintain a unitary executive branch. Both maintain a bicameral process with demographic representational coefficients. Both grant legislators a six-year term but the Unitary Presidential Macro State Partition holds elections every 3 years on the federal tier. Elections in other years only pertain to local and state offices.

It is much safer to divide the states up with state median, so that half of the seats are always found in the below median chamber and half are found in the above median chamber. This limits the concentration of districts from one state in one median chamber, reducing the odds of conflict originating from a specific region. The states are split between the two chambers resulting in a lower order of organization across the chambers. Secession or civil war is still possible but far less likely than when a macropolitical median partition uses a state median to allocate districts to the adversarial chambers

Unitary Presidential Macro State Partition

Primary Traits:

- Unitary executive

- Median income partition with state median

- Macropolitical partition

- Demographic representational coefficients

Advantages:

- This configuration also used six-year terms to protect itself against populism. There is no difference between the below median and above median chamber in this regard, so no status is lost when choosing to run in one and not the other. There are no eligibility constraints, nor differences in salaries, eliminating most of the other concerns candidates may have.

- The state median values split every state into equal parts below median and above median. This will diversify the electorates in the chambers when the below median districts from wealthy states have higher liability thresholds than the above median districts from poorer states. This protects the nation from extreme divergence in policy preferences of the chambers despite the parties remaining highly partisan.

- The six-year terms are intended to break any populist movements emerging after momentary economic disruptions or changes in immigration rates. More importantly, if an executive has authoritarian tendencies, they will break against a legislature that can't be easily removed, replaced, or coerced easily.

- Half of the chamber is elected every 3 years, with both chambers holding elections the same year. This guarantees issues that motivate one chamber are also voted on in the opposite chamber. This will help ensure that populism doesn't grip the nation as easily as it does in conventional democracies with two-year term chambers.

- Representatives gain significantly more experience over a six-year term than a two-year term, which may improve the quality of legislation and regulation. The longer terms insulate representatives from corruption. When elections are held six years apart, there is less need to appease lobbyists and influencers for private campaign finance.

Disadvantages:

- There is no advantage for the above median liability chamber when it comes to institutional protests. Each state is split in two with half the seats allocated to the above median chamber and half the seats allocated to the below median chamber. The states which sacrifice the most in taxes will be evenly represented in both median chambers.

- The six-year terms will protect against authoritarianism: More of the representatives will have confidence to wait out a protest without the fear of losing an election just a few months or 2 years later.

- The terms for legislatures may be cause for alarm when voters have access once every third years. This could breed disdain and mistrust in the electorate, especially during economic down turns or periods of excessive wealth inequality.

Executive;

- **2.i (Unitary Executive),** 5.a (National), 6.a.iii (6 year terms), b.ii (2 terms maximum), c.i (lifetime maximum, d.ii (sum of elected), 7.a.i (publicly funded), **b.ii.xxxx (One citizen = One** vote), c.x (direct elections), 8.a.v.b (Citizen), bi.ii (to vote and hold office) c.i (exclusive), 10.b (voluntary voting), 14.1.a.2.a (Macropolitical vote, Veto)

Legislative

- 1.i.xxx.z (Multi-cameral legislature, 1st House), ii.x (Representative), iii.1.2.a.3.7.a.b.i.13.a.ii.b.i.c.i (Laws, Oversight over Unitary, Ratification, Appointments, and Amendments), iv.1.b.2.d (Independent, proportional, one for one, rotating), 5.a (National), 6.a.iii (6 year terms), b.i iv (unlimited terms), c.i (lifetime maximum, d.ii (sum of elected), **e.1.i.2.iv.3.ii. (eligibility determined by median value, full terms, averaged values), 6.f.i (Wage set by chamber),** 7.a.i (publicly funded), b.ii.xxxx (One citizen = One vote), b.i.x (Presidential), c.x (direct elections), **8.a.iv.b.i.b.ii.z.d.zz.b. (Liabilities below median, aggregate), zzz.ii.zzzzz.iv (state median, eligibility by term),** v.b (Citizen), b.i.ii (to vote and hold office), c.i (exclusive), 10.b (voluntary), 12.b (Districts), **13.a.i (Representative of Population)**

- 1.i.xxx.zz (Multi-cameral legislature, 2nd Chamber), ii.x (Representative), iii.1.2.a.5.10.13.a.ii.b.i.c.i (Laws, Oversight over Unitary, Appropriations, and Taxes), iv.1.b.2.d

(Independent, proportional, one for one, rotating), 5.a (National), 6.a.iii (6 year terms), b.i iv (unlimited terms), c.i (lifetime maximum, d.ii (sum of elected), **e.1.i.2.iv.3.ii. (eligibility determined by median value, full terms, averaged values), f.i (Wage set chamber),** 7.a.i (publicly funded), b.i.x (Presidential), b.ii.xxxx (One citizen = One vote), c.x (direct elections), **8.a.iv.b.i.b.ii.z.e.zz.b. (Liabilities, above median, aggregate), zzz.ii.zzzzz.iv (state median, eligibility by term),** v.b (Citizen), b.i.ii (to vote and hold office), 10.b (voluntary), 12.b (Districts), **13.a.i (Representative of Population)**

Judicial:

- 3.A.i (Judicial, Hierarchical), b.i.a (Judicial powers only, general), c.ii.x.2 **(appointed by the Prime Minister),** 5.a.(National), 6.a.iv (Unlimited), b.iv (unlimited), c.iii (Unlimited), d.ii (sum of elected), 8.a.v.b, b.ii (citizen to hold office)

State medians do expose the nation to an entirely different risk. When states are evenly split between the two chambers, the culture of debt default threats and government shutdowns is equally likely to appear in both chambers. The above median chamber may be just as susceptible as the lower median chamber. The individual states will retain their public finance advantages during conflict, but they won't be able to depend on extra representation to defend themselves. Most of the protections against default threats and shutdowns are only acquired with straight representational coefficients.

The only issue with a macropolitical median partition using a state median income is assigning the odd district to one of the two classed chambers. Not all of the states will have an even number of seats. To remedy the situation, each of the odd seats will be included in a list with its own median partition. The aggregate liabilities for the districts are summed and a median value will split the group into two equal parts. Half are assigned to the below median chamber and half are assigned to the above median chamber. Both chambers will receive an equal number of seats even if the total number of seats in each chamber are odd.

The last median partition system to be described is the **Bipartite Micropolitical Parliament.** This system was chosen to specifically highlight the difference between a conventional majoritarian system and one that employs a median partition. Most majoritarian systems discriminate against minorities by allowing the demographic-majority to dictate most electoral outcomes. This process is disrupted by a median partition splitting the electorate into a below median group and above median group. It is much more likely that minority groups overcome the majoritarian threshold in a below median chamber if there is a larger concentration of them voting in the same election.

A minority group of 30% won't win any state-wide elections if the demographic majority votes as a group against candidates favored by them. However, if 85% of the minority group is found in the below median chamber, they will acquire 51% of the vote and dominate every state-wide election. The roles will be reversed and a demographic majority may be locked out of every seat in the chamber. This isn't ideal but it is much more equitable for minorities participating in a conventional majoritarian electoral system. This over-representation will enhance the ability of minorities to acquire more labor and civil rights protections, mitigating the discrimination, and resulting in better economic outcomes and a sounder distribution among the two median chambers.

Majoritarian systems are a lower quality form of democracy and should be avoided. Once the economic inequality is mitigated, the minorities stand to lose all of the representational advantages and risk being under-represented again. In district wide elections, minorities will still gain some direct representation when they are concentrated in certain towns or counties. This is not true in state-wide elections. Terrible things happen in countries where minority groups are not provided representation. They continue to suffer enough insults to their civil rights and labor rights even with constitutional or statuary protections. It's not hard to image how much worse it will be in majoritarian systems.

Bipartite Micropolitical Parliament

Primary Traits:

- Each chamber is parliamentarian, allowing the majority party to elect their own leader.

- Bipartite prime ministers; One Attorney General and one President

- The two median chambers acquire executive functions that switch every census year.

- Each chamber has oversight and conformation powers over the other chamber's appointment and executive powers.

- Micropolitical partition with a state median.

- State-wide elections for both median chambers.

- Demographic representational coefficients

Advantages:

- There are state-wide elections for all elected offices making this system majoritarian. However, because the two chambers are split by median liabilities, there is a strong likelihood that minorities in the below median chamber will have a majority. It only takes a margin of 26% to control more than 51% of the below median chamber. If discrimination is present, minorities may easily overcome this threshold. State-wide elections are a lower quality form of representation than district-wide elections, but it can be adequate when used in conjunction with a median partition.

- Each of the two median partitions will be responsible for one executive function for a total of ten years. Afterward, the executive functions switch between the institutions. At first, the below median chamber will acquire domain over the Attorney General functions (law enforcement, treasury, and industrial regulation) while the above median chamber will acquire the Presidential functions (military, intelligence, and judicial appointments).

- The census year occurs every 6th election cycle, with each chamber managing five full two-year terms with each executive specialization split between the parties winning majorities in each parliament. The Attorney General executive performs the census but oversight is provided by the opposition party and the other chamber.

- Rotating control of the two executive offices will matter less when both chambers has competitive elections between political parties. Each party will have an equal chance to earn the majority and control over the office in any given election year. This isn't a rule. It is a tendency. Control over the executive offices will be within the grasp of a party although they aren't guaranteed access. When the two chambers switch executive offices every census year, the likelihood of majority control increase and the political parties and chambers will average out to equal opportunities for control.

- In order to provide a check to the majority party of each median income chamber, the committees with executive responsibilities are staffed in a more competitive process that gives minority parties more power. Committees are staffed by political parties appointing legislators on a one for one basis until no seats remain. A minority party can acquire a majority in a committee by seating that function first. As a result, majority parties will control a majority of the cabinet level positions but minority parties will capture control of the committees they value most.

- Not only are there opposition parties within the parliament performing the duties, but the other chamber has primary role in providing oversight over those roles. The opposition party may have more information but the other chamber will have the necessary majorities needed to investigate and prosecute illegal or improper activities.

- A state median splits the state electorates into two nearly equal parts. This contributes to more competitive governor's elections. It also results in a more balanced political identity with equal representation in the two median income chambers.

- These are state-wide elections so the constituents will represent a cross section of incomes. Each office is an aggregate of all residents within the state but constrained to either the below median or above median liability electorates. This provides a diverse electorate within each chamber, if not by income or class but rather race and religion. Diverse electorates are more likely to be more productive than homogenous electorates.

Disadvantages:

- Majoritarian political systems are sources of abuse to minorities in most circumstances. Unless there are large proportions of discriminated minorities, the state-wide elections within the median partition chamber will produce homogenous electoral results all favoring the demographic majority. This does comport with the one person one vote standard for democracies but it is a much lower quality than district-wide elections.

- Majoritarian systems do have advantages in nation building, if the occupying nation needs to overcome strong sectarian divides. The demographic majority may pursue this option when selecting their next constitution and contemporary democracies can't really challenge their authority. Many contemporary democracies currently rely on state-wide elections for most of the presidential, gubernatorial, and senatorial elections. It's not out of the ordinary for a demographic majority to also pursue state-wide elections for a median partition, as long as the constitution includes strong protections for minorities.

- The increased protections for minorities may actually result in worse outcomes, if the demographic majority relies on violence to win political contests. If the majoritarian system produces a minority majority coalition in the below median chamber when discrimination is present, the below median chamber may start embargoing or boycotting laws coming from the above median chamber until the discrimination is addressed. This could provoke conflict. Unlike other liability-based systems, neither chamber has a superior position in terms of federal tax dollars so neither can discourage a commitment to violence or rebellion.

Executive;

- 2.iii (Abolished Executive), 5.a (National)

Legislative

- 1.i.xx.z (Bi-cameral legislature, 1st House), ii.x (Representative), iii.1.2.c.d.4.b.5.7.a.b.iii.iv.10 (Laws, Oversight over Attorney General and Treasurer, Presidential Executive Powers, Appropriations, Appointments, and Taxes), iv.1.b.2.d (Independent, proportional, one for one, rotating), 5.a (National), 6.a.iii (6 year terms), b.i iv (unlimited terms), c.i (lifetime maximum, d.ii (sum of elected), **e.1.i.2.iv.3.ii.**

(eligibility determined by median value, full terms, averaged values), 6.f.i (Wage set by chamber), 7.a.i (publicly funded), b.i.xx (parliamentary), c.x (direct elections), **8.a.iv.b.i.b.ii.z.d.zz.b (Liabilities, below median, aggregate), zzz.ii.zzzzz.iv (state median, eligibility by term)**, v.b (Citizen), b.i.ii (to vote and hold office), c.i (exclusive), 10.b (voluntary), 12.b (Districts), **13.a.i (Representative of Population)**

- 1.i.xx.zz (Bi-cameral legislature, 2nd Chamber), ii.x (Representative), iii.1.2.c.3.4.c.d.7.b.ii.13.a.ii.b.i.c.i (Laws, Oversight over Presidential, Attorney General and Treasurer Executive Powers, Treaty Ratification, Appointments over Presidential and Amendments), iv.1.b.2.d (Independent, proportional, one for one, rotating),.a (National), 6.a.iii (6 year terms), b.i iv (unlimited terms), c.i (lifetime maximum, d.ii (sum of elected), **e.1.i.2.iv.3.ii. (eligibility determined by median value, full terms, averaged values), f.i (Wage set chamber)**, 7.a.i (publicly funded), b.i.xx (parliamentary), **8.a.iv.b.i.b.ii.z.e.zz.b. (liabilities, above median, aggregate), zzz.ii.zzzzz.iv (state median, eligibility by term)**, v.b (Citizen), b.i.ii (to vote and hold office), 10.b (voluntary), 12.b (Districts), **13.a.i (Representative of Population)**

Judicial:

- 3.A.i (Judicial, Hierarchical), b.i.a (Judicial powers only, general), c.ii.x.2 **(appointed by the Prime Minister)**, 5.a.(National), 6.a.iv (Unlimited), b.iv (unlimited), c.iii (Unlimited), d.ii (sum of elected), 8.a.v.b, b.ii (citizen to hold office)

Splitting the executive functions between the two median chambers helps alleviate the majoritarian properties of the chambers only when there is discrimination present. If there is no discrimination, the majority demographic groups will have insurmountable electoral advantages in all state-wide legislators' offices and executive decisions. This is a terrible outcome and a no-win situation for minorities. Either they suffer wage discrimination and employment discrimination that concentrates them in the below median chamber, or they lack the opportunity to elect people that resemble them. However, majoritarian elections typically dominate executive election in conventional presidential democracies. It is actually a major reform and improvement to allocate half of the executive powers to the below median chamber, if that chamber does elevate minorities when discriminated against. It's the best possible worst-case scenario.

There is nothing more sinister than majoritarian parties cloaking their abusive policies and motivations in democratic process. Most elections in contemporary democracies are majoritarian. Majoritarian elections have two properties. They are always state wide or national elections based on simple majorities. State-wide elections will reward majority demographic groups with political power until the moment another demographic group overtakes them in size. This imparts a winner take all mentality, where more majoritarian parties will seek anti-democratic policies to retain majority political power despite losing the numerical superiority. In a state-wide election, it only takes 51% of registered voters to win election. This disenfranchises the 49% who are not in a majority. If one ethnicity has a majority of 65% and another just 35%, the majority demographic group will dominate almost all of the state-wide elections in every election year.

Winning isn't guaranteed but it is very predictable. There is no power sharing between parties. If one political party dominates the majority demographic groups preferences, then most of the executive and legislative races will be determined by sectarian properties like ethnicity or religion. These outcomes may be inevitable for governor elections and presidential elections, but it also presents strong arguments that all legislators should be drawn from districts and not state-wide elections. Districts distribute more political power to minorities when they are concentrated by neighborhood and incomes. This power sharing improves the accountability of government. Minority party legislators will have more oversight responsibilities to check authoritarian or majoritarian policies. They will be in a position to debate and publicly challenge the demographic majorities judgement and motivations.

Democracies should be evaluated by the number of state-wide elections they have on the federal and state tiers. If most of the offices are state-wide, they should be considered a lower-quality form of democracy. The whole concept of democracy is dependent on the belief majority rule is the highest standard for entitlements. However, but this heuristic fails to account for less competitive political markets. Democracies must value numerical superiority as a determinant for authority but too much information is lost when state-wide elections are held. Nations with more state-wide elections should be evaluated as riskier for demographic violence. If the minority groups do protest the deteriorating conditions, the majority will likely retaliate with violence. They should be carefully watched to see if the democracy acquires defects like deregulated campaign finance, voter ID laws, partisan redistricting, regressive taxes, and a lack of corruption controls. If they do, it should be interpreted as moving towards conflict.

Median partitions mitigate the worst effects of state-wide elections by splitting the electorate. When discrimination is present, minorities are more likely to have lower incomes and thus more likely to have majorities in the below median chamber. It only takes 26% of the population to have a majority in one chamber. This will counteract the typical majoritarian properties of state-wide elections and deliver power sharing to minority population. For example, if in 20 years the United States has a Hispanic population of 20% and African American population of 13%, and Asian population of 10% and where only 60% were located in the below median chamber, then this plurality would acquire a majority advantage in state-wide elections in the below median chamber. The plurality would win most state-wide elections in the below median chamber providing a representational advantage over district-wide election which offers minorities only an average of 43% of representation.

In general district-wide elections more power sharing and minority representation with other representational coefficients. If the median partition used district-wide elections, the 43% of minorities will control 86% of the districts. This is the exact opposite effect of majoritarian systems that normally exclude a margin less than 50% from achieving any state-wide electoral wins. Majoritarian chambers require just 51% of the majority to control 100% of the electoral output in less competitive political markets. The possibility exists for one party to dominate most state-wide elections for governors, federal senators, and other offices. If a demographic group suffers from mass incarceration and lack of access to IDs or voter registration, one demographic group could effectively retain majoritarian political power even when their numerical superiority ends and are technically a minority.

Election security must also be considered. It is far too easy to suppress minority voters in state-wide elections. It is too easy to suppress voters in a state-wide election. Preventing even small numbers of potential voters in large states could have significant outcomes in state-wide elections. This is less true of district level elections. There are many more district level elections with many more stakeholders watching to ensure due process is followed. Each district would have to be tampered with opposed to just one state-wide jurisdiction.

Look at the United States as an example of how majoritarian electoral systems can fail. The Senate provides 2 Senators to each state regardless of population. There are roughly 30 states that predictably vote Republican and 20 that vote demographic. The Senate assigns nearly 60% of its seats to a collection of states that has only slightly more than 50% of the population. The Senate is a majoritarian institution that exploits population differentials between the states, and state-wide elections to preserve single party rule. The situation is compounded by the filibuster which has made it nearly impossible for the opposition party to pass any laws regulating wealth inequality, election security, voting rights, and civil rights. Now the nation is beset by threats of debt default and government shutdowns on an annual basis, and the probability of the demographic shift from majority Caucasian to majority minority diminishes every year.

The impact of majoritarian politics doesn't end with the filibuster. If 50% of the electorate controls 60% of the Senate seats it could seriously erode the checks on the Presidency. Look at the inverse, this means the other 50% of the population only has access to 40% of the seats in the Senate. That is a 20% advantage for seats favoring rural, poorer, and less education states. States with this architecture are much more prone to populism. Worse, if presidents are immune from federal prosecution, and impeachment is the only way to remove them from office, a majoritarian senate can make this remedy impossible to achieve. In institutions like the U.S. Senate, this insulates one political party from the consequences of oversight and extends the other party to an excessive risk of impeachment.

If one looks more closely at the U.S. Senate in current conditions, it is much easier to reach a margin of 67 if it is a minority-party candidate impeached, and nearly impossible to breach it if majority-party. Elected officials from the majority-demographic party will not fear prosecution, nor impeachment. This may embolden them to interfere in other investigation or elections. They may pursue personal enrichment from office. They may even commit war crimes and other abuses with an expectation of avoiding removal from office and jail. The odds change during the course of a nation's history, but it is often during the more vulnerable periods, like periods of demographic shift and wealth inequality, where these defects can be exploited. Populism is always a risk but when demagogues are rendered immune to prosecution and impeachment, the risks of authoritarianism rise considerably.

There are other consequences to majoritarian institutions like the Senate. If federal judges always require confirmation by the Senate and the Senate is usually associated with one party, it will move the entire Judicial branch to one part of the spectrum. Without much effort, the 33% of voters controlling 60% of the Senate seats, can impact all federal judges, cabinets, and executive level appointments. These voters will resist any reform or movement that challenges their authority. This includes demographic shifts. They will rely on mass incarceration, voter suppression, partisan redistricting, and deregulation campaign finance to preserve power despite slipping into a demographic minority position. If they see the loss of power an inevitability, they will likely act on a debt default or government shutdown to successfully secede. Only then, can they protect their near despotic control over the legislative system, the judicial system, and state-level politics. The longer they remain in power preceding a transition, they more likely they will act on a threat to preserve power.

Majoritarian systems should be viewed with suspicion when used in nation building efforts to impose sectarian controls over an electorate despite a veneer of democracy. If there were large minorities in a nation, the demographic majority could seek state-wide elections for more local, state, and federal offices, effectively marginalizing the growing minority groups. Occupying nations, could impose a system of majoritarian elections on a satellite state with the express intent of elevating an allied demographic group and oppressing all other minority groups. This could be accomplished under the guise of the democratization movement. The majority demographic group of the occupying nation certainly wouldn't object to these conditions, and it is unlikely the minority groups from the occupied nation could object to the conditions. A more imperial and majoritarian democracy could invade and occupy other nations to set up allied demographic groups in seriously flawed democracies. Most democracies are flawed and not considered the highest quality so it may be a moderate improvement in conditions, but it otherwise should be viewed as racially motivated and dangerous.

Majoritarian system also carries an increased risk of authoritarianism. If more of the state-wide elections are determined by the electoral performance of one party or one demographic group, that group is more likely to accept anti-democratic policies in a deteriorating political process. A larger proportion of the majority-demographic group will see advantages in continuing to support an authoritarian candidate or party as the nation undergoes a demographic transformation. More importantly, a larger number of majoritarian offices shifts the risks of mortality or incarceration to minority populations, making them less likely to organize protests and object to the current conditions. State-level executives can ruthlessly put down otherwise lawful protests, and even the possibility of such a response will discourage the public from resisting authoritarianism.

If a much smaller proportion of the public will view authoritarianism as a risk and they won't protest a decline in conditions. If the people don't show up and protest, opposition parties can't gauge their chances of winning subsequent elections. If people don't publicly display their disapproval, other members of the community will assume support for the new regime. If nobody says anything, it is implicit support for a new social contract defining expectations for voting rights and civil rights. Once the expectation disappears, governments won't try to uphold the law. They will pursue their own interests, preferring to stay out of trouble and not take risks protecting minority populations with less political power and less economic resources.

When a demographic majority group has 60% control over a senate in a bicameral process, they can completely inhibit and obstruct any effort by a minority party to protect elections or civil rights. The quality of democracy is dependent on trust in valid elections and if laws can't guarantee accurate elections, then you don't have a democratic nation. Elections laws must be adjudicated in the courts and enforced by the executive branch. Majoritarian political systems are less likely to deliver on a quality product. When the senate has exclusive confirmation powers over the federal courts, it removes any recourse the opposition party and minorities have in the court system.

The longer the minority party waits, the more it favors the majority-demographic group. Every time a precedent is set for less oversight and more executive power it gets riskier for the minority party. As the nation descends into the malaise of corruption, it is more and more likely the majority-demographic group has the confidence and opportunity to install an authoritarian regime. Each new election brings new risks. There is always the risk of compromised election, where one candidate challenges the outcome, or where anti-democratic polices force out the opposition party eliminating any chance of institutional protest or organized resistance. The one unavoidable risk in waiting for new elections is the irresistible tendency for the other party to win after an incumbent is term limited. Every 4 or 8 years, depending on term lengths, the office tends to switch parties.

If an opposition party waits another 4 or 8 years, it is very likely that their governors are out of office in a year it is necessary to provoke an institutional protest after a compromised election. Any governors remaining may be unsupported by the legislature after several electoral cycles where corruption and anti-democratic policies marginalize the opposition party. If an institutional protest with government shutdown or debt default is not available, the smaller number of governors will be severely handicapped when attempting to resist an authoritarian. They will have to go up against a fully funded and supported federal government when their peers are out of office and the marginal number of legislatures can't invoke public support. As the odds of success diminish, so will the courage and incentives to resist, and within just 8 years (or two 4-year terms) a formerly robust democratic republic could be firmly under an authoritarians' control.

The biggest risk is that the majority-demographic groups can rely on more uniform support by state-level officials like governors during constitutional crises, to put down protesters or rebel states rejecting an authoritarian regime. If a president can rely on a larger number of governors to support the regime during an institutional protest, there is a better chance for overcoming resistance. If the rebel governors are fewer in number there is a lower chance of successfully preserving democratic process. Even the perception of weakness if dangerous, and majoritarian systems allocate more state-level executives to less populated states giving them the people a perception of more tacit support for the authoritarian regime. It's not only a perception of more power, a larger number of governors increases the odds of support for a regime. There will be more variance between regions for support. Just a small number of governors could provide the authoritarian the credibility and public support, they need to discourage resistance.

Governors from more populous states may have greater capacity to resist the authoritarian, but they will have less leaders to model their behavior on. If the more populous states have a fewer number of governors, this increases the chances that they collaborate and cooperate with the regime, there are fewer governors and thus a smaller probability any will demonstrate courage during the crisis. In fact, most of their peers may support the current administration. This cohort won't have the variability in experiences and perspectives to accommodate their electorates. It makes it more likely, that the Governor continue to wait out the regime as conditions deteriorate, looking for sympathies from other governors, but not willing to make public statements or take any actions that could get them arrested. Despots have always imprisoned their political opponents and the governors or legislators from the opposition party will be primary targets. Each conviction or resignation opens up an opportunity to install a more regime friendly state-level official and further consolidate the authoritarian's power.

The majority-demographic group can wait out administrations that don't produce the returns they expect. Every year, their numbers may wane, but they will have plenty of opportunities to elect an authoritarian through legitimate elections. However. the demographic-minority party relies on valid elections and won't seek to compromised outcomes. They have much more to risk, with fewer state-level executives, smaller and less capitalized electorates, with vulnerabilities to mass incarceration and other forms of disenfranchisement. As the demographic shift ages, the pressures on the majority-demographic group will exacerbate, and it will become more and more likely to support a populist candidate that quickly resorts to fascism and anti-democratic policies to prevent the previously inevitable shift in political power between demographic groups. The media and political parties must scrutinize every act, speech, and behavior during this period were elections are an asset on the balance sheet of the minority-demographic group but a liability on the majority- demographic groups balance sheet. Every policy will be cloaked in incentives to manipulate the electorate and preserve power. If the elections are unsound and not trustworthy, there is an even more extreme risk in waiting for electoral solutions to creeping authoritarianism.

10 LIABILITY COEFFICIENTS

The median partition is not the only way tax liabilities can be used to build representational systems. The most conventional way is through straight representational coefficients. The aggregate tax liabilities of one state can be compared to another with the ratio determining the number of representatives allocated to each. A slightly less conventional method used per capita liabilities to create an arbitrary system of representation with a range of representatives instead of a single number. The per capita chamber is a more acceptable substitute for a senate when negotiating concessions to rural states. It still provides them a representational advantage but a much smaller benefit than conventional senates. The last option available is net-tax chamber. It distributes representation to only those states that pay more taxes than rebates received. States that receive more rebates than pay in taxes don't receive any representatives in the chamber. Occupation governments may prefer this institution.

Straight representational coefficients are a direct form of wealth-based representation. They strongly favor the states with higher GDP or those that pay the lion share of taxes. They are a lower quality form of democracy but they still have a place in contemporary nation-building efforts. These institutions are a better foil to a demographic chamber than a senate when taking into consideration or the extra stability they provide less mature and less stable states. If newly incorporated states with higher GDPs last longer than states with lower GDP, coupling representation to states paying higher tax liabilities may extend the life of the democracies[81]. It will certainly make the nation less resistant to public finance crises like debt defaults and government shutdowns in the first few years of incorporation. As demonstrated in the United States, those regions with higher GDP tend to favor stronger labor laws, higher minimum wages, and more progressive tax laws[82]. The evidence is lacking simply due to there being no current cases of states employing econometric systems of representation.

When newly incorporated states give more representation to the states with higher GDP there is more implicit support for the establishment, with more capacity to put down rebellions, revolts, and secession movements. If the political parties rely on the higher GDP states for majority power, the states are more likely to support the regimes during crises. More progressive taxes ensure a larger portion of the population pays fewer taxes. This will help minimize resentment of the new democratic regime in developing economies. Stronger labor laws and higher minimum wages will also contribute to robust popular support for the administrations providing those benefits. An improved capacity to put down rebellions combined with fewer rebellions creates a positive feedback loop that may contributing to extended longevity for the newly created states.

One of the more important properties of straight representational coefficients is the ability for political parties and states to control the representation earned by states through fiscal policy. States will be less likely to pursue policies that reduce their tax liabilities out of fear of losing political power. States will be more supportive of policies that increase taxes when it contributes to more political power. The nation will then benefit from fully funded budgets, with less debt accumulation, with stronger welfare and regulatory sectors. Nations with straight representational coefficients will be more fiscally fit and sounder in their public policy.

Progressive taxes are the best check to aristocracy or authoritarianism and tax-based systems of representation offer incentives to citizens to maintain them. If the wealthier states help pass progressive taxes, they can expect to benefit with more representation. This benefit is gained by the median voters in the state rather than the wealthiest making it far more likely to be supported by a majority of

---

[81] Adam Przeworski, "Minimalist Conception of Democracy: A Defense." *Democracy's Value,* edited by Shapiro, I. and Hacker-Cordon, C. *(*Cambridge: Cambridge University Press, 1999), pg. 16

[82] Lyman Stone, 9/24/2014, accessed 10/21/2019, retrieved from https://taxfoundation.org/which-states-have-most-progressive-income-taxes-0/

voters in the state. If this incentive is not enough to promote progressive taxes, then the simple positive gradient in the wealth: representation curve will help ensure aristocratic wealth in controlled by progressive taxes. Current progressive taxes make it more likely that more progressive taxes will be passed, as those taxpayers immediately receive more representational influence and increase the odds of passing more laws supporting their preferences.

There will be an incremental power creep towards more progressive taxes and this will help ensure the state is more insulated from debt default threats of government shutdowns. The self-reinforcing process begins, where wealth inequality initially creates the momentum for progressive taxes, and then the representational shift to wealthier states helps ensure they protect those policies, and a more durable state is formed with better economic outcomes for residents and fewer and less severe public finance crises.

In tax-based systems of representation, the wealthier states have more influence over the legislative chambers and are more likely prevent these situations. The welfare states are less likely to organize the electoral support of an authoritarian regime. They are far less likely to enforce austerity measures they can exploit with debt defaults and government shutdowns. The nation will have stronger progressive taxes to control wealth inequality and better labor conditions resulting in higher wages and more satisfied constituents. It's not like these situations can always be excluded, but tax-based system offers more protections to the states that make more economic sacrifices for the nation. If an opposition party is intent on offering an institutional protest and committing to rebellion, they can despite all of the apparent obstacles. Where there is a will, there is a way.

The **Presidential Liability Republic** resembles a conventional Presidential system with a bicameral legislature but it substitutes a straight liability chamber for the senate and imposes state-wide jurisdictions on all legislators. This system qualifies as majoritarian and thus should be considered a lower quality democracy. However, in environments where populations are more homogenous and there is a less risk of abusing minority populations, this republic offers a more efficient alternative to conventional democracies. The legislative broker powers will make passing laws easier when parties negotiate with a smaller number of power brokers. The two-year terms within each chamber will make it far more likely that a single party captures a majority in both chambers allowing for more opportunities to pass high- quality laws. The liability-based representation will help insulate the republic from public finance insults and threats of debt accumulation. If the republic can better guarantee minority rights through a strong Constitution, maybe the state-wide elections for legislators can be ignored. If not it can easily be converted to district-wide elections.

Presidential Liability Republic

Primary Traits:

- Unitary President

- Bicameral legislature

- Straight liability coefficients in lower house

- Demographic-based coefficient in upper house

- Legislative broker powers in upper house

- Legislative broker powers in lower house

Advantages:

- The upper chamber uses a demographic-based coefficient and has primary oversight over the executive branch. The upper chamber has confirmation powers over the cabinet level positions in the executive branch. It also has sole access to treaty powers, and amendment powers.

- The upper house uses legislative brokers and allows their candidates to run for any number of seats within the upper chamber.

- The upper chamber uses state-wide jurisdictions rather than districts to increase the multicollinearity in electoral outcomes.

- The upper chamber uses a two-year term to ensure that the representatives are more responsive to voters. The whole chamber is elected every two years making it more susceptible to short-term political incentives.

- The lower chamber uses a straight liability coefficient to determine the number of representatives allocated to each state. Larger states with higher median tax liabilities will receive the lion's share of representation. Authoring fiscal bills and appropriations are the exclusive authority of the lower chamber. It retains oversight responsibilities over the executive, albeit in the inferior position when shared with the upper chamber.

- If GDP parity can be achieved between the states, the liability chamber will regress back to a demographic-based coefficient. This will leave the nation with two demographic-based chambers producing an extremely high-quality democratic entitlement for all citizens.

- The lower chamber has two-year terms that are elected in the cycle opposite that of the upper chamber.

- The lower house uses state-wide jurisdiction and authorizes legislative brokers. This allows their candidates to run for any number of seats within the lower chamber.

- The straight liability chamber will minimize the threat of populism by over-representing the wealthier states. This property disappears when GDP parity between states is optimized.

Disadvantages:

- Populism is a concern with two-year terms in both chambers and the legislative broker powers may transform it into a long-term risk.

- The most glaring defect in this system is the majoritarian elections in the federal legislature. Both chambers have state-wide elections from all seats. Majoritarian elections are one of the lowest quality ways democratic elections can be distributed to the electorate.

- This configuration can be made more conventional by making both chambers elected in districts with no legislative broker powers. If this path is followed the Presidential Liability Republic is transformed into of the more secure systems, with high quality representation and significant benefits for the public finance system.

- Direct democracy invites unbridled populism that can't be held accountable. Sure, blame can be assessed to the majority which passed the law, but there is no recourse for minorities to challenge the implicit majority rule.

Executive:

- **2.i (Unitary Executive),** 5.a (National), 6.a.iii (6 year terms), b.ii (2 terms maximum), c.i (lifetime maximum, d.ii (sum of elected), 7.a.i (publicly funded), **b.ii.xxxx (One citizen = One** vote), c.x (direct elections), 8.a.v.b (Citizen), bi.ii (to vote and hold office) c.i (exclusive), 10.b (voluntary voting), 14.1.a.2.a (Macropolitical vote, Veto)

Legislative:

- 1.i.xx.z (Bicameral legislature, 1st chamber), ii.x (Representative), **iii.1.2.3.5.7.a.b.10.13.a.i.b.ii.c.ii (Laws, Oversight, Treaties, Appropriations, Confirmations for judicial and executive, Taxes, Unilateral Amendments with supermajority),** iv.1.b.2.d (Independent, proportional, one for one, rotating), 5.a (National), 6.a.i (2 year terms), b.iv (unlimited terms), c.iii (unlimited); d.iv (no restraints), **f.i (Wage set by chamber), 7.a.i (publicly funded, citizens), ii.xxxx (Universal Suffrage),** b.i.x (Presidential), c.x (direct elections), 8.a.v.b (Citizen), b.i.ii (to vote and hold office), c.i (exclusive), 10.b (voluntary), 12.a (Jurisdictions), **13.l (Straight Median Liability), 13.h.b (Legislative Brokers, Intra-brokerage).**

- **1.i.xx.zz (Bicameral legislature**, 2nd chamber) , ii.x (Representative), iii.1.4.a.f.5.iii.iv.10. (Laws, Unitary Executive Powers, Appropriations), **iv.1.b.2.d (Independent, proportional, one by one, rotating),** 5.a (National), 6.a.iii (6 year terms), b.iv (unlimited terms), **f.i (Wage set by chamber),** c.iii (Unlimited), d.iv (no restraints), **7.a.i (Publicly Funded),** b.i.x (Presidential), c.x (direct elections), 8.a.v.b (Citizen), b.i.ii (to vote and to hold office), c.ii (non - exclusive), 10.b (voluntary), 12.a (jurisdictions), **13.a.i (Representative of Population), 13.h.b (Legislative Brokers, Intra-brokerage).**

Judicial:

- 3.a.i (Judicial, Hierarchical), b.i. Judicial powers only, c.ii.x.2 **(appointed by the President),** 5.a.(National), 6.a.iv (Unlimited), b.iv (unlimited), c.iii (Unlimited), d.ii (sum of elected), 8.a.v.b, b.ii (citizen to hold office)

Direct democracy governs through majority rule but suffers from a lack of expertise and professionalism found in representative democracies. To temper the wild nature of direct democracy, this government imposes a bicameral process through a second chamber with liability-based representational coefficients. Wealthier states have more representation on committees and general votes, but the all of the laws must be passed by the democratic chamber. The democratic chamber is as imperfect as the liability chamber but each offsets the inherent deficiencies of the other chamber. Direct democracy is less stable and less productive than the proportional representation found in demographic-based representation, but it still comports to the highest standard for democratic entitlements.

Wealth-based regulation is far from an ideal form of democracy. It can regain some authority and legitimacy by incorporating a democratic chamber as part of the bicameral process. The **Presidential Liability Democracy** resembles a conventional Presential democracy with bicameral legislature but replaces the senate with direct democracy. It may substitute one lower-quality institution for another but this may aid nation building efforts. Many more people will have more faith in a system of direct democracy that places emphasis on participation with easily measurable performance. When the senate relies on arbitrary forms of representation, they become disconnected from popular support by virtue of their infrequent elections. Direct democracy cures this defect by requiring votes every week or two.

Presidential Liability Democracy

Primary Traits:

- President

- Bicameral legislature

- Straight Liability representational coefficient

- Democratic chamber – executive filter

Advantages:

- The upper chamber uses a straight median liability to determine the number of representatives allocated to each state. The states that make more sacrifices by paying higher taxes, earn more representation. This method is slightly different than the Gross Tax Liability coefficient by multiplying the median tax liability by the population to arrive at the predicate of the representational coefficient . This correlates the number of representatives to population and average economic performances which may be more appealing to a larger number of citizens.

- The wealth-based representation in the upper house is checked by a democratic chamber with executive filter. The democratic chamber provides states with larger populations will still have proportionally more representation than states with smaller populations.

- The executive filter acts like a veto and limits the populist properties of a demographic chamber. This makes it far safer to employ than other methods of direct democracy like ballot measures or unfiltered democratic chamber.

- The executive filter places a tremendous amount of political power in the office of the president. The president can withhold votes and determine the order of votes presented to the public. All laws will require confirmation by the two legislatures to be ratified. However, if the president regularly withholds laws, the public will likely vote them out of office in the next election.

- The democratic chamber offers the legislature an opportunity to coordinate the federal legislature with the state and municipal legislatures Laws voted on by the democratic chamber can be used to pass laws on the lower levels of government, even if they don't pass on the federal level.

- The democratic chamber can only vote on bills authored by the legislature, restraining the issues the public has access to.

This constraint protects the nation from presidents pursing populist or nationalist policies.

- The straight liability chamber retains all confirmation powers making it an excellent check to an executive office with increased legislative powers. It also exercises oversight powers over the executive, ensuring that the office does not over-reach with agency laws or actions.

- The straight liability chamber has a more competitive committee selection process. The number of committee seats apportioned to the parties is in proportional representation to the number of seats they manage. The parties take turns appointing members to the committees of their preference. This allows both parties to acquire majority control over a number of committees.

- The straight liability chamber can pass laws unilaterally when they have a super majority of 60% support. This checks authoritarian executives who may be withholding too many votes from the public.

Disadvantages:

- The weekly referendum requires citizens to be more informed of issues and to set aside time to vote. This may be a huge benefit to the nation. A more informed and engaged electorate will produce better legislative outcomes. However, it may also be an opportunity for special interest groups and more radicalized citizens to gain more influence in the political system.

- The democratic chamber makes the nation more susceptible to populism while the econometric system insulates it from demographic instability. The frequency of events may be reduced but the severity may get worse due to the ability of state and municipal governments to pass bills voted on in the democratic chamber.

- Smaller less developed states will be under-represented in this system. They won't have significant representation in the straight liability chamber and they won't have a major impact in national elections or the democratic chamber.

Executive;

- **2.i (Unitary Executive)**, 5.a (National), 6.a.iii (6 year terms), b.ii (2 terms maximum), c.i (lifetime maximum, d.ii (sum of elected), 7.a.i (publicly funded), **b.ii.xxxx (One citizen = One vote)**, c.x (direct elections), 8.a.v.b (Citizen), bi.ii (to vote and hold office) c.i (exclusive), 10.b (voluntary voting), 14.1.a.2.a (Macropolitical vote, Veto)

Legislative

- 1.i.xx.z (Bicameral legislature, 1st Chamber), ii.x (Representative), iii.1.2.a.3.5.7.a.b.i.10.13.a.ii.b.i.c.i (Laws, Oversight over Unitary, Ratification, Appropriations, Appointments, Taxes, and Amendments), iv.1.b.2.d (Independent, proportional, one for one, rotating), 5.a (National), 6.a.iii (6 year terms), b.i iv (unlimited terms), c.i (lifetime maximum, d.ii (sum of elected), **e.1.iii (none), 6.f.i (Wage set by chamber)**, 7.a.i (publicly funded), b.ii.xxxx (One citizen = One vote), b.i.x (Presidential), c.x (direct elections), **8.a.1 (none)** v.b (Citizen), b.i.ii (to vote and hold office), c.i (exclusive), 10.b (voluntary), 12.b (Districts), **13.l (Straight Median Tax Liabilities)**

- **1.i.xx.zz** (Democratic chamber, 2nd Chamber) ii.ixxxx (Direct Democracy), 1.a.i (Mono-chamber, straight), 2.b.ii.x (Executive Filter), iii.xxx (federal), 2.a.iii (Referendum monthly), 3 b.ii (confirm laws bicameral), c (Repeal legislation), 4.a (municipal jurisdictions), 8.a.v.b (Citizen), b.i (to vote), 10.b (voluntary)

Judicial:

- 3.A.i (Judicial, Hierarchical), b.i.a (Judicial powers only, general), c.ii.x.2 **(appointed by the President)**, 5.a.(National), 6.a.iv (Unlimited), b.iv (unlimited), c.iii (Unlimited), d.ii (sum of elected), 8.a.v.b, b.ii (citizen to hold office)

The real strength is giving the President exclusive authority to set legislative agendas through the democracy chamber. The liability chamber will have to comport to the expectations of the president or no laws will pass. However, the president can't originate any laws from the democratic chamber. They are wholly dependent on the liability chamber to author laws. The President is more susceptible to blame for the lack of legislative production and should bend to the will of the liability chamber. The more populous and wealthier states will promote laws that protect against wealth inequality and forward civil liberties. More urban populations are more diverse and take into account more perspectives, be they poor, rich, minority, or majority demographic. Denser populations distribute more information more quickly and generally promote more mature labor laws and tax laws.

The democratic chamber is a foil to the liability chamber, but at its core is an implicit agreement that majority rules, and the more urban states preserve a significant advantage in this chamber too, larger populations are more easily organized and mobilized during elections, especially when their numerical superiority is not checked by an institution with arbitrary representation. A unicameral parliament internalizes executive functions within a unitary legislature. In many respects, this is the penultimate government, where a ruling party has implicit control over all legislative and executive functions. A minority party must win elections to have an authority to investigate and challenge the current majority party. The majority party can easily pass any laws it chooses, as long as they don't contradict the constitution or judiciary. The **Unitary Liability Parliament** combines these inherent properties of unitary parliaments with liability-based representation.

The wealthier states have complete control over the government. They have the greatest number of seats in the parliament and can command leadership within the dominant parties. More populous states that are poor are less represented than wealthier and less populated states. This does not qualify as high quality democracy but many contemporary democracies fail this test as well. Democracies that suffer from private campaign finance, gerrymandering, and use conventional senates are all flawed. In this environment, a wealth-based system may earn the legitimacy it needs to sustain itself across generations. The Unitary Liability Parliament certainly protects itself against rebellion and revolts started with debt defaults and government shutdowns, so it stands a chance of lasting for more than just a few years.

Unitary Liability Parliament

Primary Traits:

- Unitary legislature

- Straight liability representational coefficient

- Parliamentary executive

Advantages:

- States with higher tax liabilities will gain advantages in proportional representation. This is not checked by an additional legislative chamber. Those states that pay the majority of taxes will control the majority of laws and oversight committees.

- The unitary parliament avoids the pitfalls of traditional Presidential systems with bicameral legislatures. The legislative output of Presidential systems can be stalled by filibusters, vetoes, and split congresses. Newly incorporated nations may benefit from avoiding these conflicts until a more robust history of success is manufactured.

- The Nation is really secure against debt defaults or government shutdowns by marginalizing the more rural and poorer states. The poorer and more rural states are more susceptible to influencers that advocate for these policies. The wealthier better represented states will never see debt defaults or shutdowns as an option when they are the primary beneficiaries of the system. Even when opposition parties are competitive, there will be a strong tendency to protect against insults against the public finance system.

Disadvantages:

- Rural districts with lower tax liabilities will be at an initial disadvantage when forming the political union. They may not want to participate.

- Unitary Parliaments may provide advantages to newly incorporated states by avoiding partisan conflict but they are far more susceptible to authoritarianism. A political party could gain control over the institution, install their own principle, and then pass anti-democratic reforms lowering the quality of civil rights and voting rights. The opposition party will not have access to institutional protests unless they are very competitive in the denser and wealthier jurisdictions.

Executive:

- 2.iii (Abolished Executive), 5.a. (National)

Legislative:

- **1.i.x (Unicameral legislature)**, ii.x (Representative), iii.1.2.a.3.4.a.5.7.10.13.a.i.b-.ii.c.i (Laws, Oversight, Ratification, Unitary Executive Powers, Appropriations, Appointments, Taxing, Unilateral Amendments with supermajority), **iv.1.b.2.a (Independent, 3/5ths rule, majority party),** 5.a (National), 6.a.iii (6 year terms), b.iv (Unlimited), c.iii (Unlimited), d.iv (no restraints), e.1.iii (none) **f.i (Wage set by chamber), 7.a.i (Publicly Funded),** b.i.xx (parliamentary), **ii.xxxx (Universal Suffrage),** c.x (direct elections), 8.a.v.b (Citizen), b.i.ii (to vote and to hold office), c.ii (non -exclusive), 10.b (voluntary), 12.b (Districts), **13.c.i (Gross Tax Liabilities)**

Judicial:

- 3.A.i (Judicial, Hierarchical), b.i. (Judicial powers only), c.ii.x.1 **(appointed by the Prime Minister),** 5.a.(National), 6.a.iv (Unlimited), b.iv (unlimited), c.iii (Unlimited), d.ii (sum of elected), 8.a.v.b, b.ii (citizen to hold office)

Unitary Parliaments are more susceptible to authoritarianism because the legislative majority also controls all executive powers and with no second chamber to provide oversight. The older and less efficient Presidential systems break more often but they are a hedge against authoritarianism. A bicameral legislature protects against political parties passing laws that can interfere with accurate and honest election. It also provides a check on the power of the legislature to regulate itself and the nation. However, senates invite a terrible consequence when they elevate the poorer and more rural states above more populous and wealthier states. This isn't necessary. Per Capita representation preserves the bicameral process while slightly improving the quality of representation in the senate.

The **Bipartite Presidential Per-Capita Republic** uses a per capita chamber with a demographic chamber to form a bicameral legislature headed by a bipartite executive branch. The two executive branch offices hold confirmation powers which allows the government to overcome the inherent deficiencies of bicameral legislature with an arbitrary senate. To further reduce the drag produced by a senate, the demographic chamber has legislative broker powers letting its members run for the state-wide senate seats. More alignment between the senate and the demographic chamber will result in higher quality laws and more robust oversight

Bipartite Presidential Per Capita Republic

Primary Traits:

- Bipartite president with confirmation powers

- Bicameral legislature

- Demographic upper chamber

- Per Capita lower chamber

- Legislative brokers powers in demographic chamber

Advantages:

- Splitting the executive branch into two separate offices will reduce the threat of authoritarianism in young democracies. When one office is compromised, the public can rely on the other to protect its interests. The frequency or severity of events will be lower after each office sees a significant reduction in the number of powers they have.

- The two executive offices allow them to confirm laws from either of the two legislatures. This will accelerate the number of laws passed and produce higher quality laws.

- The upper chamber uses a straight demographic coefficient to determine the number of representatives. This provides the high-quality representation to use in conjunction with the per capita representation in the lower chamber.

- Although senates can be counter-productive due to their arbitrary representation, they are effective tools for union formation. The per capita chamber is a counter-offer to the senate. They provide slightly more representation to the states that pay more federal tax liabilities but not an insurmountable amount. Nations with stronger economies may demand concessions from the smaller, poorer, and less educated states, which require more tax subsidies. The smaller states are still protected by an arbitrary system of representation.

- The demographic representatives have legislative broker powers. This entitles them to win election as senators from the per capita chamber. They are eligible to run for any office within the state-wide jurisdiction.

- The demographic chamber has a term of six-years while the Per Capita (Senate) has a term of two-years. This allows the demographic majority to be the stabilizing force instead of the arbitrary chamber. Demographic chambers have more implicit legitimacy and will be more reliable.

- The six-year term allows the demographic representatives to occupy offices in the Senate, lose them, and then run for them again in subsequent elections. If the representatives lose one, they will be able to run for another office in a subsequent election cycle. The demographic representatives could hold one, two, or any of the per capita seats available.

Disadvantages:

- The two executive offices can confirm laws coming out of the per capita chamber. The executive must be wary of circumventing the demographic chamber. When the upper chamber is bypassed, there is no consent by the majority.

- Giving the legislative broker powers to the demographic representatives will extend their terms by keeping them in office beyond years they lose election. They could lose the demographic chamber and win a one more per capita chamber elections, putting them back in the running for the same demographic seat.

Executive;
- 2.ii.x.c. (**Executive Presidential**), 5.a (National), 6.a.iii (6 year terms), b.i (1 terms maximum), c.i (lifetime maximum),

d.ii (sum of elected), **7.a.i, b.i., ii.xxxx, c.x (publicly funded, presidential, one person = one vote, direct elections),** b.i.ii (eligibility for voting and holding office), 10.b (voluntary voting), 14.1.a.2.b (Executive, Confirmation)

- 2.ii.x.cc.ccc **(Executive Attorney General and Treasury),** 5.a (National), 6.a.iii (6 year terms), b.ii (2 terms maximum), c.i (lifetime maximum), d.ii (sum of elected), **7.a.i, b.i., ii.xxxx, c.x (publicly funded, presidential, one person = one vote, direct elections),** 8.a.v.b (Citizen), b.i.ii (eligibility for voting and holding office), 10.b (voluntary voting), 14.1.a.2.b (Executive, Confirmation)

Legislative:

- **1.i.xx.zz (Bicameral legislature,** 2nd chamber) , ii.x (Representative), iii.1.2.a.5.10.13 (Laws, Oversight, Appropriations, Taxing, and Amendments), **iv.1.b.2.d (Independent, proportional, one by one, rotating),** 5.a (National), 6.a.iii (6 year terms), b.iv (unlimited terms), **f.i (Wages set by chamber),** c.iii (Unlimited), d.iv (no restraints), **7.a.i (Publicly Funded)** b.i.x (Presidential), c.x (direct elections), 8.a.v.b (Citizen), b.i.ii (to vote and to hold office), c.ii (non -exclusive), 10.b (voluntary), 12.a (districts), **13.a.i (Representative of Population), 13.h.b (Legislative Brokers, Inter-brokerage).**

- 1.i.xx.zz (Bicameral legislature, Senate), ii.x (Representative), **iii.1.2.3.7.a.b.i.13.a.ii.b.ii.c.i (Laws, Oversight, Ratification, Appointments),** iv.1.b.2.a (Independent, 3/5th rule, majority party), 5.a (National), 6.a.i (2 year **terms**), b.iv (unlimited terms), c.iii (unlimited); d.iv (no restraints), **f.i (Wage set by chamber), 7.a.i (publicly funded, citizens),** b.i.x (Presidential), **ii.xxxx (Universal Suffrage),** c.x (direct elections), 8.a.v.b (Citizen), b.i.ii (to vote and hold office), c.i (exclusive), 10.b (voluntary), 12.a (Jurisdictions), **13.j.iv.b (Senatorial, per capita)**

Judicial:

- 3.a.i (Judicial, Hierarchical), b.i.a (Judicial powers only, general), c.ii.x.2 **(appointed by the President),** 5.a.(National), 6.a.iv (Unlimited), b.iv (unlimited), c.iii

(Unlimited), d.ii (sum of elected), 8.a.v.b, b.ii (citizen to hold office)

Per capita chambers are only slightly more accurate than conventional senates. Political architects should avoid them unless absolutely necessary during the negotiation phase of the nation-building efforts. Nation-building is often made of concessions and the per capita senate is still a better answer than a conventional senate. There will be enough variation in the apportionment of senators to reduce the advantage rural states have over urban states but the institution won't have anywhere near proportional representation. Most states will still fall within the range of 1-3 senators producing a nearly arbitrary system of representation.

Per capita senates remain a lower quality democratic institution and will expose the nation to risks of populism, authoritarianism, wealth inequality, and the threats of default and government shutdown that accompany them. The per capita Senate will still be an easily exploitable weakness that may result in long periods of legislative obstruction, poor performance e during impeachments, and imbalanced judicial appointments. The per capita senate will continue to provide rural and poorer states a representational advantage. Per capita senates don't provide the nation any extra protection from debt default threats and government shutdowns, except for a slight modification in arbitrary representation.

Debt defaults and government shutdowns introduce probable outcomes that can abruptly end the authority of a government. Their presence indicates a tolerance for outcomes that include a premature dissolution of the nation. The best metaphor is suicide. When an individual considers suicide, just the prospect of an attempt can change the decision process making it more likely. Bad outcomes have an attractive force, especially if they are permanent and product of public policy. While, many people have diminished inhibition, larger groups of people had even fewer inhibitions. Electorates are especially susceptible to these suicidal episodes and ideation because the consequences are distributed among a large and diverse population, with blame obfuscated through due process.

There are public policy solutions to threats of default and government shutdown. By making two simple changes, democratic nations can better ensure their own durability. The first act of a new legislature should be to eliminate a debt ceiling measure if one exists. It is unnecessary and dangerous. If the spending was previously authorized by the legislature, then there should be no second authorization necessary. The debt ceiling can be automatically raised afterward. Government shutdowns can also be eliminated. If the legislature can't decide on a new budget deal, the prior year's budget should be extended with funding levels increased by the inflation rate. This eliminates most of the risk of failed budget negotiations and gives ample opportunity for the parties to negotiate new terms. By eliminating the threat of violence, it will force both parties to the negotiating table and more substantive agreements will be reached.

If the budget is not indexed to inflation, there are incentives to not agree to budgets in order to cut spending across the board. A party could refuse to budget negotiations for 4 years and capture 10-15% cuts to all programs. This overwhelmingly benefits political parties pursuing austerity measures and those trying to deregulate the economy and eliminate the government as a viable alternative to the private sector. Indexing budgets by inflation is a neutral position that only preserves the current spending previously agreed to by the parties. Indexed budgets still provide debt relief by increasing slower than the growth in the economy. A larger economy should produce larger tax revenues which can be used to repay debt faster than if it were simply depreciated through inflation.

Parties will still have an opportunity to reduce spending and change priorities but it will take positive control and require majorities in the legislature to enforce. This is an expected outcome in most contemporary democracies. Most laws are passed with majorities and this should include budgetary laws. It would be absurd if that changes to the laws and programs require majorities to pass, but the budget itself is negotiated through threats and failures in due process. Budget negotiations occur every year and disdain will build after every shutdown. Resentment will make parties less likely to make concessions and the tension will become more severe. By eliminating the two most frequent sources of conflict, the nation makes it more likely that the parties negotiate and accept the terms of agreements. When the risk of default or permanent shut down is eliminated, the parties will act more rationally and make more investments into the future of the nation.

These budgetary changes increase the risk of authoritarian creep. Without a government shutdown, an opposition party can't protect their voting rights and civil rights. The automatic budgets will ensure the government runs for years even without the consent of an opposition party. Within just a short period, the despot can install their agents in most agencies and judicial circuits. Elections become dangerous misadventures when the legislature can't regulate the process and the federal government refuses to enforce laws. The opposition party will eventually find themselves on the wrong side of an election cycle and they may never recover.

Most democracies should not have automatic budgetary systems. The risk of authoritarianism is too great. Nations can go decades or hundreds of years without the political parties threatening dissolution through defaults and shutdowns. These risks are very infrequent, which is one of the reasons why they are leading indicators of conflict. Nations suffering under a demographic shift or significant wealth inequality are more at risk of conflict and will experience reoccurring threats of default and government shut down typically present. Most nations will only experience a single threat of default during an economic crisis. Usually, the crises subside and the threats aren't acted on. If a political party fears marginalization after a demographic shift, they may act on those threats to preserve political power. The frequency and severity of threats always depends on context. The cure is worse than the disease. Instead of eliminating the risk of secession, automatic budgetary systems embolden authoritarians who can't be forcibly removed by institutional protests.

One of the ways a nation can protect itself from debt default threats from populist parties is incorporating a third legislative chamber that apportions representatives proportional to the amount of surplus revenues they donate to the federal system. States must receive fewer federal subsidies than tax dollars contributed in order to sit within the chamber. This will give them an opportunity to shape the nation into an image of itself. The donor states will earn representation in a triangulation chamber that is only authorized to pass laws originating from either of the two other chambers. The net-tax chamber will also regulate agencies or institutions related to appropriations, public finance, and central banking.

The **Presidential Tax Republic** overlays a Net-tax chamber over a conventional bicameral presidential republic. It marries a demographic chamber and senate with a net-tax chamber to improve the legislative production rate and insulate the nation from threats of default and government shutdown. The senate remains an arbitrary form of representation, favoring the poorer and less populated states, but it is implicitly checked by the net-tax chamber favoring the wealthier and typically more diverse states. The demographic chamber will remain the primary legislative chamber by virtue of implicit popular support. Democracy is predicated on majority rule and the net-tax chamber protects the nation from abuses stemming from the senate.

Presidential Net Tax Republic

Primary Traits:

- President with Veto powers

- Multi-cameral legislature

- Demographic upper chamber

- Arbitrary lower chamber

- Net-Tax Chamber with triangulation powers

Advantages:

- The three legislative chambers ensure that a political party will have a majority in at least two chambers every year (in most two-party systems). There will never be an occasion where the bicameral legislature is split between two parties and no laws can be passed. This should not be confused with the 100% legislative production rate found in unitary parliaments. The president maintains veto powers and in at least half of the electoral outcomes, allowing the executive office to check the legislature.

- The upper and lower houses in the legislature have two-year terms for their representatives. This allows for all of the representatives or senators to be elected in a single year. The political markets will be more responsive and more accurately reflect popular sentiments. For better or for worse, short term political incentives will have a significant impact on elections.

- The two-year terms in upper and lower houses allow for a full election in each chamber every alternating year. So, every year offers the electorate an opportunity to change the current political disposition of the legislature.

- The net-tax chamber is intended to be less responsive and its elected representatives have 4-year terms. This is more acceptable because the Net-Tax chamber can only pass laws that originated in either of the two other chambers.

- The net-tax chamber has limited oversight powers over Treasury related issues, the Central Bank, and all matters pertaining to taxes, appropriations, and subsidies. It has no authority to investigate other federal agencies. It doesn't contribute to the confirmation of judges or cabinet-level officials. Nor is it involved in treaty ratification.

- In the year of the census, an accounting audit of federal taxes paid versus federal subsidies earned is conducted. The number of representatives allocated to each seat depends on the result of the audit. If a state is to lose a seat, those seats with elections the same year are eliminated first. If a seat is to be eliminated and there is a current incumbent, the seat remains until the next election where it is simply not refilled.

- The senate preserves an arbitrary system of representation, giving an advantage to the less populated states. This checks the natural advantages earned by the wealthier states with a net-tax chamber. The two will counteract each other, and working in concert, produce a 50% raw propensity for passing laws.

- This Republic is extremely resistant to threats of debt default and government shutdown. The states that pay the majority of taxes will have the greatest probability of passing laws to ensure highly progressive taxes, balanced budgets, and protect voting rights and civil rights.

Disadvantages:

- The senate is a majoritarian chamber and retains exclusive appointment confirmation powers over the judiciary and presidential cabinets. This is a source of weakness that could be exploited by parties looking to take advantage of voters in poorer and less educated states.

Executive;
- **2.i (Unitary Executive),** 5.a (National), 6.a.iii (6 year terms), b.ii (2 terms maximum), c.i (lifetime maximum, d.ii (sum of elected), 7.a.i (publicly funded), **b.ii.xxxx (One citizen = One** vote), c.x (direct elections), 8.a.v.b (Citizen), bi.ii (to vote and hold office) c.i (exclusive), 10.b (voluntary voting), 14.1.a.2.a (Macropolitical vote, Veto)

Legislative:

- **1.i.xxx.zz (Multi-cameral legislature**, 1st Chamber) , ii.x (Representative), iii.1.2.5.10. (Laws, Oversight, Appropriations, and Taxes), iv.1.b.2.d (Independent, proportional, one by one, rotating), 5.a (National), 6.a.i (2 year terms), b.iv (unlimited terms), **f.i (Wages set by chamber)**, c.iii (Unlimited), d.iv (no restraints), **7.a.i (Publicly Funded)** b.i.x (Presidential), c.x (direct elections), 8.a.v.b (Citizen), b.i.ii (to vote and to hold office), c.ii (non -exclusive), 10.b (voluntary), 12.a (districts), **13.a.i (Representative of Population),**

- **1.i.xxx.zz (Multi-cameral legislature** 2nd Chamber), ii.x (Representative), **iii.1.2.3.7.b.1.13.a.ii.b.ii.c.i (Laws, Oversight, Ratification, Appointments, Amendments),** iv.1.b.2.a (Independent, 3/5th rule, majority party), 5.a (National), 6.a.i (2 year **terms**), b.iv (unlimited terms), c.iii (unlimited); d.iv (no restraints), **f.i (Wage set by chamber)**, **7.a.i (publicly funded, citizens)**, b.i.x (Presidential), **ii.xxxx (Universal Suffrage),** c.x (direct elections), 8.a.v.b (Citizen), b.i.ii (to vote and hold office), c.i (exclusive), 10.b (voluntary), 12.a (Jurisdictions), **13.j.ii (Senatorial, two)**

- **1.i.xxx.zz (Multi-cameral legislature**, Triangulation Chamber), ii.x (Representative), **iii.1.2 (Laws, Oversight)** iv.1.b.2.a (Independent, 3/5th rule, majority party), 5.a (National), 6.a.iii (6 year **terms**), b.iv (unlimited terms), c.iii (unlimited); d.iv (no restraints), **f.i (Wage set by chamber)**, **7.a.i (publicly funded, citizens)**, b.i.x (Presidential), **ii.xxxx (Universal Suffrage),** c.x (direct elections), 8.a.v.b (Citizen), b.i.ii (to vote and hold office), c.i (exclusive), 10.b (voluntary), 12.a (Jurisdictions), **13.c.ii.x (Net Tax)**

Judicial:

- 3.a.i (Judicial, Hierarchical), b.i.a (Judicial powers only, general), c.ii.x.2 **(appointed by the President),** 5.a.(National), 6.a.iv (Unlimited), b.iv (unlimited), c.iii (Unlimited), d.ii (sum of elected), 8.a.v.b, b.ii (citizen to hold office)

Legislation is the sword but the net-tax chamber is the shield. A more efficient legislative system is the best protection against authoritarianism. Higher wages, fully funded governments, and working regulatory regimes will limit wealth inequality and protect voting rights in the nation. This will make the political markets more honest and more accurate. The people will be better able to identify the issues and move to correct them peaceably through due process. While legislation can cut away the deficiencies of a market-based economy, the net-tax chamber can also take defensive maneuvers to block debt default threats and government shutdowns. There will be fewer opportunities to use fiscal policy as a weapon against the state with higher legislation production rates, and each is more likely to fail because the donor states will more easily pass budgets during emergency periods. The combination of higher wages, more progressive taxes, and an easier path to passing budgets will make republics with net-tax chambers far more durable than conventional democracies experiencing similar conditions of wealth inequality and demographic shifts.

Ordinary presidential democracies rely on electoral outcomes to protect themselves from fiscal crises during demographic shifts. Functioning democracies will see majorities switch from party to party every few years, confusing the role identities of both rebel and institutional powers. Political parties will seek a superior position if they believe conflict is near. Their strategies will be a blur of expectations and fears, with parties seeking to empower their current perspective. The leadership won't know which party will occupy the presidency or have a majority in the legislature, but they will want to exploit any advantage of the position they find themselves in. For this reason, parties won't condemn threats of default or government shutdown, despite the ambiguous legitimacy of their claims. They simply can't risk vacating a superior position or weakening a future inferior position. This causes an escalation in rhetoric and increases the possibility of an event. Fear is the primary diver of institutional protests but opportunity is a close second.

Predicting events around demographic shifts will always fall short because of their long durations. There are many opportunities for a demographic-majority to consolidate power through authoritarian policies or declare a secession with a debt default or government shutdown. If the opposition party watches too closely, they will convince themselves they are safe as the number of potential events and nonevents grows without a precipitating act. These nonevents are not evidence of inaction, they are evidence of consideration and planning. The majority demographic group has every advantage and can patiently wait for the best opportunity.

The very presence of threats of debt default and government shutdown is evidence enough of a plan. Democracies rely on tradition and respect more than we care to admit. They can be broken fairly easily when one party is intent on exploiting all of the deficiencies in its due process and laws. Tradition is the practice of respecting previous behaviors on the expectation of reciprocity. When this reciprocity breaks down, it can expose gaping holes in the checks and balances protecting civil society and discourse. Authoritarians leverage this inherent flaw in democracy. Democrats are dependent on it, and this hesitation can easily be exploited. This is especially true in environments where debt default threats and government shutdowns are part of the regular course of business. What might have been less likely under different conditions, suddenly becomes plausible or expected after the new election cycle.

Authoritarians will act without the consent of legislature while the legitimate democratic regimes are more likely to abide by the shutdown on any court orders. A group of rebel states can easily secede from a democratic government while the same is not true for democratic states using these strategies to protect against an authoritarian. During the interim, the despot can remove obstacles like institutions, laws, or persons resisting the regime, and consolidate power around their dictum. When a court case proceeds through all of the different circuits and levels of a court system but still supports an autocrat's position it can cripple a resistance movement. Authoritarians are not constrained by the same expectations. Their biggest advantage is contradicting tradition ignoring precedent. The institutional protest is still the best strategy to force a resignation of an autocrat or a peaceful dissolution of a political union, before the authoritarian can consolidate power.

There is a definite tradeoff between certainty and effectiveness. As the certainty of authoritarianism decreases, the capacity to remove them safely diminishes. This inverse relationship is found in physics as the Heisenberg principle. As the uncertainty decreases and certainty increases, the people are moved to action as in other force equations. The quicker the change, the more force that is applied. Democracy simplifies this process, by adding weight or mass to the calculation by measuring the popular support in voters. When and if certainty increases, it will move more of the people to action. This makes change more likely. If the situation remains uncertain, then there is less impetus to cause change. There is less force behind a change in regime, or quality of democracy.

An increase in certainty works both ways. It may motivate more voters to come out and remove the despot in the next election. It may also force governors and legislators to remove the despot However, the despot is certainly aware of this condition. In fact, the despot has insider knowledge to the incentives and motivations, the despot knows exactly how far they will go to retain power and avoid incarceration or any other sanctions applied after removal. This is why the despot may act first to protect their superior position. In terms of orders of operation, by the time the opposition party recognizes the inherent risk in the situation, they are in an inferior position.

Democracy is not always the cure. Democracy entails risks. Nobody knows how future elections will turn out. The demagogue may have popular support and win any elections intending to check his aspirations. The electoral system may be rife with inaccuracies resulting from deregulated campaign finance, purging registered voters, or suppressing minority and poor voters with voter ID laws. Opposition parties are in the inferior position and have less to lose by waiting until the next election, but they could also lose all initiate and end up in a supine position. Elections are one possible solution but they carry a lot of risk in situations where there is high certainty of authoritarianism.

Uncertainty is dangerous too. If there is an authoritarian in power and the opposition party doesn't strive for information symmetry, then the public cant price in an accurate assessment of the risk. Political systems are not as reliable or measurable as physical systems, and if the certainty is not publicly recorded with rhetoric and argument by the opposition party, there might not be any rebound in the next election. Elections happen fast. A year or two may seem like a long time, but the public is often distracted by work or not engaged fully in the process. If they don't have time to appreciate the elaborations on risk, they won't act on it during an election. People generally rely on concrete or applied examples to base their judgements on, and in politics this is extremely dangerous as these experiences often entail the loss of civil liberties and voting rights. Experiential decisions in democracy can result in long periods of authoritarian regimes as the learning curve corrects itself.

The other greatest risk is uncertainty in coordination and response to an authoritarian regime. The opposition party is already in inferior position and will have to rely on a number of states and cities rather than a central government. This increases the risk of inaction or ineffective action. If the opposition party is uncertain of reliable support by its own members or the public, they are less likely to speak up and demonstrate leadership in the face of authoritarianism. This will produce a negative feedback loop or social proof system that results in appeasement or collaboration with the authoritarian regime. Any information asymmetry between the expected outcomes of the political castes and the public will cause hesitation and a failure to intervene before the authoritarian consolidates power.

Political parties have different policy preferences and a tendency to base their predictions on those behaviors. This is a fatal error for more moderate and patient parties. More aggressive political parties will price in worse outcomes and violence into their predictions and seek to optimize those returns. The more aggressive party will be creating their own opportunities while the more moderate party will deny the possibility of conflict. The more aggressive party will also tailor their belief systems and policies to maximize the chance of success during secession or usurpation. The moderate party will assign no blame as it will see a rational pursuit of profits and self-interest rather than open rebellion.

The more aggressive party can control outcomes by initiating conflict, where they have rehearsed more solutions to those scenarios. The moderate party will be conflict adverse and try to avoid all sources of conflict. This will limit the moderate party's ability to legislate and regulate away the threat, presenting the greatest risk the minority party becomes collaborators rather than resistance. Any retreat by the minority party will be intended to delay or avoid conflict but this will be characterized as appeasement. Democracy makes appeasement more likely, more excusable, and more dangerous. The minority party may hesitate to deal with the aggressors when they are in office, and once removed by legitimate elections, they may never get another opportunity to win office or resist the authoritarianism. The authoritarians can pursue anti-democratic policies like voter suppression, indefinitely extend their terms in office, or even refuse to leave office after the term expires. Appeasement by the minority party creates the opportunity to improve outcomes by avoiding conflict but they also invite disaster by putting them in an inferior or indefensible position.

The more aggressive party will earn better outcomes in more if the possible outcomes. This produces a higher average than a party relying on less likely but optimized outcomes. Outlier results tend to get buried in long histories of zeros and other more numerous and lower quality outcomes. Those zeroes may be important, as it could be equivalent to political despotism or population collapses. They can determine more of the variables and produce a higher average return than the moderate and conflict avoidant party. All of this contributes to the rational the minority party uses to appease or collaborate. When the minority party hesitates, their odds of successfully defending themselves diminish, and the value of cooperating despite the loss of democratic entitlements increases. It is a positive feedback loop majority-demographic parties can use to preserve power and bully the opposition parties.

The worst outcomes occur when the minority party does not adequately explain the circumstances to their constituents. There is virtually no benefit to appeasing the aggressor with new elections, if the electorate can't price in the likelihood of conflict into subsequent elections. In fact, any delay in response to a threat that does not include complete disclosure to the public must be considered appeasement. If the opposition party ramps up rhetoric prior to an election, in anticipation of conflict, it cannot be considered an appeaser. If it does not, the party will be deemed as either incompetent or a collaborator. The most responsible response is to fully inform the public and let them price the threat into the elections. They can even lose the election and it will still not be considered appeasement.

Democracies greatest advantage is its deliberative process and its ability to translate political will into laws and leadership. This is also its greatest weakness as it requires long periods of debate and discourse before action. Bad actors can move faster the legislative process. They can act faster than the courts can respond. They can talk faster than the fact checkers can sort through accusations or claims. When the political process breaks down, it is usually accompanied by a disrupted media and low confidence in the courts or democratic institutions of a nation. When tradition is not respected it opens up the nation to risks and crises it has no real capacity to deal with when the legislative process is obstructed and the nation's institutions fail.

The nation is at the greatest risk during the period where all of the democratic institutions have faltered, and it has been demonstrated that there is no recourse or consequences for bad action. If this is accompanied by the lack of coordinated leadership from the opposition party, all parties will be keenly aware of the opportunity presented. Political parties will know, the public will know, and so will all of the nation's adversaries and allies alike. Their allies may not talk openly about the risk but the weakness will be evident in their foreign policy Allies won't be able to rely on the nation and its political parties and will seek alternative relationships. The adversaries won't talk openly about the opportunity but that is because they want to exploit it. They will seek to marginalize the nation by corrupting its political process and compromising its elections. Everybody will be aware of the circumstances and be either too fearful to say something or too smart to say something.

Wars or conflict are often unilateral. One principle or party decides to act in a way that excludes all other possibilities. This can be a change to election laws, a prolonged government shutdown, or a preemptive military strike. The other party doesn't have to consent to it. They don't even have to believe it is possible or likely. History is a litany of those victimized by the unilateral actions of mobs and despots. It is dangerous when a political party's preference for inaction becomes a belief system unsupported by evidence. The lack of good outcomes is not a sound argument to dissuade another party from acting aggressively. Incentives matter and a nation with competing political parties have a number of different specials interest groups, each with their own set of priorities and goals. Often these incentives are set in direct opposition to other groups so there is never a single solution that satisfies all of the stakeholders. This reduces the ability of political parties to effectively predict the actions of another party. This fog of war can shroud the real risks inherent in demographic shifts or periods where excessive wealth inequality persists.

Neither the federal government nor the state governments will be acting legally or constitutionally, which reduces all justifications for the behaviors to discretion. If both are in the wrong, citizens are free to choose who to support. it is a wrong decision regardless of the position expressed. This is a fundamental aspect of all crises and conflicts, and which ever group can support their conclusions with revenues and labor will eventually win out. This will pass the priority to states, which collect the taxes and are more proximate in residency. All of the state's revenues collections, personnel management, and appropriations will remain unchallenged placing them in a superior position. The more the electorate relies on discretion the more likely one party deems elections invalid. Once government's behavior is determined to be illegitimate and its elections invalid, the threat of permanent separation becomes more immediate.

11 ENGINEERING

Modern political systems are complex and dynamic institutions, but they can still be reduced to a relatively small number of fundamental attributes. These characteristics can be recombined into a large variety of more specialized or more practical systems. The refined systems can then be engineered for integration within even larger unions. This chapter lists all of the most relevant and useful of attributes in outline form and briefly describes each one. The order of the attributes is arbitrary, but the outline still serves a purpose in making a quick translation of property to code for more efficient substitution and re-organization. Although disparate and seemingly unconnected when presented within the individual system designs, they will coalesce to form the most important themes contained within the other chapters. Most of the attributes are self-explanatory but in cases of ambiguity, the term and definitions can be referenced with ease in this chapter.

The first aspect of government to be explained will be the legislatures. Their most fundamental characteristics are the number of chambers contained within the institution. This book will focus on three broad types; unicameral, bicameral, and multi-cameral. Unicameral legislatures are the most efficient where laws can be passed with least effort and with greater frequency. It is the most basic and prototypical form of majority rule. This speed allows the nation or jurisdiction to adapt to critical environments quickly and with implied consent. The velocity at which legislation can be passed might also be viewed as a negative; changes may be made too hastily and require reversal. However, reversals are also much easier to achieve due to the fact that only a simple majority in one chamber is necessary to unwind previous legislations. This too has its dangers as a generation worth of progress can be undermined by a relatively few numbers of politicians in a very short time.

Bicameral legislatures actively inhibiting reversals but the pace at which new legislations are passed is much slower by virtue of two complementing majorities are needed within the two chambers. It is actually much more likely that a bicameral legislature is split between the parties reducing the possibility of passing significant bills while diluting their strength and integrity. Bicameral legislatures are a factor of 3x more conservative in this respect. This can have a terribly corrupting effect as the regression will produce ample opportunity for institutional powers to monopolize market share in politics and economy.

1.) Legislative
    i. Organization
        x) uni-cameral
        xx.) Bi-cameral
           z. 1st camera
           zz. 2nd camera
        xxx.) Multicameral
           z. 1st camera
           zz. 2nd Camera
           zzz. 3rd Camera
           zzzz 4th Camera
        xxxx.) Abolished (usurped by executive,
           administrative laws only)

Another danger exists. Bicameral Legislatures are slow and ponderous and can be unresponsive during crises. Not only are the chances of passing a reactionary law much lower but it will take much longer. Doubling the number of politicians will triple the number of debates. This gives rise to the possibility that the Legislature not act fast enough or strong enough when a crisis presents itself.

Multi-legislatures can be as fast and nimble as unicameral chambers while as thorough and secure as bicameral chambers. The third chamber increases the chances of passing laws while still requiring two chambers to repeal. Their greatest asset is their ability to assume the responsibilities of other branches and reserve powers from each other. A multi-legislature, or complex legislature, could combine a unicameral structure for the chambers assuming executive or judicial powers with bicameral structures for those retaining legislative powers. Complexes permit multiple segments of the population to be individually enfranchised which offers opportunity for concession as well as specialization. Multi-cameral structures are more compatible with reserve system structures, triangulation powers, and legislative equivalents to tripartite executive structures all of which will be explained in more detail in subsequent chapters.

The entry of abolished legislatures is useful for manufacturing political systems where the executive branch or judicial branch usurps the legislative primary responsibilities. During emergencies, it offers significant efficiencies. Nearly half of the laws governing a nation and its economy are administrative laws derived from executive authority. With a more specialized executive department it might be able to develop the entire legal canon. This is especially true with configurations where there is no unitary order within the executive branch but rather discrete and independent parts that act as checks on the other parts for a more distributed and balanced structure.

For the contemporary history of democracy certain executives have had veto powers over the legislature. This reinforces the dictatorial aspect the original founders intended. They modeled the Presidential office on a monarchy burdened by parliament. However, this has conspired to produce some of the worst outcomes for democracies when employed with bicameral legislatures which already inhibit regulatory initiatives and reform movements. The odds of passing a significant piece of legislation are already minimal and made much less frequent when a veto adds to the number of negative solutions already produced by bicameral legislatures with opposing majorities.

It is unlikely that executive officers will abandon veto powers but there is a more appropriate substitute. Macropolitical votes allow the executive branches to interact with legislatures and other branches and triangulate between multiple legislatures to confirm one version of legislation over another version. Instead of inhibiting the legislation process, the Macropolitical vote would increase the number of passed bills. It is simply a much more productive power than the veto, acting like a one-way valve towards more progressive regulatory and civil rights environments. The body politic still has the opportunity to repeal legislature but this requires the cooperation of the entire legislature. In cases of tripartite executive structures, the macro political vote would offer confirmation of the legislation created through agency laws in order to check each individual executive branch's accumulation of power over the others.

Another important qualifier for legislative branches is whether they are representational or tyrannical. If another branch or chamber appoints legislators, it qualifies as tyrannical. It is expected that terms continue to apply to the officers serving in the chamber despite its classification as autocratic. Tyrannical appointments can come from any number of executive, judicial, or legislative branches from the same tier or adjacent tier of government. Appointment powers are very common even in the most progressive of democracies. One of the more common forms of tyrannical appointment is an executive's access to the court systems. Judges are often appointed to permanent tenures on federal courts, appellate courts, or supreme courts. Another example of appointment powers comes from the original structure of the US Senate. All of the Senators were originally appointed by the various state legislatures rather than being elected directly by the population.

The term representative implies that the number of representatives elected are correlated to a proportion of the electorate. This will result in a legislative body that imparts a number of legislators to each state or region equal to its population in proportion to the other states or regions. Larger states will have proportionally more legislators. The representational option refers to both proportional and non-proportional allocations of legislator members. Non-proportional representation includes stipulated and arbitrary representational coefficients. This means that the number of representatives can be fixed in non-proportional ratios to populations. A non-proportional legislature might assign two senators to every state regardless of its size.

Non-proportional representative criteria have their uses but is the weaker of the two forms of representational coefficients. It is also a clear depreciation of universal suffrage and typically produces a government which is which is more easily exploited by the owner's class or the politically enfranchised. Imbalanced systems of representation can still work but they require offsetting powers between demographic or economic criteria so that more segments of the populations are empowered than those disenfranchised. This is the primary source for political concession during moments of crisis.

    ii. Attributes
        x. Representative
        xx. Tyrannical
                a.   Appointing Tier
                   1.   Same Tier
                   2.   Lower Tier
                b.   Appointing Agent
                   z. Appointed by Exec
                       1. Unitary Executive
                       2. Presidential
                       3. Attorney General
                       4. Treasurer General
                 zz. Appointed by legislators
                 zzz. Appointed by judicial

zzzz. Appointed by Reserve
Chamber
c. Proportion (remaining are elected)
z. minimal 3%
zz. Optimal 10%
zzz. Total 100%

Tyrannical systems are qualified by the branch or tier making the appointments and produce the political levers for manufacturing extra-national tiers of government (central, federal, or economic unions). Tyrant appointment powers occur within the same tier or lower tier. Same tier appointments are more acceptable for executive officers controlling their own branches, but control can be extended to limited degrees within the legislative branches. Often this will be a predetermined proportion of representation. The portion of legislators not appointed are then elected and representative of the population. When there are multiple executives, each appointing authority will be able to install 3% or 10% of the seats, depending upon the appointment authority.

Tyrannical appointments are also useful for emergency governments and for configurations that demand greater control over a specific tier or branch of government. One example is a President appointing the members of Congress during an occupation. This will be temporary with the seats eventually transferred to democratic control when elections are more secure. This way the government can organize the political system prior to its acceptance by the occupied people so that all of the infrastructure can be created. This should maximize the probability of success after the occupation ends.

Tyrannical systems have practical use but otherwise introduce many of the same flaws non-proportional representative appointments endure. Appointed legislatures can be representational of population in the same respects that elected legislatures can be which will impart more legitimacy to the institution as the individual senators will be accorded a proportion of power equivalent to the scale of part: whole in regard to population, GDP, or tax liabilities paid.

Atomized configurations dictate that the members of lower tier legislations appoint, by consensus, the members of the higher tier legislatures. Terms will insulate current higher tier legislatures from political turnover occurring too quickly and too often. The atomized structure operates across tiers rather than chambers. The Atomized attributes permit appointments to be made by either the executive branch or the legislative branch which will be incredible useful for constricting extra regional or extra-national governmental institutions like economic unions and satellite systems.

xxx. Atomized (lower tier governments appoint representatives in higher tier, lowest tier elected by popular vote)
   1. Legislators (Council members) appoint representative in federal tier
   2. Executives (mayor or governors) appoint representatives in federal tier

Democracy is a misnomer for many nations in the West. Most contemporary democracies are actually republican forms of governments and not traditional democracies. However, modern technologies in communication and information distribution might accommodate true democratic reforms. Nations can adopt reforms that imitate the first instance of democratic government found in Ancient Greece. The term direct democracy typically implies an entitlement for citizens to vote directly on the issues in front of the body politic. Historically, this has had disastrous consequences, but the Greek empire did persist for hundreds of years and thrive for much of it. Corruption eventually set in and an endless period of warfare followed. Only then did the empire recede. Modern economy, society, and technology is much more sophisticated than the ancient era of Greece and might contribute to a more effective deployment of True Democratic reforms.

Direct democracies can be implemented in a popular form with no restrictions on access or without voting based on rigid economic or demographic criteria. Direct democracies can also be improved with an auxiliary chamber meant to filter the legislation for popular voting. These filters can be subjected to eligibility criteria and refined with procedural rules to ensure the locus of power remains with the larger voting body. More mature postal systems, telephone systems, and internet systems provide the necessary communication infrastructure permitting the true democratic structure to be distributed among a much larger population over a much larger area. Independence from a physical building allows for larger populations to participate efficiently with enough checks on voter fraud to provide a secure voting system.

The most obvious criticism of democratic reforms is the access it grants to the general public. The best way to diffuse the potentially devastating consequences is to restrain or restrict their powers and responsibilities. Many of the responsibilities maintained by the republican legislature could easily be transferred to a democratic chamber without endangering the state or nation. Direct democratic formats might be more acceptable within multi-legislatures where responsibilities can be delegated to the popular chamber without diluting the specialized leadership professional politicians provide.

Democratic chambers can be premised on different methods for vote calculation. Function can be engineered into the chamber by allowing the results within the individual jurisdictions to earn values not predicated exclusively on the number of affirmative votes for the measures or laws. Systems can be made more stable by reducing the standard deviation away from actual votes or by maximizing it with an averaged value from a midpoint. Predictability is an important part of engineering political systems but sometimes the measure of change itself produces more change. Producing a variable mechanism should motivate more participating from the public with incentives for public planners to actively promote more registration and active involvement. There are five primary vote calculation methods.

    xxx. Direct Democracy (non-republican)
        1. Structure
            a. Echo-chamber
                i.   Straight
                      1.   Representative
                      2.   Winner Take All
               ii.   Leverage
              iii.   Cumulative
              iv.   Registered
               v.   Senatorial

Straight voting is what one would expect. The number of votes earned by the winning argument is tallied with the other jurisdictions and the combined figure determines the outcome of the election or vote. This is also a winner take all election. Only the values for the winning argument are tallied with the other values. It is the most conventional of vote counting methods with the most familiar of voting processes. If a jurisdiction with a population of 100 residents holds a vote and only 60 people cast a ballot, with 40 affirmative and 20 contraries, 40 votes will be tallied with the affirmative votes of other jurisdictions. If the same town voted and the result was 20 in the affirmative and 40 negatives, then only the 40 No votes would be tallied. The total number of Yes votes and No votes from the various jurisdictions are compared with the result dependent on answer with the larger figure.

It is what one expects within a popular democratic election. A slight variation on this method involves counting all answers in all jurisdictions and using that figure to determine the outcome of an election or vote. For instance, if in town A 100 people vote, with 60 voting affirmative and 40 voting contrary, and in town B 80 people vote, with 40 voting affirmative and 40 voting negative, the final result will be 100 voting affirmative and 80 voting negative. This looks to have the same result of a winner take all system, but this method is much more accurate when polling larger populations.

If town A has 100 voters, when only 40 votes affirmative, with 20 voting contrary, when only the 40 affirmative votes count it has a much more dramatic impact on final results than if the 40 affirmative votes were offset by the 20 negative votes. In one instance, the difference is 40 votes and with the other method the difference is only 20 votes. This could be pivotal in closer votes where the difference in votes excluded could have an impact on the final result. A Representative tally would ultimately contribute more accurate information to the analysis occurring after the vote. It would be supported better by actual demographic and ideological partitions.

Leveraged voting is only slightly more complex. Instead of tallying only those votes that carried the measure the value is comprised of total of number of residents within the jurisdictions. If a population of jurisdiction of 100 residents holds a vote and only 60 votes with 40 for the measure and 20 against the full 100 population is applied in the affirmative when tallying the result with other jurisdictions. Likewise, if 60 vote with 40 voting against and only 20 voting in the affirmative, a "No" vote captures the entire 100 votes prescribed to the jurisdiction. There are deficiencies with this method, especially when large populations have low voter turnout, but the advantages are that votes and elections can be more easily predicted with the fixed value of leveraged population used in the calculations.

A cumulative voting method is similar to the leveraged method except that it only tallies active participants. If a population of jurisdiction of 100 residents holds a vote and only 60 votes with 40 for the measure and 20 against the combined figure of 60 votes is applied in the affirmative when tallying the result with other jurisdictions. Only active voters are counted but this process provides a significant advantage to more active and larger jurisdictions. It acts as a force multiplier with advantages scaled up in accordance with population by a factor of activity.

The registered method a hybrid between the cumulative method and the leveraged method with only registered voters being applied to the result. The figure will be much smaller than total populations but larger than participating voters. It will motivate city and state planners to pursue maximum registration rates in the jurisdiction. This will improve the jurisdictions influence within the election system and will contribute to a more informed electorate.

The senatorial methods allow individual jurisdictions to come to a conclusion on a vote and translate it into a fixed figure or ratio applied to the entire system. There are varieties of senatorial democratic voting that can be applied. The first applies one fixed value to each jurisdiction regardless of the population or other attributes. The second established an average or ratio of votes per population similar in republican chambers

If a population of jurisdiction of 100 residents holds a vote in an arbitrary senatorial system and a total of60 persons vote with 40 for the measure and 20 against, an arbitrary value of 1 is applied in the affirmative when tallying the result with other jurisdictions. Obviously, this method overwhelmingly favors low population and more numerous municipalities. Larger jurisdictions will be under-represented if it captures an arbitrary value rather than a ratio value. Despite this failure in accuracy, Senatorial forms of representation are extremely popular in most contemporary democracies. This demands its inclusion within direct democratic chambers.

The frequency of votes matters when determining the scope of responsibility of the democratic chamber. A monthly voting schedule won't be able to accommodate legislation confirmation duties as the number of laws passed during a month will make the monthly vote too cumbersome when information distribution is considered. It may be appropriate for confirmation of appointments, treatise, or excising as they occur much less frequently. Weekly votes will be necessary when the democratic chamber is part of a bicameral legislative process. The schedule will accommodate more votes when needed and can be scaled down when less are needed.

    2. Components
        a. Echo-chamber (all functions usurped
      by referendum)
        1. Voting Schedule
            i. Referendum weekly
            ii. Referendum biweekly
          iii. Referendum monthly

Democratic chambers draw their issues from outside sources. There are two options. The first is by ballot. This imitates the conventional way most state government currently use direct democracy. A petition circulates among the residents and those with a number of signers in excess of the statuary threshold are put onto the ballot for the annual election. The public then votes on the issue and if more than half the voters support the measure it becomes law. The other option for issue selection is assigning each law passed by the republican chamber to a vote in the democratic chamber. There is no direct filter. Instead, the public has the opportunity to vote up or down every law passed by the republican chamber.

2. Issue selection
      i. by ballot
      ii. bills passed by legislature

The success of a voting schedule will be dependent on the method used to distribute information regarding the votes. Democratic chambers with no auxiliary chambers or professional politicians will be exposed to information deficiencies. However, ballots allow a small measure of control which provide a moderate amount of control on which issues are presented for votes. Often, ballot measures must overcome thresholds for signatures before the can be considered. This implies public support for the ballot measures before they can be voted on. Still, it is very possible that deleterious or counterproductive ballots are supported by the public and passed.

There should be little doubt that checking the power of a direct democratic chamber is necessary. One option is to only permit those ballots gaining the majority support of the legislature. In this respect, the public assumes the role of checking the legislators' powers. All of the ballot measures are vetted and supported by legislators with the legislators held accountable for the consequences of the ballot measure. Only those bills passed by the legislature considered in the democratic chamber. BY regulating the number are and quality of ballots, the democratic chamber needs no other controls. As long as each citizen has access to voting in the chamber, it will be considered a valid part of the legislative process.

Another option exists. The democratic chamber can be staffed by elected or appointed officials who dictate the pace or quality of bills considered. The auxiliary chamber can be delegated presentation powers where they dictate which legislation is tabled for popular voting. Procedural rules will protect the franchise of the public in their responsibility for voting on the most important issues. A filter will only allow for more order with issues prioritized and emphasized according to the needs of the nation or state rather than the individual. If necessary, auxiliary chambers can be relegated to deliberation only with the tools necessary to research and argue the issues prior to a popular vote but where no filibuster controls are authorized.

           b. Auxiliary Chamber
             i. Legislators charged with
                      presentation/filter
             (veto & Schedule)
             x. Elected advocates (by popular
                      vote)
            xx. Appointed (by chamber
                      leadership)
                        1. Upper house
                        2. Lower house

The most obvious choice for electing auxiliary officers is to resource the legislators for candidates. They are more familiar with the process and they already have a working relationship with the public. It would not be hard for an elected legislator to act in the capacity of distributing information to the public for use in a democratic chamber. The elections should remain separate but double coverage is acceptable. It would certainly be a major benefit for the legislators to be able to prioritize the voting schedule and control the filter for the democratic chamber. Those legislators working for the Democratic chamber would have more access to the media and have many more opportunities to address the public. This could translate to more successful elections.

Legislators can come from the either the state tiers or the federal tiers. Both have their advantages. Legislators from the state tiers will align the state governments with the federal democratic chamber. Legislators from the federal tier will align the democratic chamber with the republican legislature. This is a significant decision for political unions and nations. Those unions that favor stronger state rights will benefit from state legislators appointed to the auxiliary chamber. Those nations with federalist characteristics will favor federal representatives acting in the capacity of filter for the democratic chamber. \

Legislators can be elected by the democratic chamber through a popular vote or they can be appointed by the leadership within a designated republican legislature. The majority party will decide which legislators staff the auxiliary chamber and control which ballot measures to consider. This is more complicated in triangulation chambers with multiple institutions to choose from. Either the upper house or lower house can control the auxiliary chamber but the balance of power should be checked with other responsibilities given to the chamber lacking oversight over the democratic chamber.

> ii. Executives act as filter (veto &
> Schedule)
> x. Unitary
> xx. Presidential
> xxx. Attorney General
> xxxx. Treasurer.

Democratic chambers can be found on all levels of government. They are most effective on the federal tier where their votes can be tallied and used by lower level governments as part of the legislative process. However, direct democracy is a productive form of due process that lends credibility to state governments and urban government. It represents the highest quality of democracy where popular support of measures ensures their passes. Most other institutions are based on representatives which may pass laws lacking the public support of the people or pass laws in direct opposition to popular will.

> iii. Tier
> x. municipal
> xx. state
> xxx. federal

All of the powers of a true democratic legislature imitate those of a republican legislature except they are much more limited and specialized. The fact that most powers are predicated on triangulation and confirmation makes it a powerful partner for other government branches. The powers focus on legislative responsibilities including appointment powers, treaties, and laws. There are five principle domains of power within the democratic chamber. The democratic chambers can excise, appoint, pass legislation, repeal legislation, and confirm treatise.

> 3. Powers
> a. Excising
> i. Appointments
> ii. Legislators
> iii. Executives
> iv. Judicial

Excising politicians is a potent power and should be restricted in most charters. It should demand a super majority in support from the popular chamber as simple majorities will make it too accessible and destabilize the government branches. The power can be reformed to only apply to appointed executives rather than any elected officials. This might just inhibit government rather than decimate it. The only other ways a people can exert control over appointed officials is during the legislature's appointment process and this this only proactive.

There is no real way to censure appointments after they are in office. Executive elections are too far in between to be an effective means to reform wayward appointments and the executive is not likely to be swayed from public opinion only. The dilemma is a double-edged sword in that both the status quo and the reform are unsatisfactory. Prohibiting excising exacts too loose of a control and permitting it applies to much scrutiny with too much volatile. Still, the option for entitlement should be available to the electorate and body politic.

The power to excise elected officials is partitioned into executive, legislative, and judicial aspects to add specialization in the checks and balances between the different institutions. Excising can be an important aspect when dealing with longer term limits and unregulated terms for legislators. Excising may be critical in dealing with those appointed to Supreme Courts with no term limits. It would also be an effective tool to reign in wayward or overly ambitious Excising does not require confirmation from any bicameral process, but an executive might be given veto power in lieu of a supermajority needed.

> b. Confirms Legislation
>   i. Triangulation
>   ii. Bicameral
> c. Repeals Legislation

Confirming legislation is a major component of democratic chambers responsibilities. It is certainly the least controversial. It is important to determine whether the duty can be discharged by virtue of a bicameral process or a triangulation process. Triangulation chambers are generally much more productive than bicameral chambers by virtue of the increased likelihood of successfully passing legislation.

Repealing legislation is more akin to the excise power in that supermajorities should dictate access to this powerful tool. The loss of legislation can leave a vacuum in regulatory power or taxing power that can cripple a state or administration. It can deny citizens access to voting entitlements or welfare benefits. It can also be a powerful measure to check the animal spirits of an earlier legislative session. If reckless legislation is passed in a prior year the recourse to correct must be available. Repeal powers will be a potent power to check dangerous advances in powers from the other chambers or government institutions.

d. Confirms Appointments (Circuits)
i. Exclusive
ii. Bicameral

The democratic chamber can be given exclusive responsibility for confirming or it can be relegated to just one part of a two-part bicameral process. Appointment powers often preside over executive agency employees as well as over judicial circuit allocations. Most appointments should proceed without much resistance and a simple majority vote will suffice. This will aid the nation by producing seamless transitions from one administration to the next. A bicameral process for appointments will slow it down tremendously if the public is less cooperative than the republican senators but otherwise the up and down vote can be scheduled immediately after the vote in the republican chamber. Even if debate is necessary it should be shorter and more concise having occurred subsequent to the Republican legislature which already dedicated significant resources to the debate.

Confirmation of treatise must occur within a bicameral or triangulation process. Most are simply too complex for a democratic chamber to consider in entirety without the help of a republican chamber. However, by virtue of a treatise's intent most should be reviewed by the masses with access to a popular vote to confirm the agreement. This is a check on the alignment of commercial interests with political interests at the expense of consumer or employees. It is never acceptable for a trade agreement or defense pact to be agreed to without public discourse and popular consent.

e. Confirms Treaties
i. Triangulation
ii. Bicameral

Oversight is another typical legislative power that isn't readily compatible with true democratic chambers. No discrete committees are formed with the intent to scrutinize over the executive branch's agencies. It is possible that the appropriate infrastructure is created and that oversight powers can be earned but then the chamber begins to blur its intent and organization with that of more conventional republican chambers.

The same limitation applies to a democratic chamber's contributions to taxing and public finance. Future evolutions and improvements to the true democratic chamber can include powers over budgets and taxes but they can produce more disastrous results more quickly where a span of misallocated budgets and ill-conceived taxes cripple a nation or states within just a few years.

    4. Jurisdictions (zones for tallying votes)
        a.   Municipalities
      a.   Counties
      b.   States

One of the most important properties of the democratic chamber is how the voting jurisdictions are organized. It complements the voting method in almost every respect. The nation is already dissected into discrete parts with each state divided into counties which are further divided into municipalities. In order to have a competitive democratic chamber all state must employ the same system for voter demographics. It is unacceptable for one state to organize around counties and another by municipalities. For this reason, the attribute list was paired down into only states and municipalities. States can be combined into regions of equal size, but consideration must be made on how to apportion the distinct populations among the jurisdictions.

Jurisdictions must satisfy the lowest common denominator in terms of population or size. This is important for alignment between the cities or counties within the participating state. It matters less to maintain an equivalent sized unit between the states, but each jurisdiction should be paired with a legislature or committee that can use the result of the democratic institutions vote. Each vote produces recordable data for use in future legislation production and confirmation processes. Even if measures fail on the national level, there may be enough votes to pass in a majority of lower level jurisdictions.

The city or state legislatures can pass legislation using the democratic vote as a triangulation measure. All it needs is an affirmative vote in the majority for the democratic chamber to be used as confirmation. Most legislature chambers are bicameral, and this mechanism gives either chamber the opportunity to circumvent the other. This will maximize legislation production within all of the city, state, and federal tiers. This brings an amazing component of popular will and momentum to the legislative process. It allows for parties to expand politics from 2 dimensions to 4 dimensions with leadership declared from within the federal tier. This could be an incredible accelerant to an amendment process with a huge reservoir of votes being accessible to parties seeking reforms within the Constitution or federal system.

xxxxx. Abolished
1.   Executive assumes Legislative Powers
a.   President
b.   Treasurer
c.   Attorney General
2. Authoritarian (Unitary)

An important aspect of a government's structure is whether the legislature has been abolished and which institution assumes the responsibilities. Although this stands to be updated, the two current options are assumption are truncated executive officers (tripartite, bipartite, fractal, etc.) or an authoritarian system (unitary). Executives can always legislate through agency law. The more successful variation will be when individual components of the elected executive branch all have their own agency powers with a means to check each other. Executive law is a potent force in most contemporary democracies and it will translate to an acceptable substitution if due process is temporarily interrupted. The worst-case scenario is when only one primary executive has control over agency law. This is far from optimal but for most of human history this was a legitimate form of law.

The powers of the legislative branch are also enumerated within the attributes list so they can be delegated between the chambers. Many of the powers are self-explanatory. The powers are;

iii. Powers
1. Laws
2. Oversight
a. Unitary
b. Judicial
c. Tripartite Presidential
d. Tripartite Attorney General
e. Tripartite Treasury
3. Ratification (Treaties)
4. Executive
a. Foreign (President/ Military/
Intelligence/Alliances)
b. Domestic (Attorney General/
Law enforcement/ General
Administration)

       c. Commerce (Treasurer/Central Bank &
            Banking/Insurance Agencies,
            Commerce).
       d. Fractal (all executive functions
            assumed by separate
               committees)

5. Appropriation (Budgets)
6. Removed
7. Appointments (confirmations)
       a. Judicial confirmations
       b. Executive confirmations
            i. Unitary
            ii. Presidential
            iii. A.G.
            iv. Treasurer
8. Direct Democracy Role
       a. Presentation (Filter)
       b. Deliberation only
       c. Ratification (within the same branch)
9. Triangulation
       a. Stipulated (Powers apportioned to the
            chamber)
       b. General (Powers apportioned to the
            other chambers)
10. Taxing
11. Appointments (Direct, by Majority leader)
12. Elections
13 Amendments
       a. Scope
            i.   Unilateral
            ii. Bicameral
       b. Width
            i.   Simple Majority
              ii. Supermajority 60%
       c. Depth
              i.   State affirmed
              ii. Democratic chamber

    Enumerating the different powers is really important for all systems that maintain more than one or two chambers. The separation of powers is also necessary when the executive branch is divided into multiple branches or fractal (departmental) structures. Executive powers can easily be assumed by committees within legislatures with the chairperson acting as CEO and the remaining legislators acting as a corporate board. This permits the most interesting and possibly most useful combinations and intersections of power within democratic systems of representation and governance.

In most conventional democratic systems, the majority party automatically receives chairmanship of all committees (and majorities on all committees) while the political parties independently determine members appointed. The current committee allocation system reinforces the majority status of the majority party by imposing its will on all of the chambers committees. In order for a political system to provide opposition parties or minorities parties more influence in or control over legislatures the committee selection process can be better regulated and provide more opportunity for leadership.

Committee selection is more critical in prime ministerial systems where committee chairs have access to executive responsibilities and true power sharing will result from the improved process. By allocating one member at a time in a rotation the parties have to decide which committee is important and which they want to staff in higher numbers. The allocation process can result in unequal or disproportional numbers of staff on each committee and it can result in opposition parties acquiring majority in select committees at the expense of representation on other committees.

       iv. Committee Selection
1. Composition
    a. Coalition
    b. Independent
2. Order
    a. 3/5ths rule: the majority party and chamber dictate how committees are formed (conventional).
    b. 3/5ths, one for one, rotating
    c. 3/5ths, incremental, rotating
    d. proportional, one for one, rotating
    e. proportional, incremental, rotating

The current committee allocation systems can contribute to sectarian or partisan tension if the proportion of demographics is stable and they are one of the more important factors when determining elections. A minority will feel as though the government isn't favorable to them when most of the federal elections result in majorities favorable to the other demographic groups. When the minority has less faith in the government it can result in obstruction, dysfunction, and worse. The best way to diffuse this is with a more competitive committee selection process. \

There are two methods for allocating seats within coalitions. The first is grouping all of the parties forming the coalition together and forcing them to coordinate their appointments as one organization. Order of rotation is still dependent upon size of party. The winning coalition makes the first pick with the largest component getting the first pick, the second largest getting the second pick, and so on and so on. This continues in order until each individual party's runs out of seats or the coalition runs out of seats. The minority party is comprised of all parties not included within the majority coalition.

They apportion their committee seats by size and number as well. Smaller parties are given a slight advantage in that they have access to better committee selection earlier on. Coalitions often form through concessions and minority parties can take committee selection process into account before staking out a claim. Ordinal picks are important, but the size advantage is much more critical. A larger presence on a committee greatly improves chances of the party producing legislation that it supports.

The second method allows each party to be evaluated in terms of its actual size (number of seats won in the election) with the rotation going in order from greatest to least. This might result in the winning coalition having the first two or three seat allocations but that would only allow the minority party to consolidate seats in other committees. The largest party may not be in the majority coalition and this method will allow it to pick first despite not allocating the largest number of seats.

Current committee staffing processes don't permit any order or number variation. They simply permit the majority party to appoint 3/5ths of the committee seats in any manner they wish. This can be improved by establishing an order to the committee selection process. Order can't be equivocated with equality, as the process can result in either under-representation on certain committees and over-representation on other committees. However, establishing a regimented order will provide opposition parties the opportunity to secure majority positions on several committees - an opportunity they would otherwise be excluded from in conventional processes.

The majority party in the legislature will still control the order of voting and be more likely to control the passage of bills but at least the minority party could expect to pass more bills from committee to the general legislature. In executive legislatures (parliamentarian governments) the majority party will have oversight over the committees they staff in minority proportions granting them recourse when minority parties staffing executive committees with majorities.

The 3/5ths rule is meant to maximize cooperation. If there are 20 committees each staffed with 9 members then the chamber will allot 180 members to committees where the 3/5th rule permits the majority party to allocate 108 members (60%) to the minority parties 72 (40%) in a 435-member chamber (can be scaled up or wound down, depending on the number of committees and the size of the chamber). The majority party will have a hefty advantage despite the small margin of seats over the minority.

A proportional system is meant to impose conditions on membership that reflect the actual ratio of seats owned by each party. If the 435 seats of an institution are split 235 to one party and 200 to the opposition party, this ratio is imposed onto the 180 open committee seats so that 54% of the seats will be apportioned to the party with 235 seats and 46% of the seats will be apportioned to the party with 200 seats. The majority party will only have a slight numerical advantage over the minority party.

The five methods of distributing committee membership will provide varying degrees of opportunity to the participating parties. With a one: one rotating appointment process the majority party maintains the most control over the process and the number of party chairs, but minority parties will still have the opportunity to acquire chairmanship of 20% of the committees if they abandon significant representation on the other committees. Most opposition parties will distribute their representatives over the largest number of committees to gain access to the debate and discussions relevant to each committee. However, a small minority of opposition parties will favor a majority position on a few committees at the expense of representation on the other committees.

An incremental selection process starts with one appointment and adds one after every rotation so that it progresses from one, to two, to three, to four, and ongoing until all of the seats are exhausted. An incremental selection process will allow a party more strategic maneuvering with the ability to quickly staff 4/5ths of a committee or as a means to quickly distribute its members to as many committees. In an incremental process, the minority party stands the greatest chance of securing a chair or majority control over a committee they deem more valuable than others. This will be the most successful method in environments charged with sectarian or partisan divide as it produces the most power sharing without seriously compromising the legislature or government. The 3/5ths rule applies to the number of candidates available for appointment to committees.

If a party acquires the opportunity to appoint multiple seats but can't due to limited members, then those additional seats are forfeited with the next party in order assuming the next value in the individual or incremental allotment of seats. This provides smaller parties a modest efficiency in the process for incremental allotments as they will have access to a larger number of allotments earlier on and able to exhaust only after gaining appointment to the committees of their choice. This is a minor check on the power of larger majority parties who will earn earlier appointments at a lower value.

There are fewer options for Executive branches, but most combinations are more potent in regard to changing the function and essence of a government. Most executive branches emphasize top down control which means considerable power is concentrated within a single individual. Executive Branches have direct access to military assets and law enforcement officers which allows them to defend their policies and priorities much better than a legislature which is often divided by party and split into a large number of districts or jurisdictions.

    2.) Executive
        i.) Unitary (standard) – Primary determines
            subordinates

The most common, earliest, and simplest of configurations is the unitary structure where one executive maintains complete and unchallenged command over the entire executive branch. This permutation offers incredible efficiencies regarding coordinating internal policing with external intelligence and actions, especially regarding foreign policy and treaties but also between commerce and economy. Efficiencies come at a cost with no significant internal check on the abuses of power. This can occur within the domain of economy as regulatory agencies and or legal through policing agencies. One of the most frequent abuses is the refusal to enforce regulations and previously enacted laws. This is exacerbated with free market ideologies which in limited party systems produces an environment where regulations are ignored or enforced for periods of equal length resulting in unpredictable markets.

To mitigate this natural flaw in political science Executive branches can be separated into multiple parts to preserve the net advantage of the branch while introducing internal checks on power. The simplest division is into three parts. A President maintains control over foreign policy, militaries, state departments, and intelligence agencies. An Attorney General maintains control over internal domestic law enforcement and regulatory agencies. And finally, a Treasurer General to focus on the Federal Reserve, economic stimulus, permanent funds or sovereign wealth, sciences, R&D, and infrastructure. The divisions mitigate accumulation in powers during states of emergency or in erosions of system balance between the legislature and executive departments.

More complex systems can marry one component with another, so combinations of Presidential/Treasurer, Presidential/Attorney General, or Attorney General/Treasurer occur. These may introduce efficiencies without devolving back into a unitary structure. These combinations can be labeled tripartite, bipartite, or bifurcated and may offer more flexibility when married with more sophisticated legislature or judicial systems. Not only can the powers be assigned on a permanent basis, but more complicated multiple executive systems can manufacture for themselves a system to delegate or auction executive powers between the executives during or between election years, possible as a system of competitive budgeting or corporate governance.

    ii.) Divided; all individually elected, primaries determine subordinates

        c.) Treasurer/Central Bank, Science,
            Permanent Funds, Commerce,
        cc.) President/ Military/ Intelligence/
            State,
        ccc.) Attorney General/Law
            enforcement/ Regulatory/
        General Administration
        cccc.) Fractal – each department or
            agency elected or appointed
            individually
          a. Division
              1. Departments
              2. Individual Agencies

The fourth option is a Fractal structure (departmental) which provides an opportunity for the public to elect each agency or department director independently. It should be noted that this differs from an Executive Legislature because the agencies are not governed by committees but rather specific individuals. The Fractal structure eliminates almost all concerns of individuals assuming too much power during states of emergency. A fractal system permits leadership to be tailored to the agency rather than the party allowing for a more flexible election process. In contemporary liberal versus conservative political divisions, it would permit the electorate to install more conservatives within the military and law enforcement agencies with liberals retaining executive control over the regulatory and economic agencies. This might result in significant advantages for the state or nation.

      iii.) Abolished (Congress assumes responsibilities and
            internally determines agency chairs or
            department secretaries)

Executive branches can be abolished with the powers and responsibilities usurped by legislative or judicial branches. The function will be dictated by the powers prescribed to the branch within that section's options. Executive legislatures are just one possible solution with executive powers able to be apportioned to judicial branches or reserve branches as well. Less mature federal systems and economic unions may incorporate legislatures and court systems without an independent executive branch. It would then be the responsibility of the member states and nations to enforce any of the laws and regulations established by the legislature.

Judicial Branches need not necessarily maintain the contemporary structure of interlocked and hierarchical circuits. Instead, Justices can be appointed or elected to congresses, representative of population or some other criteria, with an annual internal vote determining which judges are appointed to which committee. Committees will replace the different hierarchical circuits within the court system. This permits the judicial congress to rotate individuals within committee to minimize abuses of power, be it on an annual basis, a term basis, or life tenure basis (i.e., permanent). It limits the monopolization of a circuit or court by a party due to specific appointments with the new majority granted authority to adjust every year. This can accommodate changes in voting preferences of the public while preserving the inherent stability court systems need.

      3.) Judicial
         A. Structure
                i.) Independent Circuits (like family/ criminal/
                        superior/ supreme)
                ii.) Congressional structure with internal votes forming
                        committees
        B. Powers.
                i.)   Judicial
                ii.)   Legislative Sub Routine
                iii.)   Executive Sub Routine

iv.)   Reserve Sub Routine

The number of justices in a congress can be determined by population or made representative of some criteria like number of states or counties, GDP, or a jurisdiction's tax liabilities. This is of critical importance as the caseload should normally determine the number of judges. A larger number of justices do not dilute the prestige of the court system. In fact, it makes deliberation more effective and minimizes the impact of outlier verdicts and opinions. It reduces the negative consequences of a bad appointment or an ineffective judge. A congressional structure naturally allows for more points of view from more demographic groups, with more research performed, and more facts to be presented. More judges within larger populations will speed up the time it takes for civil and criminal matters to be processed with due diligence. More importantly, a larger number of judges allow more specialization within the courts for more precise and accurate verdicts.

Most judicial branches will be pre-occupied with discharging the typical responsibilities of justice and law but there will be times that they assume individual responsibilities from the other three branches. The attribute matrix provides the flexibility to attach powers through subroutines. This can occur during periods of emergency, the powers can be prescribed at the inception of the institution, or they can be bestowed by some other branch by amendment. Many of the tripartite executive branches assume appointment powers over the Judicial which might legitimize justices assuming more specialized executive functions. In other instances, the judicial department should be granted access to traditional legislative powers like oversight or confirmation as they fall within similar domains of authority

C. Transmission
   i.) Elected
            x. Representative of population (like
            House) tethered to individual
            jurisdictions
            xx. Unrepresentative (like US Supreme
               Court, or Senate) with a stipulated
            number of justices untethered to
            jurisdictions

After the number of justices is determined, it must be stipulated whether the group is elected or appointed, and if appointed, appointed by whom. With more complicated political systems come more sophisticated appointment powers. Specific circuits and committee can be appointed by specific executive or legislative branches. This is especially useful in tripartite executive structures where judicial appointment powers can provide a check to domestic policing powers with the President or Treasurer General delegated authority while excluding the Attorney General from the process.

      ii.) Appointed
           x.) By executive
              1. Unitary
              2. Presidential
              3. Attorney General
              4. Treasury
              5. Determined by the
              committee/ circuit
          xx.) By legislature
              x. Terms
                  i. 4 years
                  ii. 6 years
                  iii. 10 years
              xx. Permanent (life tenure)

Elections for judges do mitigate the threat of conflicts of interests within political appointments. They also guarantee that the court's ideology keeps pace with the general population's ideologies. Both impart a measure of stability that is lost when other elected officials appoint judges for indefinite or permanent terms which causing a dislocation in representation and execution within government institutions.

Reserve branches offer a government the invaluable opportunity to recycle previously elected officials and preserve their years of experience within the government within an institution with abbreviated powers. Reserve branches can be relatively simple with all public officials maintaining eligibility or they can be partitioned into separate parts for different party or branch members. Admitting all retired officials is the easiest method to immediately constitute a Reserve body for a new government institution. A greater number of participants do imbue greater legitimacy as it is harder for one party or one generation of officials to dominant the dialogue or powers of the branch. For maximum utility, the Reserve branch can be composed from previous elected officials from different tiers and branches of government so that more precise checks and balances can be installed.

Even more sophisticated reserve branches can be self-admitting with current members authorizing new memberships based on terms.

This better ensures the highest quality of official is admitted within the Reserve branch rather than opening membership up to one term retired officials who demonstrated no particular affinity for politics or integrity. Reserve branch members can even be appointed so that the number is naturally measured, and the participants can be vetted.

    4.) Reserves (continuing to use retired political
    representatives)
       i.) members
              a.) all retired elected officials
              b.) self-admitting (internal party vote)
                    i. Terms
                    ii. Permanent
              c.) appointed (determined by previous
              position, speaker, whip, president)
                    i. Term
                    ii. Permanent

Reserve branches offer an incredible opportunity to continue regulating political officials after their terms expire. With reserve branch responsibilities come restrictions on employment and permanent salaries. This can mitigate the more corrupting forces within a democratic government where private sector companies can coerce politicians with lucrative positions after they are unelected from office. The reserve branch members will continually draw a public salary and be precluded from employment in the private sector. The incentive to forward the agenda of powerful corporations is diminished with the permanent salary and permanent oversight over politician's finances. If there are no elections for reserve branch members corporations can't exert pressure through campaign contributions. This will provide an interesting check on the other elected branches of government which might still be influenced by businesses or the wealthy.

There are powers that are indigenous to reserve branches and those that can be borrowed from the other branches. The traditional Reserve powers are the power to repeal, excision, excommunication, and triangulation. With a consensus between a two chambered Reserve branch, a simple majority in a unicameral structure, or most chambers within multi-cameral structures, the reserves can employ the repeal, excise, or excommunication powers. The reserve branch acts as the rear guard and protects the body politic from outlier political maneuvers or unwarranted pieces of legislation. These actions should not occur at a high frequency and will require a bi-partisan effort among different chambers and retired party members, but they can be instrumental in the institutions self-regulating itself. The Reserve Branch should have considerably more experienced career politicians within its ranks which justify their high caliber powers.

If the traditional powers of the reserve branch are not adequate, new powers can be prescribed to the Reserve branch or it can assume those of other chambers and branches. Most executive and legislative powers can be delegated on an individual basis or in lots of traditional groupings. The reserve branch can more easily assume legislative powers with the ability to confirm appointments, write and confirm legislation, oversight, ratify treaties, and the other responsibilities ordinarily delegated to similar bodies. Judicial powers aren't transferred too easily but in moments of crisis concessions can include reserve branches with access to appellate courts or lower level circuits.

    ii.) Powers
        a.) Executive (sub routine)
        b.) Legislative (sub routine)
        c.) Judicial (sub routine)
        d.) Exclusive Reserve (Supermajority)
            x.) Repealing; Legislation
            xx.) Excising;
                    i.   Executives
                    ii.   Legislators
                    iii.   Judges
        xxx.) Excommunication; removing
        reserve branch eligibility
        xxxx.) Triangulation (can confirm laws
        from one of two other chambers but
        can't write laws).

Repealing legislation is a powerful check on the legislature's authority. Repeals can occur immediately after the passage of a bill or years later after the consequences have been deemed dangerous or detrimental. This will make the overall political system more conservative with the number of passed bills and legislations subjected to the threat of repeal from both the reserve chamber and general legislatures. Executive branches with triangulation powers instead of veto powers would accelerate the rate of passed laws warranting a more mature repeal process and allowing the two to offset each other's advantages.

With a super majority within one chamber or consensus between multiple Reserve chambers the institution can Excise currently elected or appointed legislators, executives, or justices from office. Reserve branches should not agree very often considering the natural split in party or regional affiliation so when consensus is earned it implicitly authorizes the severe actions. Fear of retaliation should limit the number of unjustified excising attempts with the other party or parties likely to gain consensus in a counter-movement and orchestrate similarly aggressive maneuvers.

According to a sum over histories explanation of history for prediction of behavior, these episodes will be unavoidable but that doesn't mean they can't be checked by a veto by the executive. The instances where an opposition party maintains a supermajority in the reserve branch will be small and the frequency will be even less when the executive branch won't be able to defend against these episodes with a veto. Most excised legislators will immediately gain access to voting within the reserve branch which inherently diminishes the majority abusing the excise power. There are many self-limiting attributes which make the Excising powers more acceptable than first impressions typically impart.

Excommunication is a similar power to excision although it only concerns members of the reserve branch. This allows the chamber to self-regulate and disjoin members guilty of crimes or misdemeanors that embarrass or threaten the body politic. This power must be restrained to super-majority proportions as well to help ensure that one dominant party does not overwhelm a smaller less relevant party and exclude them unjustly from the Reserve system. This is true even in cases where one political party has been relegated to history with no active members in the General Legislature or Executive branches to defend them.

Triangulation is a power that permits one branch to confirm the actions of another branch but where there are multiple chambers or branches each vying for confirmation in competition with the others. The institution with triangulation powers will usually be the odd member so that it can select legislation from multiple sources to confirm. Generally, this pertains to legislation with an executive branch or reserve branch confirming legislation passed by one chamber of a multi-chamber legislative branch at the expense of dissent from the other chamber or branch. Repeal powers might slow the pace of legislation, but triangulation powers will accelerate the number of passed bills.

    iii.) Structure
        a. Bifurcated by party (multi-Cameral);
        b. Unicameral (indiscriminate)
        c. Fractal; organized by decade (or increments

that produce odd numbers, singularly or in
tandem by position within boards and legislatures (with a
delay in activation of the reserve body politic until the
imbalance is achieved if necessary, to perpetuate the ordinary
progression of politics).

Consensus is necessary to deploy any of these powers and that
completely depends on the structure of the reserve branch. Unicameral
systems allow for a more dynamic interface between retired politicians
and currently elected government with less of a check on the powers of
the reserve branch. Unicameral structures should be used more often
when the reserve branch assumes those powers of other conventional
branches of government and less often when apportioned the special
repeal, excise, and excommunication powers.

Multiple chambers for reserve branches provide innate checks on
the powers of the branch by making it much less likely that consensus
is reached. The reserve branch should be an auxiliary part of the
government with its most important powers used during crises or where
most retired officials agree they should be used. Chambers of reserve
branches can be dedicated to individual parties (or coalitions of parties)
so that its members with self-admitting or appointment powers
primarily influence their own parties Reserve powers.

Fractal organizations allow for multiple chambers to be
engineered around decades, parties, branches, or other indices to
produce an odd number for convenience in authorizing reserve powers
or for a more precise control over the reserve boards. Increasing the
number of reserve components might improve the likelihood of
achieving the consensus necessary to implement any of the powers.
Different generations of the same party may have different intentions or
preferences imparting some predictability or flexibility within the
branch. Peer pressure is always a factor and a majority should be easier
to earn with smaller and more distinct groups of retired politicians.

It is very important to stipulate the exact pool of retired officials
eligible for election or appointment to the reserve branch. The specific
branch and tier of official can be determined in accord with the
apportioned powers so that a pool of retired state level governors
acquire powers to check an executive branch or a pool of state
legislators can apply continual oversight over the currently elected
federal Congress. Retired officials need not be constrained to the same
branch they served in.

iv.) Pool
   1. Tier

        a.) National
        b.) State
        c.) Local (county + municipal)
    2. Branches
        a.) Executive
        b.) Legislative
        c.) Judicial

When necessary the reserve branches can be engineered with a parameter or time frame requiring a confirmation from the legislature for continued use; this would permit governments to experiment with different combinations of reserve branches knowing they are temporary in nature unless re-confirmed. This allows for older nations to introduce the reserve boards within the framework of its constitution or government without disrupting the current checks and balances within the system. A system of temporary authorizations will increase the number of different Reserve Boards created within the reserve branch maximizing the likelihood of successfully integration and minimizing the occurrences of failures due to abuses in powers.

Term lengths are one of the most important attributes for reserve members. Reserve members aren't elected. When legislators lose an election or are forced to retire, they earn a term in the Reserve chamber. These terms are of variable lengths determined by the length of service of the legislator in their primary chamber. The term length for reserve members can be set at single equivalency allowing the member to serve a term equal to that of one normal term in the legislature. Double and triple equivalency is acceptable too. The reserve chamber can have a total equivalency so that legislators who serve multiple terms capture the entire length of service in the new reserve chamber term. A legislator who served for 18 years in the upper chamber would gain 18 more years in the reserve chamber. If a half total equivalency term is used, the legislator would earn only half of their total service in the other legislature. A permanent term allows the former legislator to serve out their life in the reserve chamber, unless they are disqualified by criminal conviction.

        v.) Terms
            a.) single equivalent
            b.) double
            c.) triple
            d.) total equivalent
            e.) Permanent
            f.) Half total equivalent

The attribute matrix allows for separate tiers to be engineered independently of each other. Most governments are composed of municipal tiers, state or regional tiers, and then federal tiers. More complicated systems of government now include economic unions. Economic Unions are meta governments that extend some regulator powers and some taxing powers to a group of participating states but where the members retaining significant independence from each other for other matters.

Many federal systems start off as economic unions and over time consolidate regulatory powers, taxing powers, and law enforcement powers. A supremacy clause is usually necessary for an economic union to transform into a more mature political union. There should be no doubt that larger single currency and single language markets are a major accelerant to economy when a universal regulatory system is applied.

    5.) Tier
        A. National
        B. State
        C. Municipal (and County)
        D. Corporate
                1. Industrial Nonprofit Regulators
                2. Employee Owned (Resident Owned,
                Socialist)
                3. (Permanent Funds) C-G/ Private
                Finance
        D. Economic Unions

Contemporary innovations in public finance allow corporations to receive the classification of government tier. Industrial nonprofit regulators are a critically important aspect of government. It permits professional with the expertise to regulate an industry the legal authority to regulate it. This is typically accomplished through licensing or some other mechanism. It is not the most effective means of regulation. The regulators will have the same education and fail in the same judgment as the members. However, it can function during periods of relative dysfunction within the Congress or legislature.

Another fulcrum for representation will be local communes with resident owned enterprises. These are less common in capitalist states but open societies should invite more diverse ownership systems which will include employee owned or resident owned companies. A larger system of representation can be extrapolated out from this organizational hierarchy. If industries can self-regulate with nonprofit associations, then the cooperatives owned locally will also be permitted to organize themselves into an institution that regulates itself. It may not be optimal but a mixed market economy should accommodate all forms of economic and political organization.

It is intended that permanent funds eventually acquire representation within the government system. The managers will be political appointments by Governors but they will be constrained by fiduciary laws and a profit incentive. This makes them an effective locus for political representation. Permanent Fund managers can be given an institution that operates as some capacity of the legislature, to confirm laws or write laws, which captures the interests of both the citizenry and industry. The permanent fund managers will also self-regulate industry through shareholder activism. The permanent fund managers can organize their ownership shares and push through reforms that benefit employees, consumers, and government stakeholders, despite losses in revenue or depreciation of assets. This should mitigate concerns that industry is unfairly represented within the institution.

Term limits are often a necessary component of all functional democracies. Term limits comes in two varieties. The length of the term is often determined independently for every institution. The total number of terms a candidate can earn office is also determined for each elected office. However, one constraint is often enough, with certain offices limited by either length or number, but not both.

    6.) Term limits
        a.) max length of term
            i.) 2
            ii.) 4
            iii.) 6
            iv.) unlimited

Term limits can be too constraining and have a counter-productive result. The deleterious effect of the abbreviated length of terms for U.S. Representatives is evidence that terms should be longer than 2 years, especially in competitive election systems that require significant effort for re-election and involve deregulated campaign finance. The short term predisposes members to way too much undue influence from wealthy contributors and corporations. It has an incredibly corrupting force on contemporary politics with members often required or incentivized to neglect voting constituency interests in favor of corporate or wealthy donors.

Shorter terms favor corporations who can entice representatives with high salaries after public service ends. The shorter terms and more frequent elections make it much more likely that a politician's career ends earlier making them aware of the opportunities available in the private sector. The high salary and low effort company positions are repayment for the unprofessional and untrustworthy representation provided to constituents during the short term.

Terms of only 2 years also depreciate the labor involved in performing the public service as half of their appointment is spent campaigning for the next election which imposes serious constraints on time and effort. Candidates and officers don't develop the intellectual capital to discharge their duties until much later in their careers. However, this is made far less likely with shorter terms and more frequent elections. Terms of six years are more adequate for managing the time and effort constraints installed within election-based systems of representation. They also mitigate some of the undue influence corporations have over the chamber by making the election more infrequent. More importantly, public policy requires time to be expressed in economic terms and longer terms allow for more accurate evaluations of efforts. A public won't be as susceptible to the animal spirits when terms are generally longer than the medias' short attention span.

Those national representatives sitting on intelligence committees or armed services committees should have years of dedicated experience to maximize benefits to the country in regards to national security and oversight. A nation certainly wants their politicians to develop the necessary political or intellectual capital to discharge their duties. However, establishing a maximum number of terms makes it harder and more costly for corporation to unduly influence politicians with lucrative post career positions for large sums of money. Corporations will have to make more investments into new campaigns for more members unlike successful career politicians who can leverage institutional election advantages to minimize corporate campaign donations by attracting a larger number of donors.

Legislators should not have unrestricted access to terms as it predisposes the nation to terrible generational imbalances in cultural and ideology. Labor environments change, demographic environments change, and economic environments change. All of which makes one representative more qualified and more useful than another. This exposes the nation to imbalances in representation despite numerical parity or accuracy. Instead, a system should be developed to encourage politicians whose careers end due to limits to pursue other chambers or offices within the federal, state, or local tiers. Reserve Branches adequately conserve the political capital (experience) while enforcing the pertinent restraint on accumulated power.

    b.) max number of terms
        i.) 2
        ii.) 4
        iii.) 6
        iv.) unlimited

It is possible for a politician to acquire significant expertise over the course of 8 - 16 years or longer with moderate term lengths and term number limits. The typical length of service for a working adult from age 25 to retirement is only 40 years which sets an ordinary ceiling or threshold for maximum term length and numbers. Most citizens are only eligible for election at a more advanced age, which is appropriate considering the maturity or experience necessary to author legislation, and provide oversight on executive functions. This gives legitimacy to the argument that shorter terms and fewer consecutive terms are more appropriate. It is also precedent for establishing a ceiling or retirement age for politicians. Senior representatives don't have the same sympathies or interests as younger generations, and this could contribute to a serious imbalance in representation.

    c.) constraints on number of terms
        i.) Lifetime Maximum (sum)
        ii.) Intermittent (reset after absence)
        iii.) Unlimited

There is an important distinction between consecutive terms and total terms. Consecutive terms are only those were re-election is earned immediately after the preceding term. This usually determines institutional advantages, which makes a lower number of consecutive terms safer regarding maintaining accurate representation between demographics and generations. Establishing a threshold for total terms allows an elected official to leave office after defeat or a switch between government roles and then return but with an extension of maximum number of terms. Establishing controls on both consecutive terms and total terms so that officials can be forced out of office for a few terms to return with only a slightly higher threshold of remaining terms of eligibility is appropriate to conserve political capital and expertise while mitigating the threat of excessive accumulation of institutional power.

d.) restraints on terms
    i.) Sum of both elected and appointed
    ii.) Sum of all elected
    iii.) Per individual office/region
    iv.) None

One of the more important properties of econometric systems of representation are the income eligibility requirements that can be placed on elected officials. The income eligibility will typically be based on the median wage with some variability in the frequency of the measurement. Most measurements will be based on the median income value because it splits the population evenly in two. This is the mechanism by which electorates are generally organized in the econometric systems. However, districts or states may choose to use an averaged value to provide a small improvement in the candidate's income. Higher compensation will attract more ambitious candidates or those with better economic outcomes.

e.) Income Eligibility for Representatives
    1.) measure
        i.) mean
        ii.) median
    2.) parameter
        i.) Annually
        ii.) Every 3 years
        iii.) Every 5 years
        iv.) Equivalent to terms
    3.) output
        i. single year
        ii. averaged

The second most important component of income eligibility for candidates is the testing parameter. Eligibility can be tested on an annual basis, every 3 years, every 5 years, or after every term. There are tradeoffs between each parameter with shorter periods resulting in more disqualifications. More disqualifications result in more appointments by regional governors and this could be problematic. There is another benefit. A larger period will allow for candidates to adjust their own income levels to meet the eligibility requirements. This is especially true if income eligibility is averaged across the period rather than using a single year. If a single year is used to determine eligibility, the test is conducted in the year of the election and then according to the parameter. Otherwise, the income data is collected every year and the output is averaged by the parameter. This permits individuals or families to adjust their incomes in expectation of passing future eligibility tests.

It may be obvious to set a limit of the median wage on all incomes for representatives from the below median wage chamber but other institutions may also want to set wages for their members. Likewise, it may be prudent for states to set the wages for their representatives as elected officials may habitually raise their own wages despite letting the minimum wage or median wage deteriorate from inflation for everybody else. If states use an adjusted gross income figure, they can force candidates to donate income in excess of their income eligibility requirement. If wages are determined by the mean wage of a state, that median wage can be based on wage earners or entire labor force (working and non-working). The value will be much lower if the zero values from all students and non-workers are included.

    f.) Representative Compensation
        i.) Set by chamber
        ii.) Set by State
        iii.) Dependent on median wage of district/jurisdiction
            z. Income earners only
            zz. Entire labor force

The structure of the election is incredibly important for determining how the government is modeled. Democratic elections involve many variables including campaign donation regulations, election coordination (Presidential or Prime Ministerial), and whether they are popular elections, or are more insulated with electoral colleges or appointed representatives. Most elections involve competitive campaigns with multiple opponents pitted against each other in public debates and T.V. advertisements. Whether these contests are funded by public sources with prescribed tax contributions or by private more competitive sources determines how susceptible the system is to corruption.

These attributes can make one system magnitudes more conservative than other systems. They affect how quickly the government apparatus adapts to crises and circumstances, how fast it progresses towards labor rights, and how likely it is to adopt civil rights protections and Universal Suffrage. They can also dictate how susceptible they are to corporate money, government money, or foreign money. Most citizens make policy choices based exclusively on how popular the options are in their immediate vicinity and culture. They are in fact mirrors of either restrictive or progressive policies meaning that they conditioned by exposure to favor either political inclination.

    7.) Elections
        a.) Campaign Donations
                i. Publicly Funding
                ii. Privately Funded
                        x.) citizen only
                        xx.) corporate
                                c. domestic corporations
                                cc.. foreign corporations
                        xxx.) government (corporate)
                                c. constrained to jurisdiction
                                cc. constrained to nation
                                ccc. none (foreign government)
                        xxxx.) open (citizen, corporate, and
                                foreign entity)

The soundest way to organize democratic elections is through public campaign finance. It helps the nation to develop diversity in candidates that might otherwise be compromised in a private campaign finance system. Many of the best examples of democracies all employ public campaign finance and it is arguable that their citizens enjoy more equitable economies with stronger labor protections, more civil liberties, with higher voter turnout, and less institutional corruption.

Corruption is less of an issue when corporations can't use their incredible economic power to win themselves less regulated labor markets and lower taxes to earn more profits and distribute more campaign donations to protect those privileges. When economic conditions deteriorate the enticements by corporations appear larger and become more effective. Moneyed politics is a "Might Makes Right" system where poorer citizens are less represented and therefore are less likely to acquire the economic opportunities and capital in the future. It's a vicious cycle that leads to wealth inequality, political instability, and eventual decline. However, there are democracies that choose to open their elections to private campaign contributions.

No doubt there will still be examples of democratic governments that accept the risks of private campaign finance. If this is the case the estate or nation must first decide whether its independent citizens can participate. Then it must decide whether corporations can. If Corporations can make campaign contributions, there should be discussion of what boundaries and conditions exist for the entitlement. The last possible source for political donations is governments. They too should be constrained by reasonable laws to protect the integrity of elections.

Corporations can be both privately owned or publicly owned and those that are listed on the stock exchanges or have multiple owners should take the diversity of those owners' political beliefs into question prior to donating to a party or candidate. It should be unlawful for management to transfer corporate dollars to political candidates unless they are in proportion to the listed affiliations of stock holders with management shares redistributed by the same proportion a second time. There should be no concessions made on this issue as executive's incentives aren't completely aligned with shareholder preferences especially if they come from different demographics, income brackets, and where a nearly half of all securities are typically owned by pension funds including public pensions.

Politicians construct tax policies, trade policies, and regulatory systems which make any political donation by the corporation more potent than the initial intent. The use of shareholder equity to forward the designs and ambitions of company executives is unwarranted and closer to theft than any legitimate representation of interests. The best examples of this are public and private pension fund investments into companies favor candidates that don't synch up with pensioner beliefs. Most pensioners are not aligned with management regarding the labor policies they enforce, the fiscal policies they advocate for, and the misuse of natural resources, and especially the forceful deregulation stance posited. When political contributions are involved the fiduciary duty encompasses more than profits as the costs include tax penalties, subsidies, or remediation and often accumulate in amounts greater than the original investment.

Unrestrained corporate campaign donations set precedents for state governments and local governments also making campaign donations. Corporate charters should be given no powers that municipal charters and state charters don't have. Other governments are actually more responsible political donors than corporations which are far from representative of the populations employed by them or which purchase their products.

Government campaign donations may be one of the only ways a democracy can protect itself from the coercive effects corporate access to political contribution. A party pledging better labor rights, unionization, more regulations, and progressive taxes would improve its chances for beating a party espousing pro-corporate policies including deregulation and regressive taxes, despite their advantage in corporation donation, when they can distribute state or city tax revenues through the various allied Governors offices and Mayoral offices. It is a source of political contributions that can rival corporate donations when combined with donations from employees and consumers.

       b.) Structure
          i. System
               x. Presidential (antagonistic or
                    unsynchronized with legislature)
                xx. Parliamentarian (majority in
                       legislature determines executive
                       officer)

Many citizens don't recognize the difference between Presidential Elections and those with Prime Ministers. Presidents are typically elected independently from their legislatures resulting in scenarios where the President can win office but then face a Congress where the Opposition Party is a majority. When Prime Ministers are elected, they implicitly have the support of the political party winning most seats in the primary legislature. Prime Ministers can enact reforms more easily and have the political power to enact laws that coincide with campaign promises and agendas. Parliamentarian governments are much more efficient passing laws more quickly and in greater numbers.

Presidents can sit idle for years prior to earning the political support for a mandate. Inefficiencies in the system of representation are abused more easily as it is far easier to limit the rate of progress or reform simply by refusing to enact new legislation. Take for example a bicameral legislature in combination with a Presidential Veto. The likelihood of successfully passing reforms is minimal with a split congress occurring half the time, an antagonistic congress occurring one in four times, and majorities in both chambers having a frequency of only one in four instances. This contributes to a 25% chance to pass legislation before the Presidential Veto is taken into consideration. A Veto changes the frequency of passing laws to 1 in 8 or approximately 15%. During crises, this could spell doom for the nation. Worse, is that this innate inefficiency causes parties to seek compromises and to give concessions that seriously undermine the strength of all regulations and tax systems. The low legislative production rate results in a lower number of lower quality laws rather than a moderate number of more reasonable laws.

Coalition governments improve this ratio to nearly 1 in 1 with only one chamber of congress and no self-limiting Veto power necessary. With a 100% success rate the quality of regulations improves as well as increasing the frequency of passed laws. There is no evidence that suggests that these systems are prone to frequent and disruptive repeals which would be the single best argument for maintaining an antagonistic bicameral legislature. There is also no evidence that Parliamentarian systems are more prone to despotism or political fanaticism which was the philosophical underpinning for a bicameral process with presidential veto. More representative governments are sounder governments with more equitable economies and more moderate populations.

Universal Suffrage is an ideal. Voting systems need not be relegated to one vote for every eligible person. Instead, votes can be distributed according to the value of asset, number of stocks, number of acres, or in relationship of part to whole, or some other pre-set calculation. As previously discussed, many of the more successful democracies formed as the result of hundreds of years of reform. These nations started with land based or wealth-based systems of representation and only recently required Universal Suffrage.

    ii. Vote

        x. Number (One stock or One Acre = One vote or Ratio)

        xx. Part: Whole (Asset Value = Number of Votes, coefficient)

        xxx. Combinational (Weighted Part: Whole)

        xxxx. One Citizen = One Vote

Although not always a political reality, Democracy is premised on one vote per citizen. It is an exceptionally good measurement for a legitimate and efficient government. However, more complicated governments with more branches and departments might actually gain efficiencies by introducing variations in voting systems for those particular parts. It might be more convenient to permit one chamber of a bicameral legislature to be determined by stock ownership and the value of bond assets in order to introduce significant corporate and economic interests into government while simultaneously eliminating private campaign finance and maintaining the standard one person one vote mechanism for the executive branch and second legislative chamber. It might even be more appropriate for new institutions to be incorporated with the enhanced voting entitlements so that older power bases remain intact. A third legislative chamber with triangulation powers and premised on wealth representation might be a serious improvement to a bicameral process, as long as those wealth-based entitlements distribute voting rights to a diverse cross section of citizens or residents.

All senate structures are direct arguments and contradictions of the primary premise of democracy as majority rule. Senates aren't representational of populations as each city or state is afforded and equal number of senators regardless of population. Obviously, the one person one vote rule is violated when comparisons are made in regard to ratio of senators to represented citizens. However, senates can be an effective hedge against abuses levied by a majority but are more easily abused by minorities gaining a disproportionate amount of influence in the nation or union. Minorities can be extremely effective at obstructing government and the progress of civil rights, economic rights, and developing well-funded and strong public sectors. Political Systems with too many protections against majority rule are prone to extreme periods of dysfunction and susceptible to instability.

If one readily accepts the deficiencies involved in Senatorial representation, then one must as earnestly consent to the deficiencies of wealth-based representation. Wealth based representation can be manipulated to a greater extent than Senatorial representation providing some meaningful improvements. One such method for voter representation is value voting. Value voting assigns votes in accord with some other factor, like income or income tax. The amount of income tax paid translates to a raw figure used in tabulating elections or legislative votes. Make no mistake, might makes right with this method but most of the political force of a democracy will continue to be found in the middle class who will combine average individual values with staggering numbers of instances within the group.

Value voting can be reformed by introducing a scale of representation with brackets reflecting a static amount of representation. The premise is similar to how tax brackets are formed except that rather than producing a percentage of taxes owed an integer is substituted for vote representation. This figure conveys a numerical value for voting. Those in the lowest voting bracket would maintain a one to one ratio for votes per person, those in the middle bracket would gain a two to one ratio of votes per person, while the top income bracket would confer a vote multiplier of 3:1. Note that this ratio translates to 1 voter per person, 2 votes per person, or 3 votes per person. In other value voting systems, a larger proportion of the total vote might go to the top 10% of income earners who pay a much larger proportion of taxes in terms of the total number of payers. In effect, this would constrain the top 1% of income earners to a total of 3% of the vote where they might otherwise capture 10% or 20% with more liberal voting entitlements.

A value voting bracket should skew voting powers to the middle classes with the raw voting power of the first three income quartiles continuing to outnumber the voting power of the 4th income quartile. The middle class tend to be more representative of the whole population anyway. It includes professionals, union members, public sector employees, and small business owners. A large proportion of the 4th quartile is still considered middle income, especially by standards set by the top 1% of income earners, which will bolster the raw voting power of the middle class in the middle two income quartiles.

Combinational value is similar to value voting, but it provides individuals with a number of votes equal to the number of persons living within the jurisdiction they are in charge of, under their direct command, or within the same department or agency. In a combinational voting system, citizens would be afforded one vote apiece, their mayor would gain access to a number of votes equal to that of the town, a county executive would earn an equivalent number of votes as the number of residents in all of the participating towns, while the Governor would leverage a number of votes equal to the entire population of the state. The method is reminiscent of feudalism and can be applied to corporate, military, or governmental elections and appointments (confirmations). This is intended to be less democratic and more authoritarian in nature.

If the state had 1 million residents split into 10 counties with 100,000 residents each, for a total of 100 cities of 10,000 residents, then the Governor would have 1 million votes, the 10 county commissioners would each have 100,000 votes, each of the 100 mayors would have 10,000 votes, and all 1,000,000 residents would each have a vote. The total number of votes in the system is 4 million with the Governor only capturing 25%, the 10 County Commissioners capturing 25%, the 100 Mayors capturing 25%, and the residents capturing 25%. However, there are other constraints to this voting mechanism.

Politicians can't participate in their own election, but they can leverage their votes in elections for executives in higher echelons. For example, a mayor couldn't vote for himself in his own election, but he could vote in a county commissioner election with the full number of residents of his city. This allows executives to elect other electives in a similar fashion that parliamentarian governments allow the majorities of representatives to appoint their own Prime Minister and government. The residents can participate by electing the executives wielding the combinational vote while also leveraging their own individual votes in economies of scale.

In state elections Governors couldn't participate so 1/3rd of the vote would be earned by the county commissioners, 1/3rd earned by the mayors, and 1/3rd by the residents. If one examined national elections through this prism it would work out that the Governors would have 1/4th of the total vote, county commissioners would have 1/4th of the total vote, Mayors would have 1/4th of the total vote, and the residents would have 1/4th of the total vote. Obviously, the President would be excluded from all combinational votes by virtue of his apex position. Not all states are equal and those states with larger populations will have proportionally lager voter entitlements. Previous elections would have tremendous impact on future elections with the leverage of populations up through the ranks of executives within the state or nation.

At some future point, combinational value voting representation can be used in true democratic chambers. This will reign in some of the animal spirits that might make the institution less predictable or management than the other institutions. Combinational representation goes against the main premise of true democracy so the attributes are not currently available but that doesn't mean future evolutions can't include more executive control over the chambers. In these instances, all executive would participate allowing them to moderate the results of the democratic votes. In this respect, they could prime the legislative body with affirmative votes to confirm laws with other parts of the legislature.

Each system will have to determine how to structure its own elections. The two most common methods are direct through popular voting and indirect through systems like the Electoral College. A 3rd option is one that insulates elections from the public by relegating voting to the domain of the legislatures. This is the same mechanism by which a parliamentarian system elects their prime minister. A fourth option exists where the President is elected by a consensus of Governors. The State level executives determine the candidates from their ranks and they vote in accord to the number of votes earned by their representatives and/or senators in the federal legislature.

By far the most appropriate and effective method for voting is the most direct through popular voting. It enfranchises the entire population with majority rule which should be checked by a strong alternating binary party system or a more functional rotation in a multiparty system. There is a more practical reason for permitting majority rule to govern a nation – the people must take responsibility for the actions of the nation unlike situations where minorities are vested with the principal political power. This implied responsibility is a burden to all descendants and all voters; it persists even in cases where a minority establishes political control and usurps all the benefits of the state or wages war in the name of the state. Maintaining the integrity of majority rule is extremely important as current administrations and cultures create legacy and history with mistakes often reverberating through history for the length of the state's survival.

    c.) Intimacy
        x. Direct (Popular)
        xx. Indirect (Electoral College)
        xxx. Insulated (Legislative dictates)
            i. Upper chamber – majority appoints from their own ranks
            ii. Lower chamber - majority appoints from their own ranks
            iii. Reserves - majority appoints from their own ranks
        xxxx. Coalition (a majority of Governors determine executive from their own ranks)
            i. vote equals number or representatives in Upper chamber
            ii. vote equals number of senators in Lower chamber
            iii. each governor is afforded a single vote regardless of population.

Electoral College is an indirect method that produces inconsistent results for popular representation in elections which contributes to political instability and long-lasting feuds. Electoral Colleges are scandalous affairs in democratic countries as they remove the executive branches from popular control. Even inefficiencies as small as 4% differentials between electoral votes and popular votes between states will produce extremely divergent results in political economy over extended periods of time. As the sample size increases so do the outliers and deviance from normalized results. That figure of 4% represents an outcome of 4 times in 100 elections where the imbalance in representation likely results in an unpopular election of a politician to office.

That poor statistic is only in best case scenarios within unadulterated system where party interference isn't an obstacle. Examples of bad behavior that can exacerbate these conditions include voter suppression efforts or manipulating campaign finance laws to dilute representation. Stability is engendered by votes wholly dependent on accurate and popular elections. This does not mean there won't be failures in public finance or governance when majorities can self-regulate and self-govern themselves, but it does mean that more of the population can expect to be held responsible for their errors and mismanagement during office. Where there is inaccurate representation and excessive amounts of waste in the political markets there is less culpability and a greater likelihood of secession, insurrection, civil war, or occupation. At the very least, inefficiencies in the political market produce imbalanced wealth concentrations and poverty which can't be cured as power accumulates within the institutionally wealthy.

Insulated elections occur when democratically elected legislators hold a quorum and reach consensus on electing the chief executive officer for that tier. It's not a direct election but it's not an indirect system like an electoral college either. It is very like how parliamentarian systems elect their prime ministers except that the legislators are already elected, and the election pertains to a branch external from their own. The transitive property transfers legitimacy by prior democratic election for the legislators holding the quorum.

Likewise, a coalition of governors can be bestowed election powers over the chief executive of a federal tier in the same respect legislators can be given the power to appoint an executive. The Governors hold a quorum and the majority verdict determines the outcome of the presidential election. Each Governor can be given a number of votes equal to the number of representatives they have in the chamber that is more representative of population. This will ensure that more numerous but less populous states can dominate elections unfairly. If a nation wants rural communities or minorities to exert more political control over the government, they can elect to have the Governors leverage senatorial votes or individual votes. This is another form of insulated election that is neither direct nor indirect, but which must be considered as valid as the elections held for those individuals participating in the insulated election.

Appointment powers have been enjoyed by executive branches since they were first authorized through popular elections. A legislature typically maintains traditional oversight with all appointments conditional on a confirmation process. In more complicated systems of government, more precise declarations must be made regarding which executive branch is permitted to exercise the appointment power. This book deal primarily in Tripartite and Bipartite structures which divide the executive branch within two or three principle branches which is the main reason why three options are offered.

        d.) Appointed
             x. Tyrannical
                 1. Executive
                     a. Presidential

b. Attorney General
c. Treasury General
d. Unitary
2. Legislatures Majority Party
3. Judicial

Appointment powers can be wielded by legislatures just as effectively as executives with a majority leader allowed to install the directors of their choice. When Executive Legislatures usurp all of the previous responsibilities and charges of a unitary executive branch it will obviously need to delegate authority over the apparatus of government. In other instances, a judicial branch might have domain over an agency requiring appointment with confirmation from another branch. The delegation of appointment and confirmation powers are necessary for checks and balances between the various branches or chambers. A government can fall into complete dysfunction with the abuse or neglect of either appointment or confirmation powers. All efforts must be made to ensure they are accessible during even the most dire or stressful of circumstances.

xxx. Eligibility
1. Individual
A. Citizen
B. Resident
C. Alien

On the individual basis eligibility can be made more exclusive by citizenship constraints, residency requirements, or alien entitlements. The alien entitlement can be combined with the citizenship option so that nonresident citizens can hold office. None of the attributes are exclusive and from these three options come an almost infinite number of combinations when systems are engineered with the access provided for specific tiers and branches. Resident aliens might gain representation on the local tier but be prohibited from voting or holding office in state and federal tiers. Nonresident citizens could be an instrumental resource for governing reconstruction or occupation efforts. Other combinations might aid in imperialism and other efforts to engineer empires between otherwise disparate jurisdictions.

By designating difference between citizenship requirements, residency requirements, and alien entitlements one system can coerce compatibility with other foreign systems and larger economic unions. All of these attributes can be toggled independently to manufacture different variations of democratic governments. Governmental tiers can be dissected into city, county, state, and federal with the domains restricted by executive, representative (legislature or reserve), judicial, or by agency in either domestic or foreign jurisdictions.

    2. Governmental
        A. Tier
        i. city
        ii. county
        iii. state
        iv. Federal
        v. Union
      B. Domain
        i. Office
          x. Executive
          xx. Representative
          xxx. Judicial
        ii. Agency (Fractal)
      C. Jurisdiction
        i. Domestic
        ii. Foreign
    4. Any

If any specific quality defines a democratic nation it will be the eligibility requirements for voting. The very fabric of the society and soul of the nation is found in which demographic groups are empowered with representation, in what proportion, and combinations. Most modern democracies don't discriminate between criteria when it comes to administering a popular vote for elections but with more refined and exact systems of representation, stricter regulation of voting hierarchies can produce more efficient systems.

Certain governmental powers can be exercised with more precision and expertise from legislatures exacted from more practiced and knowledgeable legislators and voting constituents. Manipulating voting rights is a treacherously dangerous power to exercise but political engineers can ensure that privileges are delegated responsibly with adequate checks and balances. Voter rights and eligibility criteria can be re-organized according to contemporary social and economic pressures. More sophisticated governments with multiple executive branches and multiple legislative chambers will accommodate the extra specialization necessary to administer larger economic unions and empires.

8.) Eligibility Constraints

       a.) Criteria
       i.) removed
       ii.) removed
       iii.) removed

For centuries land barons dominated medieval Europe and although there was no voting with ballots, the aristocracy voted with pledged soldiers and promised military support in exchange for maintaining titles and access to taxes and income from the land. The Magna Carta was an important development towards Democracy and it was a revolt staged by the landed aristocracy within England that demanded representation in the Monarchy through a Legislature. This would be the basis of future democratic reforms despite the fact it was not a popular form of representation. The United States premised its initial democratic representation on land requirements. It was an aristocratic republic for the first few decades until protesting veterans earned universal suffrage for Caucasian adult males. Wealth based representation is a major improvement to these classical examples of democracy. Wealth based representation are high quality entitlements that protect universal suffrage and majority rule.

Wealth offers the greatest opportunity to enact voter eligibility criteria as a huge variety of different indices can be used which accommodate most citizens of the nation. Representation can be conserved within the system which makes it the perfect substitute for universal suffrage contributing to the specialization in both governmental branches and tiers. Most of the wealth-based representation relies on divisions between above median and below median so that the entire public is included within the electorate. Zero values are factored into the below median group to ensure that all citizens have an opportunity to vote. The most applicable wealth-based attributes are personal incomes, tax liabilities, and gross domestic product. Each one can be dissected into above median and below median groups. These attributes are not to be confused with representational coefficients which determine the number of representatives per district or jurisdiction, rather than participation in an electorate, despite the similarities in the values used (GDP, population, Tax liabilities, etc.).

      iv.) Wealth
        A. removed
        B. Income or Liability based
           i. Source
                a. Income (household and

family)
b. Tax liabilities
c. removed
d. removed
e. removed
f. Gross Domestic Product

All natural persons in a nation have an income, even if it is a zero value. This makes personal income an adequate attribute to split an electorate. A personal income can be compared to a national median, a state median, or a district median, and the population can be split into two parts. These parts may be equal in size depending on the jurisdiction, but two unequal parts is an acceptable outcome. Ultimately, the population will be split into two (nearly) equal parts when all of the districts or jurisdictions are tallied, depending on the median value used. Class divisions are exception themes in politics and they can improve the quality of representation with role identity and more accurate self-interests.

Tax Liabilities can apply to individuals, corporations, or governments. Individuals can be split into above median and below median groups as easily as income earners. This includes non-tax payers who will be allocated within the below median group. Citizens may pay different amounts of taxes depending on the instrument used and this may differ from the group they would be normally allocated when income is used. When governments pay taxes, it is usually to a higher organizational tier. A municipal government would pay taxes to a state by virtue of its residents paying taxes to the state. A state would pay taxes to a federal tier by virtue of its residents paying taxes to the federal tier. The total tax liability of a jurisdiction or district can be tallied and then separated into above median and below median.

Correlating representation to GDP captures a fair proportion of representation by population but has extracurricular benefits by exporting the region's more successful economic policies through the increased political influence. Large population bases can have lower GDP than small efficiently managed population bases. GDP representation is a measure of the differential and a way to distribute the efficiency across jurisdictional borders. There is the danger that a jurisdiction will vote in accord to its own self-interest and take advantage of other cities, counties, or states but that gross behavior already occurs in most contemporary political systems. Senatorial representation has propagated within most democratic systems and is predicated on disrupting majority rule and providing inaccurate representation.

The term political-economy predates both modern democracy and modern global economy and was used specifically to illustrate the very intimate and intricate relationship economy has with politics; Modern states should employ more precision in defining the roles and powers of the different facets of government in accord with the powers and privileges of the classes of individuals working as legislators or voting for representation within the chamber or branch. The species entertains most ideologies in binary opposition with unchecked capitalism rivaled by ominous communism where both are extremes within one spectrum of political economy. Generally, neither satisfies all that the citizenry require. However, they still introduce significant themes that ultimately benefit the growth of theory and practice which will help leaders and voters navigate the tumultuous exchange of sacrifice and service across generations and national borders. The dynamism between the owner class and the labor class has entertained the race for hundreds of years and more specialized systems of political economy will empower both segments with democratic franchise through the refinement of government institutions and the reinforcing of roles.

Imagine the potential of an entire chamber representative of only employees and laborers offset by another chamber dedicated to the interests of the owners' class and leisure class (institutional wealthy and investors). Normally labor and the owners' class represent opposite positions and it would be easy to predict non-cooperation between two specialized chambers acting in opposition but if both chambers also included the professional class or middle class as a bridge in interests it increases the likelihood that moderate policies will be passed by both chambers. One chamber will admit only below median income earners and the other will admit only above median income earners; this prevents cross corruption from intermingling of campaign donations or other means of influence. The middle class typically votes in larger numbers (with a component unionized) which will be competitive with the upper class which has the capital advantage but not the advantage in votes.

When the legislators more readily recognize the class, they represent and suffer the same economic stressors they will be better advocates for their constituencies. There will be more transparency when everybody appreciates their designated roles. There will be less incentive and less opportunity for ambitious legislators to leverage their votes for another income or asset class without the camouflage of one or two ambiguous national parties with ideologies based on coalition rather than specific interests in economy or society. Multi-party systems can accommodate Income-based representation better especially in cases where multiple chambers are employed as the parties can specialize their platforms within a chamber devoted to a specific economic class and their associated legislative powers.

Bifurcating the measure into above median and below median segments is one of the most effective means to create distinct populations from one pool of eligible voters. It ensures that all segments of a population are represented and share economic interests and pressures. The more egregious forms of economic oppression through wage suppression and duress modeling must be more forcibly argued in the prism of wealth and class differences. The differentiation of population based on economic criteria will provide the specialization the chambers need to focus more intently on their own economic interests.

    ii. Attribute
        z. Value Index
                a. removed
                b. removed
                c. removed
                d. Below Median
                e. Above Median
                f. removed
                        g. removed
                        h. removed
      zz. District Index
                        a. Independent
                        b. aggregate
      zzz. Threshold
                i. national median
                ii. state median
                iii. district median

When districts are separated into above median and below median groups, the value can be based on the districts independent value or the states aggregate value. For an example in GDP based representation, if an independent value is used, the district calculates its own GDP. If an aggregate value is used the same district would use the states GDP value to calculate its position in the sequence to determine the median value. Aggregate values will generally separate districts from the same states into the same above median or below median group. Independent values will dissect a state into separate districts, part of which may be in the above median group and the others in the below median group.

      zzzz. Instrument
          a.) sales
          b.) property
          c.) income
          d.) capital gains
          e.) payroll
          f.) Total (Combined)

The representation is dependent on the type of instrument being measured. Most states use sales taxes, property taxes, income taxes, and capital gains taxes. There are plenty of other taxes not represented in this matrix and they can all be fairly easily introduced or substituted. The point is more that the representation can be tailored to a specific instrument. Many governmental tiers specialize in a tax and it would be more appropriate for the jurisdiction to utilize only that measure. Any number of instruments can be listed with the values averaged or tallied. Sometimes it is more appropriate for a jurisdiction or tier to tally all applicable tax liabilities. All of the public records and prior histories should be available to aid in organizing the voter entitlement.

If the political system is based on calculations involving income, taxes, or other variables it will require voters to be classified as below median or above median. This test can be applied every year on an annual basis or in longer periods of 3 years or 5 years. The bench marking can even be set to the length of the term for the office. Each voter will be assessed through the tax documents provided with noncompliance factored in as zero entries. The states will be chiefly responsible for determining the status of voters and assigning them to the correct chamber.

      zzzzz. Electorate Eligibility
          i.) Annually
          ii.) Every 3 years
          iii.) Every 5 years
          iv.) Equal to terms

Most nations do not control their borders with enough precision to only grant access to approved individuals. Therefore, the nation would be in a position to establish a tiered citizenship system. Resident Aliens could acquire certain rights or privileges over unauthorized aliens. Still, unauthorized aliens could gain work permits for certain industries and protections for transit or healthcare. In most cases, voting rights will be exclusive to citizens reducing the risk of an electorate shifting due immigration policies or patterns.

v.) Domicile
   a. Resident Alien
   b. Citizen
   c. Unauthorized Alien

Voting rights can be relegated to certain lower tiers or specific agency representation. Obviously, states participating in an economic union with other states could elect to empower resident aliens with special suffrage while the other states in the Union are protected by continuing to exclude the alien from federal elections or their own state votes.

b.) Action
   i.) to vote
   ii.) to hold office

Eligibility requirements can be independent, or they can be accumulative. Independent attributes are non-exclusive which means permits citizens satisfying one component of the eligibility criteria to vote or hold office when multiple attributes are listed. Exclusive domains require voters or candidates to maintain all eligibility criteria listed making the population of possible voters or candidates much smaller. More complicated systems of representation will attempt to index divergent qualities to hedge or check the influence or power of any single segment of the population. An example of this would be maintaining a domicile requirement with an income requirement. Neither are related but in exclusive systems both must be satisfied in order to qualify.

c.) domain
   i. exclusive
   ii. non-exclusive

An example of non-exclusive attributes would be indexing one legislative chamber to income earners within the lowest bracket along with income earners from the highest bracket. Obviously one resident couldn't possibly satisfy both requirements. This has an important effect on representation because it conjoins the political power of the lowest income earners who occur in large numbers with the highest income earners which occur infrequently. By offsetting this chamber with another devoted exclusively to middle class income earners it dilutes the richest segment and emphasizes the middle class without mitigating the poorest. This might be an effective check to the corrupting power of private campaign finance which overwhelmingly benefits the highest income earners.

There will definitely be times when it is appropriate for legislators or executives from different tiers of government to appoint the officers of other branches. This is true in instances of colonial or imperial rulership but also has uses for integrating more efficient command hierarchies between federal and state tiers or within local jurisdictions. Appointed officers can occur within the same jurisdiction which has the potential to maximize efficiencies in governance without depreciating the franchise of democratic rule within the jurisdiction. Political engineers should consider both top down control and bottom up control where elected municipal officers appoint state officials or where state officials appoint federal civil servants. Appointments can occur through the consensus of legislators which would imitate a parliamentarian mode of elections or an executive from lower jurisdictions can vote to install the executives within higher jurisdictions. There are a myriad of different combinations that can be explored in theory prior to implementing for self-governance or union management.

      9.) Appointed by
        a.) region
                i.) municipal
                ii.) county
                iii) state
        b.) branch
        '
                i. legislature
                ii. executive
                iii.. judicial
                iv.. reserve

Voting isn't a right it's a duty and a responsibility. Advocating for mandatory or compulsory voting for citizens is an appropriate response to the expected malaise that typically overtakes democratic societies and governments. The danger in contemporary governments is that special interest groups and other outlier populations are more likely to vote than average or lower-class citizens. This pressures government engineers into satisfying the demands of minorities rather than the base and contributes to the polarization of political-economy. The product is an unstable government, dangerous to itself as well as its neighbors and others community members.

      10.) Voting

a.) compulsory
b.) voluntary
c.) automated

Making voting mandatory is complementary when specializing eligibility criteria for voting and holding office; with greater privileges come greater responsibility. Voluntary voting is the standard for contemporary democracies, but the mode of representation and political governance is relatively new and it can be expected that as political systems evolve more will demand compulsory voting from their eligible citizens.

Mandatory voting presents an excellent opportunity for the state to enact automated voting although it can be used for voluntary systems as well. In automated voting, an individual register as an affiliate of a political party and all votes occurring within that jurisdiction are allotted towards the predetermined candidate. This will have no effect on primaries with the voter still required to make a selection unless a more exact preference based on ideology can be selected. The individual registers once and doesn't need to personally cast a vote until he elects to suspend the automated voting at some future point.

This should improve voting turnout a great deal by eliminating the effort needed to vote. Voters can be registered upon the age of majority and enrolled within automated voting system that allows the individual to vote regardless of economic or other stressors that generally inhibit voting during elections.

Democracies can suffer from periods of low voter turnout which expose the nation to extreme amounts of danger. When popular will isn't translated into political will the public will be susceptible to fundamentalist ideologies and vote against their interests. This is exacerbated when a strict voting system excludes a large number of poorer citizens. Automated voting will make these populations less susceptible to voter suppression efforts and exploitation that prevents them from voting.

Examine the United States where 75% of the citizens don't vote in 75% of the elections. A minority of 18% dictates most off year elections with off year elections describing 3 of the 4 election seasons. Even in Presidential election years only 76% of the population votes. An automated voting system wouldn't result in a 100% voter turnout, but it could double the number of off cycle voters. The US is critically sensitive to voter suppression movements with access to voting sites regularly obstructed and all efforts are at inhibiting new voter registration and prohibiting voters who actually make it to the sites. An automated voter system will make it virtually impossible for opposition parties to obstruct voting attempts for general elections although primaries will still be vulnerable.

Automated voting coordinates with value voting systems in that voting already requires for labor to be exerted on determining the number of votes cast. At the time of registration an eligible voter can select automated voting preferences and from that period on all of their re-ported tax data will translate into value voting for candidates within the appropriate jurisdiction. It will be far easier to tabulate value voting systems with the use of automated voting as the time required to process the tax information can be distributed more easily during an election period. Mandatory voting and automated voting will make election prediction much easier with turnout almost guaranteed and where prior year econometrics and tax data is available for analysis.

Most democracies won't function correctly if an oligarchy of political parties constricts the political choices voters can make. Every opportunity must be taken advantage of to ensure that binary political systems do not dominate the political markets. Multi-party systems promote more cooperation and coalition building and reduce the deleterious byproducts from peer pressure and lack of diversity. Political Parties can be regulated by size so that smaller units of similar parties exist, but their leadership is individually determined with bureaucracy limiting how efficiently they can market and organize their efforts.

If size is not an adequate limit, then each state or provincial jurisdiction must organize its own party with its own leadership and work to negotiate the regulations governing the marketing of the individual parties so that one brand name does not exist, and a national initiative is harder to organize. Most state representatives and parties have wildly different and often antagonistic interests that compete for funding and legislative priority. Requiring different party names will help identify reoccurring patterns in power distributions and profit sharing. Political parties vary within distant regions with their own conservative and liberal spectrum differentiating the members from one state and another.

    11.) Political Parties
       a.) Primaries
          i.) closed
          ii.) Open
       b.) Endorsements
          i.) Two Party System
          ii.) Multiple Party Endorsements
          iii.) Endorsement Parties

A more interesting structure for forming political parties is enfranchising the special interest groups by patenting the issues and permitting those groups to extend or retract endorsements based upon performance. The special interest group can then dictate how all endorsed politicians vote on any measure tabled regarding their interest. This will disrupt the any command hierarchies within a two party or multi-party structure while infusing more integrity within the legislature by limiting politician's abilities to claim endorsement while bargaining votes on that issue for other issues.

Endorsement party structures enables open primaries with multiple candidates to satisfy more individualized constituent groups with more specialized representation. The endorsements are individually tailored and demand performance which means voters will have more accurate representation on the issues the care most about. The endorsement parties themselves should be able to dedicate more resources to debating and deliberating the issues voted on by the professional politicians with less conflict in policy. More sophisticated endorsement systems will permit the endorsed politicians to hold a practice vote prior to the real vote with the result dictating the endorsements party formal and public position on the issue. The era of computer technologies will grant the access needed for more highly organized voting.

Jurisdictions or districts typically define a legislator's constituency. Jurisdictions tend to encompass a whole state, city, or county. For example, if a state is permitted two senators all of the resident citizens are permitted to vote for both offices. The senators are both responsible for representing the same constituency. Districts reduce the State or city into distinct regions with a dedicated constituency. If the state has three districts and three assembly members each is only responsible for representing only one jurisdiction.

The difference is access with jurisdiction wide candidates required to satisfy a larger cross section of interests and district wide candidates allowed to specialize within a smaller cross section of interest. One produces a regression to the mean (or average) while has polarizing tendencies. Both have their individual merits; however, the two methods are not equal; jurisdictions tend to promote more cooperation within a state or city while districts tend to invite political abuses like Gerrymandering.

Although contrary to most critical beliefs, a smaller number of representatives should be accorded to district representation with a greater number allotted to jurisdiction representation; this will permit faster and easier political reorganizations with more binary or symmetrical areas of representation while also dedicating more resources to the representation attempting to satisfy the averaged interests within the jurisdiction.

More complex forms of representation including Legislative Broker and Executive Representation are more accessible with jurisdictional organization which must be considered when engineering a political system. A third qualifier is presented as a means to integrate commercial interests and accommodate corporate statehood if it ever applies. When and if corporations are granted suffrage, they may need more specialized representation which does not necessarily correlate to either Jurisdiction or District but rather Industrial sector or market.

    12.) Jurisdiction;
        a. Jurisdiction wide (Senators)
        b. Districts (Representatives)
        c. Sector (Commercial)

After the criteria is established to determine eligible voters and candidates each system of representation must have a method to determine the number of representatives provided to each jurisdiction. Most Democracies correlate representation to population as it is the reasonable and balanced way to organize democratic government. The number of representatives can be correlated to other measures that have important functions within the nation state. For instance, representation based on GDP typically aggregates population with productivity producing a more practical form of representation because it can help transmit the economic ideologies that contributed to the higher economic product. Correlating representation to taxes is an even more sophisticated measure for representation because it combines population, with economic productivity, and fiscal policy. It can help ensure that one subset of the population does not exploit another through unfair gradients in tax policies or exploitative economic policies. It also positive reinforces tax collection by associating political power with the surrendered moneys.

    13. Determining the Number of Representatives
        a. Straight Demographic

Most democracies are built around the concept of proportional votes between jurisdictions which are based upon the size of the population in each. The premise of democracy is inextricably associated with popular representation. A least common denominator is calculated and then each population is divided by the figure to produce the representational coefficient. The coefficient equals the number of politicians prescribed to that region or state. This process results in representative government with all citizens earning an equal ratio of representatives: residents. It is by far the fairest and most accurate way to structure representation. Population naturally accounts for economic figures, demographic figures, and civil figures and is the basis for majority rule.

    b. GDP
        i. Straight
        ii. Per capita

GDP and similar economic indicators are substitutes to population when establishing the ratio of representatives distributed among the various jurisdictions. There are two variants in the way GDP can be used in calculating the Representational Coefficient. The first is a straight calculation using a least common denominator. The raw GDP figure is divided by the LCD to determine the exact representative coefficient for each jurisdiction. GDP can vary from jurisdiction to jurisdiction with some states being much richer and earning much more direct influence within the system. Exceptions and outliers gain proportionally more or less representation. With the straight calculation of representation, the wealthier jurisdictions can export their economic and political ideologies through the efficiency gained in representation. These are absolute terms which don't take population into account.

The second method is to average the value by dividing GDP by the population. The LCD is determined and divided into each result to calculate coefficient for representation. This is a Per Capita value. When using the Per Capita calculation, there will always be differences in the representation earned by each individual and each jurisdiction, but the variance should be much smaller than the result of the straight calculation. A Per Capita calculation will result in a more equal distribution of representation between jurisdictions. A larger component of the population may be willing to accept this form of wealth representation making it more practical for all intents and purposes.

    c. Federalist Taxes (Tax Liabilities)
        i. Gross
        ii. Net
                x. Surrendered
                xx. Minimum

Tax representation for jurisdictions can be a convenient means to establish tighter controls on federal or state budgets and check other imbalances within the system of representation. A nation that rewards tax liabilities with increased representation will be stronger and more influential than other nations. They will have better funded militaries and more equitable economies. These are huge advantages for nations over with nations that favor austerity and deregulated economies. Countries that develop cultures that resist tax policies will find their governments under siege with debt defaults and government shutdowns. Wealth inequality will grow along with political corruption, and eventually the people will sow discord and consider rebellion. A nation with more equitable economies with better funded governments with access to healthcare and education are less likely to favor regime change. Tax based representation make it far more likely that nations perform better at economic engineering and wealth control.

Tax representation can be based on net taxes paid or gross taxes paid. Net taxes paid are calculated from the previous year with the total federal or state rebates subtracted from the total remitted. This figure is not proportional representation and it is more than likely that certain jurisdictions will lose their representation due to receiving more federalist tax rebates than contributions. Gross tax representation is based on the total amount of taxes remitted to the tier of government where the representation is earned. The amounts assessed to each region are compared to each other to determine the proportional number of seats earned. The primary mechanism for establishing the comparative values is a ratio of taxes remitted: number of representatives. Each increment produces another representative. Each of the states or regions will be in ratio or proportion to one another

Federalist tax policy is necessary for stimulating lower GDP jurisdictions and should be a major component of fiscal policy. The idea is exceptional, but its application is generally flawed. It is too easy to exploit wealthier jurisdictions where there is an imbalance in representation favoring the poorer and less populous states. A political union's measure of inefficiency is huge differences within taxes paid into a federal system and rebates received. Economic Unions and most Federal governments are based on cooperation and mutual consent; these extreme differentials can exacerbate over extended periods of neglect and can precipitate premature dissolution of the organization or entity.

Tax exploitation can be compensated for by introducing representation based on net taxes paid so that those jurisdictions acting as net donors of federal taxes can leverage more political power within the system than the net welfare recipients. This will discourage the net welfare jurisdictions from perfecting their exploitative practices. It should condition them to think of the nation as a whole rather than focusing on their short-term self- interests, and develop macro-economic strategies based more on competition than federal government subsidy by reducing their net political influence and likelihood of earning future federalist government subsidies. Due to the representational deductions due to tax rebates, those states that are welfare recipients won't have any representation in that specific chamber, branch, or tier of government which should be an extremely potent and effective means to discourage tax exploitation.

In both methods, larger jurisdictions with more mature economies will have access to much more representation which is correlated to their extra contributions to federalist taxes. This will benefit the nation as population with the more specialized labor and more experienced professionals will have more representation. The regions with higher GDP and stronger economies will be able to export their economic practices and government theories. The net result of enfranchising those regions which pay more taxes should be faster economic growth and more competitive markets for export.

There is an option for regions or states with negative federalist tax contributions to continue receiving representation. It would be a bare minimum, a lowest common denominator set by the constitution that would apply every time a state would normally lose representation in the chamber due to federalist tax policy. States with positive contributions to federalist tax policy will earn that minimum representation in addition to number if seats earned by proportional positive contributions to federalist tax policy. The representation gained by positive federalist tax contributions are still based on a value equal to an LCD in ratio to itself with the coefficients then added to the primary (minimum) coefficient.

This is a significant concession, but it will improve the chances of states agreeing to representational coefficients based on net taxes. Surrendering representation in exchange for increased federalist tax contributions might be too extreme a consequence for a conventional public policy intended to build market economies and strengthen the public sector within poorer, smaller, or less capable regions.

    f. Executive Representation
       i. Registered Voters
       ii. Allied Voters
       iii. Total Voters

Executive Representation concentrates the amount of influence awarded from proportional representation within one elected office. If the popular representation would have produced 11 senators for the jurisdiction the single Executive Representative would wield the equivalent of 11 votes within the legislature. It combines the best attributes of representational government with focus. Leadership is concentrated onto a smaller number of representatives without diminishing the proportional influence the jurisdiction should have. The administrative staff of an executive representatives within the legislatures will have to bulk up to accommodate the larger number of committees they must participate in and the executive representative appoints their surrogates on any committee they sit on. Executive representation can use any representational coefficient based on population, GDP, or taxes, and any variant thereof.

Even more complicated systems of Executive Representation can predicate the votes leveraged by the position on the number of votes the individual received during election to the office, the number of registered voters in the jurisdiction, or the number of total voters in the jurisdiction. The variable figure will introduce some uncertainty in votes from year to year. This is especially true when Presidential elections affect voter turnout making those executive representatives elected during that year much more powerful. Results will be less predictable over any length term adding impetus and emergency to passing laws when the opportunity presents itself. It should make the political more responsive to popular movements and much harder to obstruct.

Executive Representation based on voter turnout requires the election system to be engineered so that the states coinciding with Presidential election and increased turnout is on a rotation that grants the extra advantage to all Executive Representatives in a cyclical manner. This can be accomplished with making sure the Presidential term is one step or two steps longer than the executive representatives terms allowing the constellation of states affected by the increased voter turnout to change every full term.

If the Presidential term and Executive Representative's terms were equal the same states would always benefit from the improved turnout making their Executive Representatives more potent. This could be purposefully engineered into the election cycle to create a two-tiered state system (imperial) where certain states had institutional advantages. Take the United States as an example with Presidential voter turnout at 70% and off years at only 30%. Those executive representatives elected during those years would have more than double the representation. The states or party with elections during the Presidential election would dominate for the next few years. This can simulate the same mechanism that provides a Prime Minister is guaranteed a majority in the Parliament.

This system of Executive Representation can be used to form empires. Instead of a rotation a pre-selected number of states would always gain the advantage of stronger presidential turnout and thus more legislative power. This would allow a democratic nation to actively seek or coerce more membership through war or negotiation with new states provided clearly stipulated but abbreviated representation in the political union. It would still qualify as democratic with each citizen gaining one voter. Contemporary democracies have many representational deficiencies that are ruthlessly exploited by opposition parties rendering any formal criticism of an imperial presidency less accurate or meaningful.

Executive Representation follows the traditional method for allocating committee representation. If an executive representative earns a total of 10 votes this translates to the equivalent to 10 separate representatives when allocating the committee seats. If the executive representation uses registered voters, raw, population, or recorded votes the process is slightly different. The total number of votes earned by each executive representative is divided by the number of committee seats available. This simulates an LCD where each Executive Representative then takes turns appointing themselves to committees until their personal store of votes is exhausted.

If there are 1 million votes in a system and only 100 committee seats each seat is worth 1000 votes. Seats can be purchased for less votes than the LCD if it represents the last of the executive representative's appointments. Any votes remaining after all seats are filled are lost. This should favor minority parties just enough to ensure that popular movements in the electorate are checked by a slight decrease in committee seats for the majority. The majority party will still own a majority of the votes in the legislature and can pass all measures escaping committees.

Representatives install themselves on committees in the order of most votes or least votes, one at a time or according to the various committee staffing procedures. It is also possible for the political parties to dictate the order of seat selection instead of individual members. Leadership will decide the candidate and the committee in the order prescribed to the system.

g. Combinational (Scale)

Scaled representation is an abridged form of democracy that can be used in occupations, empires, or for feudal variations. The population would continue to vote on a proportional basis with the majority of participants receiving a single vote. However, a coefficient is introduced to provide management representation equal to that of the number of employees or enlisted under their command. Authoritarian control is avoided by distributing votes among all levels of leaders so that the bulk of the votes remain with the lower level managers when combined with the free vote of all enlisted or employed. The top commander would have the most individual votes, but the combined total of all votes including subordinates always maintains a majority requiring all legislators to seek out coalitions within the institution or company and rule through consensus.

    h. Legislative Brokers
      a. Intra-brokerage
      b. Inter-brokerage

Legislative broker powers allow currently elected politicians to consolidate power by winning elections in other chambers of the legislature or by earning multiple seats in the same chamber. Each position permits an additional vote and access to more committees. Legislative brokers are paid for each position and can use that salary to hire the staff they need to administer to the new duties and powers. When necessary, a legislative broker should be permitted to authorize a surrogate to vote in his stead if the multiple chambers are operating simultaneously.

Successful legislative brokers are more likely to win other seats adding value to the set of appointments and making the candidate more attractive for campaign donations. In most political systems, the total number of eligible seats will still be restricted by location ensuring that the integrity is protected as one broker will typically only represent one state. Legislative brokers will vary in size, power, and party contributing to the overall competitiveness of the system.

There are two types of brokerage powers. The first allows brokerage powers within the same institution. If the chamber has state-wide elections, then a single candidate can pursue multiple seats. Districts restrict this property through residence eligibility criteria. The second brokerage power extends to external institutions. Residency requirements still apply reducing the effectiveness of the brokerage powers but a single representative from a district could run in as many state-wide elections as were available.

    j. Arbitrary (Senatorial)
           i. 1
           ii. 2
           iii. Senatorial Method of Total Proportion
           iv. Per Capita
        a.   Income
        b.   Tax Liabilities

Senatorial Representation is generally capped at either 1 Senator per state or 2 Senators per state. The ratio between states and senators should remain fixed regardless of the number of senators. For example, if there are 50 states and they are split into two groups, with one group maintain control over 20 states and the other group maintaining control over 30 states, it doesn't matter which representational coefficient is used the ratio will remain about 66% each time. If there are 1 Senator per state, it would result in 20 Senators from one group and 30 Senators from the other group. This has the same ratio of senators when there are 40 Senators in one group and 60 in the other. No matter how many Senators are apportioned to each state, the ratio remains the same.

A third option exists where a method of total proportion is used. When a method of total proportion is used for a senate the total number of seats are reduced to smaller ratio of states: seats. For example, a senate might have 50 states and only 100 seats creating a range of only 1 to 3 senators per state. The senatorial method of total proportion is compatible with population, GDP, income, tax liabilities or any other reasonable factor.

A fourth option uses per capita values to create a more flexible range for the number of senators assigned to each state. Outliers will still earn more representation but it will not be nearly as much as if they used interval level variables or conventional total proportion method. This entitlement does use method for total proportion but per capita values are used, reducing the difference between states.

    k. Straight Median Income

Not all Income-based representation splits the electorate into above median and below median groups. Income can also be used as a stand-alone representational coefficient. To calculate a straight median income coefficient, one multiplies the median income of a state by its population. This figure is summed and then divided by the number of seats in the chamber. Each individual product is then divided by this second figure producing a ratio of seats for each state. This coefficient is intended to adjust the demographic representation by the wage dispersion in the nation. If all of the states have an equivalent median wage, there would be a strictly demographic-based representation coefficient. This is the intended effect. With more wealth equality, the nation can continue to rely on simple majorities. When there is significant difference in wealth and standards in living, those states with higher median incomes will gain more proportional representation and be able to export the policies that produced those outcomes.

1. Straight Median Liability

In the exact same way straight, median income can be calculated, liabilities can be substituted for income producing a straight median liability coefficient. The median tax liability is calculated for the state, it is multiplied by the population, tallied, and then divided by the number of representatives in the chamber. Once an LCD is established, each of the state values are divided by this number, producing a discrete number of representatives for each state. Some states will round up to one representative while other states will be rounded down. No political system is perfect. The liability and population values can be determined during a census year and apply until the next census is taken.

      14. Macropolitical (Executive, Legislative)
          1.) Class
               a. alpha (primary executive or legislator)
               b. agency heads, committee heads
               (Fractal)
               c. proportional (Governors and Mayors)
          2.) Power
                    a. Veto
                    b. Confirmation (triangulation)
                    c. both.

When an Executive branch is split in multiple parts each one can be empowered with a macropolitical vote for use in negotiating with legislators. Each Executive branch or agency would have a vote in whether or not legislation passes, with each institution maintaining one vote equivalent with final vote of the legislation. It is a more productive form of a veto requiring the legislation passes by a Legislature to be confirmed by the majority of institutions including the executive branch prior to being made into law. This is a progressive reform to the contemporary single executive veto power. Increasing the number of intuitional parties with a macropolitical vote actually increases the likelihood of more legislation passing.

For example, in a bicameral legislature with unitary executive, there would be 3 total votes, with each institution gaining 1 vote, and where only a 2/3rds majority is needed to pass a law. The two institutions contributing to the passage could be both the lower chamber and the higher chamber of the legislature, or the lower chamber and the executive branch, or the higher chamber and the executive. The three permutations increase the chances of laws passing with both chambers acting more aggressively to author laws the executive agrees with.

History demonstrates that Inefficiencies in a political system are often ruthlessly exploited for personal gain and profits. Imbalanced wealth concentrations and political representation produce an environment of instability and danger. The usual symptoms are present; extreme budgetary problems resulting from low taxes and sustained government expenditures in excess of revenues, and excessive corruption in the election cycles from lack of access or excessive moneyed interests.

More obvious imbalances are evident when public sector institutions like penitentiaries and security services are privatized, and where labor protections remain diluted and ineffective. Decay occurs over the span of years and decades and is often irreversible when the population accepts and even advocates for their degraded environment – the result is always the same in that it ends in rebellion, revolt, or war as body politics suffer the same threats of injury and death as its citizens due but in economies of scale.

Political systems that resist change or impede the rate of change are subject to more threats of insolvency and dissolution. It's only a matter of time until excessively complex or rigid systems of political governance are exposed to crises which require quick decisive action but where the awkward interaction of antagonistic legislative chambers or executive branches fail to resolve a critical issue and precipitate a system ending event. More cumbersome systems, requiring more dedicated cooperation, are the easiest to exploit economically as regulations will be irregular and infrequent with institutional powers protecting current market share and monopolies rather than producing economic opportunity and fair exchanges.

Under-regulated political markets also subjected to moneyed representation based on campaign contributions rather than fixed proportions of asset or income representation is the quickest way to destroy integrity and faith in the system. Most economies have steep natural gradients towards monopolistic market share and dangerous wealth concentrations. Moneyed influence accelerates this trend and makes it more resistant to reform. Within decades, a nation could be rendered noncompetitive and irrelevant within the global theatre of political-economy.

These deficits' present opportunities for insurrection, rebellion, and reformation. Stability is the most valuable currency in political economy, but when a nation or state is in decline maintaining the current trajectory is not productive. Order can be achieved by diluting civil liberties, inhibiting organization, and enforcing property laws but this is hardly sufficient in dispelling the potential instability. Nations can continue to suppress opportunities for self-determination, but it will be a persistent ambition and goal for the population, especially when the premise of democracy exists elsewhere, and the ideas can be communicated through trade or example. Democratic societies will thrive more often simply because the communities can provide for themselves with political and economic reforms. They will naturally seek out more stability and more productivity.

<u>Bibliography</u>

"America's Choice 2012 Election Center", Nov 2014, CNN Politics,
        retrieved from http://www.cnn.com/election/201-2/results/-
        race/governor/

Carney, Jordain (March 25 2020). "Senate unanimously passes
        $2T coronavirus stimulus package". Retrieved from
        https://thehill.com/home-news/senate/489590-senate-passes-2-
        trillion-coronavirus-stimulus-package

Chafetz, J. (2011). "The Unconstitutionality or the Filibuster".
        Connecticut Law Review, Vol 43, No. 4, pp. 1003-1040, May
        2011. retrieved from https://papers.-ssrn.com/sol3/papers.-
        cfm?abstract_id=1730782

Cox, A., He, E., Mclean, A., Russel, K, Tse, A., and
        Waananen, L., (July 2011)/ "Charting the American Debt
        Crisis". Retrieved from http://archive.nytimes.com/www-
        .nytimes.com/interactive/2011/07/28/us/charting-the-
        american-debt-crisis.html

"Democracy Index 2018: Me too?", 2019, The Economist
        Intelligence Unit, www.eiu.com

Department of Treasury, "Internal Revenue Service Data Book 2017",
        Retrieved from https://-www.irs.gov/pub/irssoi/17-databk.pdf

Desilver, Drew (December 5 2013). "U.S. income inequality, on rise
        for decades, is now highest since 1928". Retrieved from
        https://www.pewresearch.org/fact-tank/2013/12/05/u-s-
        income-inequality-on-rise-for-decades-is-now-highest-since-
        1928/

Eichler, Alexander & McAuliff, Michael, "Income Inequality Reached
        Gilded Age Levels, Congressional Report Finds", last updated
        Dec 6th 2017, Huffpost, retrieved from https://ww-w.huffpost-
        .com/entry/income-inequality_n_10326

"Election 2016", Nov 2016, CNN Politics, retrieved from https://www.-
        cnn.com/-

Frey, W.H. (March 14 2018). "The US will become 'minority

white' in 2045, Census projects." Retrieved from https://www.brookings.edu/blog/theavenue/2018/03/14/-the-us-will-become-minority-white-in-2045-census-projects/

"GDP Growth (Annual %)", World Bank, Retrieved from https://data.-worldbank.org/indicator/NY.GDP.MKTP.KD.ZG?locations=US

Gill, N.S., "The Roman Republics Government", March 30th, 2019, retrieved from https://www.th-oughtco.com/the-roman-republics-government-120772

"GINI Index (World Bank Estimate)". World Bank, retrieved from https://data.worldbank.org/-indicator/SI.POV.GINI

Gruber, Jonathan (2013), "Public Finance and Public Policy", 4ed, Worth Publishers, New York, NY.

Infoplease staff (March 17 2020). "Timeline of U.S. Government Shutdowns", Retrieved from https-://www.infoplease.com/history-/us/timeline-of-us-government-shutdowns

Kong, Cameron, "Recession is Overdue by 4.5 Years. Here is How to Prepare". Forbes.com, Oct 23, 2018, retrieved from https://www.forbes.com/sites/cameronkeng/-2018/10/23/-recessionis-overdue-by-4-5-years-heres-how-to-prepare/#5710753240d8

Krogstad, Jens Manuel, (07/31/2019) "A view of the nation's future through kindergarten", retried from https://www.pewresearch.-org/fact-tank/2019/07/31-/kindergarten-demographics-in-us/?fbclid=IwAR2KUcxTv4a-V7EZH2kX-SpvEaiYmm-GvCfEa6TjdGwvqzaf4AFaq-KqvHNhy4

Legion, Thomas. "Population of the Original 13 Colonies", retrieved From http://-www.thomas-legion.net/population_of_the_orig-inal_thirteen_colonies_-free_slave_white_and_nonwhite.html

Longley, Robert, "Direct Democracy Pros and Cons", July 7th, 2019, retrieved from https://www.th-oughtco.com/what-is-direct-democracy-   3322038

Murse, Tom. Aug 30 2019, "Why the Presidents Party Loses Seats in
    TheMidterm Elections", retrieved from https-
    ://www.thoughtco.-com/historical-midterm-election-results-
    4087704

Przeworski, Adam. "Minimalist Conception of Democracy: A
Defense"
    Democracy's Value, edited by Shapiro, I. and   Hacker-
    Cordon, C. *(*Cambridge: Cambridge University Press, 1999

Politico, "Election Central", updated 12/23/2014, retrieved from https-
    ://www.politico.c-om/2014-election/-results/map/governor#-
    .XSyJkPZFz85

Rappeport, Alan (Oct. 25 2019)."Federal Budget Deficit
    Swelled to Nearly \$1Trillion in 2019". Retrieved from
    https://www.nytimes.com/2019/10/25-/us/politics/us-federal-
    budget-deficit.html

"Statistics and Historical Comparison". Gov Track. Retrieved on
    https://www.govtrack.us/congress/bills/statistics

Stone, Lyman, 9/24/2014 "Which States have the most progressive
    income taxes", retrieved from https:
    //taxfoundation.org/which-states-have-most-progressive-
    income-taxes-0/

Weisman, Jonathan, and Parker, Ashley (Oct 16,2013). "Republicans
    Back Down, Ending Crisis Over Shutdown and Debt Limit".
    Retrieved from https://www-.nytimes.com/2013/10/17-
    /us/congress-budget-debate-.html

Woods, Darian, 06/25/2019 "The Magic Number Behind Protests",
    accessed on 9/10/2019, retrieved from https://www.npr.org/
    sections/money/2019/06/25/-735536434/ the-magic-number-
    behind-protests

Zaveri, M., Gates, G., and Zraick, K. (January 25 2019). "The
    Government Shutdown Was the Longest Ever. Here's the
    History", retrieved from https://www.nytimes.com/-
    interactive/2019/01/09/us/politics/longest-government-
    shutdown.html

"2018 National and State Population Estimates", U.S. Census, accessed on 7/9/2019, retrieved from https://www.censu-s.gov/newsroom/press-kits/2018/pop-estimates-national-state.html

Table 1: Tax-based Coefficients (Democrats)[83]

State	Revenues (in millions)	# Reps Revenue in Union	%	# Reps Revenue Split	%	Party
Vermont	$4,495.28	1	0.14%	1	0.24%	Democrat
Maine	$7,464.28	1	0.23%	2	0.41%	Democrat
Hawaii	$8,221.29	1	0.25%	2	0.45%	Democrat
New Mexico	$8,969.67	1	0.28%	2	0.49%	Democrat
New Hampshire	$11,314.99	2	0.35%	3	0.62%	Democrat
Rhode Island	$14,373.32	2	0.44%	3	0.78%	Democrat
Nevada	$18,450.07	2	0.57%	4	1.00%	Democrat
Delaware	$22,640.85	3	0.70%	5	1.23%	Democrat
Oregon	$31,219.15	4	0.96%	7	1.70%	Democrat
Colorado	$47,210.72	6	1.45%	11	2.57%	Democrat
Wisconsin	$51,748.83	7	1.59%	12	2.81%	Democrat
Connecticut	$59,174.58	8	1.82%	14	3.22%	Democrat
Maryland	$63,936.80	9	1.97%	15	3.48%	Democrat
Washington	$73,334.44	10	2.25%	17	3.99%	Democrat
Michigan	$77,948.41	10	2.40%	18	4.24%	Democrat
Minnesota	$106,927.81	14	3.29%	25	5.81%	Democrat
Massachusetts	$108,049.21	14	3.32%	26	5.88%	Democrat
Pennsylvania	$136,108.81	18	4.18%	32	7.40%	Democrat
New Jersey	$153,917.57	21	4.73%	36	8.37%	Democrat
Illinois	$158,042.27	21	4.86%	37	8.59%	Democrat
New York	$269,717.00	36	8.29%	64	14.67%	Democrat
California	$405,851.30	54	12.48%	96	22.07%	Democrat
Total	$1,839,116.64	246	56.54%	435	100.00%	
Divisor	$4,227.85					

---

[83] Table created from Department of Treasury, Internal Revenue Service Data Book 2017, Accessed 7/8/2019, Retrieved from https://-www.irs.gov/pub/irs-soi/17databk.pdf

Table 2: Tax-based Coefficients (Republicans)[84]

State	Revenues (in millions)	# Reps Revenue in Union	%	# Reps Revenue Split	%	Party
Wyoming	$5,284.15	1	0.16%	2	0.37%	Republican
Alaska	$5,717.64	1	0.18%	2	0.40%	Republican
Montana	$5,805.10	1	0.18%	2	0.41%	Republican
West Virginia	$7,374.30	1	0.23%	2	0.52%	Republican
North Dakota	$7,711.24	1	0.24%	2	0.55%	Republican
South Dakota	$7,732.14	1	0.24%	2	0.55%	Republican
Idaho	$9,785.03	1	0.30%	3	0.69%	Republican
Mississippi	$11,468.66	2	0.35%	4	0.81%	Republican
Utah	$20,178.72	3	0.62%	6	1.43%	Republican
Iowa	$23,969.39	3	0.74%	7	1.70%	Republican
South Carolina	$24,086.26	3	0.74%	7	1.70%	Republican
Alabama	$25,070.26	3	0.77%	8	1.77%	Republican
Nebraska	$25,103.77	3	0.77%	8	1.78%	Republican
Kansas	$27,019.29	4	0.83%	8	1.91%	Republican
Arkansas	$32,508.76	4	1.00%	10	2.30%	Republican
Kentucky	$32,708.39	4	1.00%	10	2.31%	Republican
Oklahoma	$33,942.29	5	1.04%	10	2.40%	Republican
Louisiana	$42,628.15	6	1.31%	13	3.01%	Republican
Arizona	$42,631.32	6	1.31%	13	3.02%	Republican
Indiana	$57,972.83	8	1.78%	18	4.10%	Republican
Tennessee	$62,708.66	8	1.92%	19	4.44%	Republican
Missouri	$64,112.50	9	1.97%	20	4.53%	Republican
North Carolina	$78,736.40	11	2.42%	24	5.57%	Republican
Virginia	$80,242.85	11	2.46%	25	5.68%	Republican
Georgia	$86,446.60	12	2.65%	27	6.11%	Republican
Ohio	$140,981.15	19	4.33%	43	9.97%	Republican
Florida	$177,389.49	24	5.44%	55	12.55%	Republican
Texas	$279,904.43	37	8.59%	86	19.80%	Republican
Total	$1,413,935.61	189	43.56%	435	100%	
Divisor	$3,250.43					
Union	$3,253,052	435				
Union Divisor	$7,478.28					

---

[84] Table created from Department of Treasury, Internal Revenue Service Data Book 2017, Accessed 7/8/2019, Retrieved from https://-www.irs.gov/pub/irs-soi/17databk.pdf

Table 3: Above Median Chamber (by Population)[85]

State	Population	Revenues (in millions)	# Reps population	%	Median Partition by Revenue	Party
Massachusetts	6,784,240	$108,049.21	9	4.24%	Upper	Democrat
Pennsylvania	12,791,904	$136,108.81	17	7.99%	Upper	Democrat
New Jersey	8,935,421	$153,917.57	12	5.58%	Upper	Democrat
Illinois	12,839,047	$158,042.27	17	8.02%	Upper	Democrat
New York	19,747,183	$269,717.00	27	12.33%	Upper	Democrat
California	38,993,940	$405,851.30	53	24.35%	Upper	Democrat
Minnesota			1	0.46%	Upper	Democrat
Ohio	11,605,090	$140,981.15	16	7.25%	Upper	Republican
Florida	20,244,914	$177,389.49	27	12.64%	Upper	Republican
Texas	27,429,639	$279,904.43	37	17.13%	Upper	Republican
Total # of Seats			217			All
Total # of Seats			137	62.98%		Democrat
Total # of Seats			80	37.02%		Republican
Totals	320,226,241	$1,419,219.75				
Union Totals	320,226,241	$1,419,220				
Union Divisors	737848.482	$3,270.09				

---

[85] Table created from U.S. Census, 2018 National and State Population Estimates, accessed on 7/9/2019, retrieved from https://www.censu-s.gov/newsroom/press-kits/2018/pop-estimates-national-state.html and Department of Treasury, Internal Revenue Service Data Book 2017, Accessed 7/8/2019, Retrieved from https://-www.irs.gov/pub/irs-soi/17databk.pdf

Table 4: Below Median Chamber (Democratic, by Population)[86]

State	Population	Revenues (in millions)	# Reps population	%	Median Partition by Revenue	Party
Vermont	626,088	$4,495.28	1	0.39%	Lower	Democrat
Maine	1,329,453	$7,464.28	2	0.83%	Lower	Democrat
Hawaii	1,425,157	$8,221.29	2	0.89%	Lower	Democrat
New Mexico	2,080,328	$8,969.67	3	1.30%	Lower	Democrat
New Hampshire	1,330,111	$11,314.99	2	0.83%	Lower	Democrat
Rhode Island	1,055,607	$14,373.32	1	0.66%	Lower	Democrat
Nevada	2,883,758	$18,450.07	4	1.80%	Lower	Democrat
Delaware	944,076	$22,640.85	1	0.59%	Lower	Democrat
Oregon	4,024,634	$31,219.15	5	2.51%	Lower	Democrat
Colorado	5,448,819	$47,210.72	7	3.40%	Lower	Democrat
Wisconsin	5,767,891	$51,748.83	8	3.60%	Lower	Democrat
Connecticut	3,584,730	$59,174.58	5	2.24%	Lower	Democrat
Maryland	5,994,983	$63,936.80	8	3.74%	Lower	Democrat
Washington	7,160,290	$73,334.44	10	4.47%	Lower	Democrat
Michigan	9,917,715	$77,948.41	13	6.19%	Lower	Democrat
Minnesota	5,482,435	$106,927.81	6	2.76%	Lower	Democrat

---

[86] Table created from U.S. Census, 2018 National and State Population Estimates, accessed on 7/9/2019, retrieved from https://www.censu-s.gov/newsroom/press-kits/2018/pop-estimates-national-state.html and Department of Treasury, Internal Revenue Service Data Book 2017, Accessed 7/8/2019, Retrieved from https://-www.irs.gov/pub/irs-soi/17databk.pdf

Table 5: Below Median Chamber (Republican, by Population)[87]

State	Population	Revenues (in millions)	# Reps population	%	Median Partition by Revenue	Party
Wyoming	586,555	$5,284.15	1	0.37%	Lower	Republican
Alaska	737,709	$5,717.64	1	0.46%	Lower	Republican
Montana	1,032,073	$5,805.10	1	0.64%	Lower	Republican
West Virginia	1,841,053	$7,374.30	2	1.15%	Lower	Republican
North Dakota	756,835	$7,711.24	1	0.47%	Lower	Republican
South Dakota	857,919	$7,732.14	1	0.54%	Lower	Republican
Idaho	1,652,828	$9,785.03	2	1.03%	Lower	Republican
Mississippi	2,989,390	$11,468.66	4	1.87%	Lower	Republican
Utah	2,990,632	$20,178.72	4	1.87%	Lower	Republican
Iowa	3,121,997	$23,969.39	4	1.95%	Lower	Republican
South Carolina	4,894,834	$24,086.26	7	3.06%	Lower	Republican
Alabama	4,853,875	$25,070.26	7	3.03%	Lower	Republican
Nebraska	1,893,765	$25,103.77	3	1.18%	Lower	Republican
Kansas	2,906,721	$27,019.29	4	1.82%	Lower	Republican
Arkansas	2,977,853	$32,508.76	4	1.86%	Lower	Republican
Kentucky	4,424,611	$32,708.39	6	2.76%	Lower	Republican
Oklahoma	3,907,414	$33,942.29	5	2.44%	Lower	Republican
Louisiana	4,668,960	$42,628.15	6	2.92%	Lower	Republican
Arizona	6,817,565	$42,631.32	9	4.26%	Lower	Republican
Indiana	6,612,768	$57,972.83	9	4.13%	Lower	Republican
Tennessee	6,595,056	$62,708.66	9	4.12%	Lower	Republican
Missouri	6,076,204	$64,112.50	8	3.79%	Lower	Republican
North Carolina	10,035,186	$78,736.40	14	6.27%	Lower	Republican
Virginia	8,367,587	$80,242.85	11	5.23%	Lower	Republican
Georgia	10,199,398	$86,446.60	14	6.37%	Lower	Republican
Total # of Seats			217			
Total # of Seats			79	36.30%		Democrat
Total # of Seats			138	63.70%		Republican

---

[87] Table created from U.S. Census, 2018 National and State Population Estimates, accessed on 7/9/2019, retrieved from https://www.censu-s.gov/newsroom/press-kits/2018/pop-estimates-national-state.html and Department of Treasury, Internal Revenue Service Data Book 2017, Accessed 7/8/2019, Retrieved from https://-www.irs.gov/pub/irs-soi/17databk.pdf

Table 6: Per Capita Tax Liabilities (Democratic)[88]

State	Population	Average Tax liability (Per capita)	# Reps - Partisan	%	# of Reps - Full	%	Partisanship
Vermont	626,088	$7,179.95	13	2.92%	7	1.51%	Democrat
Maine	1,329,453	$5,614.55	10	2.28%	5	1.18%	Democrat
Hawaii	1,425,157	$5,768.69	10	2.35%	5	1.21%	Democrat
New Mexico	2,080,328	$4,311.66	8	1.75%	4	0.91%	Democrat
New Hampshire	1,330,111	$8,506.80	15	3.46%	8	1.79%	Democrat
Rhode Island	1,055,607	$13,616.16	24	5.54%	12	2.86%	Democrat
Nevada	2,883,758	$6,397.93	11	2.60%	6	1.34%	Democrat
Delaware	944,076	$23,982.02	42	9.76%	22	5.03%	Democrat
Oregon	4,024,634	$7,757.02	14	3.16%	7	1.63%	Democrat
Colorado	5,448,819	$8,664.39	15	3.53%	8	1.82%	Democrat
Wisconsin	5,767,891	$8,971.88	16	3.65%	8	1.88%	Democrat
Connecticut	3,584,730	$16,507.40	29	6.72%	15	3.47%	Democrat
Maryland	5,994,983	$10,665.05	19	4.34%	10	2.24%	Democrat
Washington	7,160,290	$10,241.82	18	4.17%	9	2.15%	Democrat
Michigan	9,917,715	$7,859.51	14	3.20%	7	1.65%	Democrat
Minnesota	5,482,435	$19,503.71	35	7.94%	18	4.09%	Democrat
Massachusetts	6,784,240	$15,926.50	28	6.48%	15	3.34%	Democrat
Pennsylvania	12,791,904	$10,640.23	19	4.33%	10	2.23%	Democrat
New Jersey	8,935,421	$17,225.55	30	7.01%	16	3.62%	Democrat
Illinois	12,839,047	$12,309.50	22	5.01%	11	2.58%	Democrat
New York	19,747,183	$13,658.51	24	5.56%	12	2.87%	Democrat
California	38,993,940	$10,408.06	18	4.24%	10	2.18%	Democrat
Total	159,147,810	$11,168.95	435	100.00%	224	51.58%	Democrat
Divisor		564.87					

---

[88] Table created from U.S. Census, 2018 National and State Population Estimates, accessed on 7/9/2019, retrieved from https://www.censu-s.gov/newsroom/press-kits/2018/pop-estimates-national-state.html and Department of Treasury, Internal Revenue Service Data Book 2017, Accessed 7/8/2019, Retrieved from https://-www.irs.gov/pub/irs-soi/17databk.pdf

Table 7: Per Capita Tax Liabilities (Republican)[89]

State	Population	Average Tax liability (Per capita)	# Reps - Partisan		# of Reps - Full		Partisanship
Virginia	8,367,587	$9,589.72	18	4.16%	9	2.01%	Republican
Alabama	4,853,875	$5,165.00	10	2.24%	5	1.08%	Republican
South Carolina	4,894,834	$4,920.75	9	2.13%	4	1.03%	Republican
Arizona	6,817,565	$6,253.16	12	2.71%	6	1.31%	Republican
Mississippi	2,989,390	$3,836.45	7	1.66%	4	0.81%	Republican
Kentucky	4,424,611	$7,392.38	14	3.21%	7	1.55%	Republican
North Carolina	10,035,186	$7,846.03	15	3.40%	7	1.65%	Republican
West Virginia	1,841,053	$4,005.48	8	1.74%	4	0.84%	Republican
Florida	20,244,914	$8,762.18	17	3.80%	8	1.84%	Republican
Idaho	1,652,828	$5,920.17	11	2.57%	5	1.24%	Republican
Alaska	737,709	$7,750.54	15	3.36%	7	1.63%	Republican
Montana	1,032,073	$5,624.70	11	2.44%	5	1.18%	Republican
Oklahoma	3,907,414	$8,686.64	16	3.77%	8	1.82%	Republican
Georgia	10,199,398	$8,475.66	16	3.67%	8	1.78%	Republican
Louisiana	4,668,960	$9,130.12	17	3.96%	8	1.92%	Republican
Iowa	3,121,997	$7,677.58	14	3.33%	7	1.61%	Republican
Tennessee	6,595,056	$9,508.44	18	4.12%	9	2.00%	Republican
Missouri	6,076,204	$10,551.41	20	4.57%	10	2.22%	Republican
Utah	2,990,632	$6,747.31	13	2.93%	6	1.42%	Republican
South Dakota	857,919	$9,012.67	17	3.91%	8	1.89%	Republican
Wyoming	586,555	$9,008.78	17	3.91%	8	1.89%	Republican
North Dakota	756,835	$10,188.80	19	4.42%	9	2.14%	Republican
Indiana	6,612,768	$8,766.80	17	3.80%	8	1.84%	Republican
Kansas	2,906,721	$9,295.45	18	4.03%	8	1.95%	Republican
Arkansas	2,977,853	$10,916.85	21	4.73%	10	2.29%	Republican
Nebraska	1,893,765	$13,256.01	25	5.75%	12	2.78%	Republican
Ohio	11,605,090	$12,148.22	23	5.27%	11	2.55%	Republican
Texas	27,429,639	$10,204.45	19	4.42%	9	2.14%	Republican
Total	161,078,431	$8,237.20	435	100.00%	211	48.42%	Republican
Union Total	320,226,241	530			1095.07733		
Union Divisor	736152.278						

---

[89] Table created from U.S. Census, 2018 National and State Population Estimates, accessed on 7/9/2019, retrieved from https://www.censu-s.gov/newsroom/press-kits/2018/pop-estimates-national-state.html and Department of Treasury, Internal Revenue Service Data Book 2017, Accessed 7/8/2019, Retrieved from https://-www.irs.gov/pub/irs-soi/17databk.pdf

Table 8: Table of Payments and Revenues 2017 (Democrats)[90]

State	Population	Total Subsidies (in millions)	Revenues (in millions)	Rev - Spending (in millions)	Average Tax liability (Per capita)	Partisanship
Maryland	5,994,983	$92,987	$63,936.80	$ (29,050.20)	$10,665.05	Democrat
New Mexico	2,080,328	$27,554	$8,969.67	$ (18,584.33)	$4,311.66	Democrat
Michigan	9,917,715	$94,014	$77,948.41	$ (16,065.59)	$7,859.51	Democrat
Hawaii	1,425,157	$19,309	$8,221.29	$ (11,087.71)	$5,768.69	Democrat
Maine	1,329,453	$16,078	$7,464.28	$ (8,613.72)	$5,614.55	Democrat
Nevada	2,883,758	$23,181	$18,450.07	$ (4,730.93)	$6,397.93	Democrat
Vermont	626,088	$6,915	$4,495.28	$ (2,419.72)	$7,179.95	Democrat
Oregon	4,024,634	$32,713	$31,219.15	$ (1,493.85)	$7,757.02	Democrat
Colorado	5,448,819	$48,664	$47,210.72	$ (1,453.28)	$8,664.39	Democrat
New Hampshire	1,330,111	$12,414	$11,314.99	$ (1,099.02)	$8,506.80	Democrat
Washington	7,160,290	$72,937	$73,334.44	$ 397.44	$10,241.82	Democrat
Pennsylvania	12,791,904	$134,989	$136,108.81	$ 1,119.81	$10,640.23	Democrat
Rhode Island	1,055,607	$11,549	$14,373.32	$ 2,824.32	$13,616.16	Democrat
Wisconsin	5,767,891	$47,735	$51,748.83	$ 4,013.83	$8,971.88	Democrat
Delaware	944,076	$9,047	$22,640.85	$ 13,593.85	$23,982.02	Democrat
Connecticut	3,584,730	$41,452	$59,174.58	$ 17,722.58	$16,507.40	Democrat
Massachusetts	6,784,240	$75,631	$108,049.21	$ 32,418.21	$15,926.50	Democrat
Illinois	12,839,047	$105,483	$158,042.27	$ 52,559.27	$12,309.50	Democrat
California	38,993,940	$343,725	$405,851.30	$ 62,126.30	$10,408.06	Democrat
Minnesota	5,482,435	$44,304	$106,927.81	$ 62,623.81	$19,503.71	Democrat
New Jersey	8,935,421	$82,573	$153,917.57	$ 71,344.57	$17,225.55	Democrat
New York	19,747,183	$195,334	$269,717.00	$ 74,383.00	$13,658.51	Democrat
Totals	159,147,810	$1,538,588	$1,839,116.64	$ 300,528.64	$11,168.95	

---

[90] Table created from Department of Treasury, Internal Revenue Service Data Book 2017, Accessed 7/8/2019, Retrieved from https://-www.irs.gov/pub/irs-soi/17databk.pdf

Table 9: Payments and Revenues 2017 (Republicans)[91]

State	Population	Total Subsidies (in millions)	Revenues (in millions)	Rev - Spending (in millions)	Average Tax liability (Per capita)	Partisanship
Virginia	8,367,587	$138,029	$80,242.85	$ (57,786.15)	$9,589.72	Republican
Alabama	4,853,875	$56,762	$25,070.26	$ (31,691.74)	$5,165.00	Republican
South Carolina	4,894,834	$48,784	$24,086.26	$ (24,697.74)	$4,920.75	Republican
Arizona	6,817,565	$67,306	$42,631.32	$ (24,674.68)	$6,253.16	Republican
Mississippi	2,989,390	$34,308	$11,468.66	$ (22,839.34)	$3,836.45	Republican
Kentucky	4,424,611	$48,027	$32,708.39	$ (15,318.61)	$7,392.38	Republican
North Carolina	10,035,186	$93,907	$78,736.40	$ (15,170.60)	$7,846.03	Republican
West Virginia	1,841,053	$21,317	$7,374.30	$ (13,942.70)	$4,005.48	Republican
Florida	20,244,914	$190,831	$177,389.49	$ (13,441.51)	$8,762.18	Republican
Idaho	1,652,828	$15,139	$9,785.03	$ (5,353.97)	$5,920.17	Republican
Alaska	737,709	$10,568	$5,717.64	$ (4,850.36)	$7,750.54	Republican
Montana	1,032,073	$10,148	$5,805.10	$ (4,342.90)	$5,624.70	Republican
Oklahoma	3,907,414	$37,851	$33,942.29	$ (3,908.71)	$8,686.64	Republican
Georgia	10,199,398	$88,532	$86,446.60	$ (2,085.40)	$8,475.66	Republican
Louisiana	4,668,960	$44,701	$42,628.15	$ (2,072.85)	$9,130.12	Republican
Iowa	3,121,997	$25,883	$23,969.39	$ (1,913.61)	$7,677.58	Republican
Tennessee	6,595,056	$64,508	$62,708.66	$ (1,799.34)	$9,508.44	Republican
Missouri	6,076,204	$65,452	$64,112.50	$ (1,339.50)	$10,551.41	Republican
Utah	2,990,632	$20,620	$20,178.72	$ (441.28)	$6,747.31	Republican
South Dakota	857,919	$8,025	$7,732.14	$ (292.86)	$9,012.67	Republican
Wyoming	586,555	$5,177	$5,284.15	$ 107.15	$9,008.78	Republican
North Dakota	756,835	$6,805	$7,711.24	$ 906.24	$10,188.80	Republican
Indiana	6,612,768	$55,496	$57,972.83	$ 2,476.83	$8,766.80	Republican
Kansas	2,906,721	$24,243	$27,019.29	$ 2,776.29	$9,295.45	Republican
Arkansas	2,977,853	$28,514	$32,508.76	$ 3,994.76	$10,916.85	Republican
Nebraska	1,893,765	$15,636	$25,103.77	$ 9,467.77	$13,256.01	Republican
Ohio	11,605,090	$101,573	$140,981.15	$ 39,408.15	$12,148.22	Republican
Texas	27,429,639	$234,459	$279,904.43	$ 45,445.43	$10,204.45	Republican
Totals	161,078,431	$1,562,601	$1,419,219.75	$ (143,381.25)	$8,237.20	

---

[91] Table created from Department of Treasury, Internal Revenue Service Data Book 2017, Accessed 7/8/2019, Retrieved from https://-www.irs.gov/pub/irs-soi/17databk.pdf

Table 10: Net Chamber Eligibility (Democrats)[92]

State	Population	Total Subsidies (in millions)	Revenues (in millions)	Rev - Spending (in millions)	Average Tax liability (Per capita)	Partisanship
California	38,993,940	$343,725	$405,851.30	$ 62,126.30	$10,408.06	Democrat
Colorado	5,448,819	$48,664	$47,210.72	$ (1,453.28)	$8,664.39	Democrat
Connecticut	3,584,730	$41,452	$59,174.58	$ 17,722.58	$16,507.40	Democrat
Delaware	944,076	$9,047	$22,640.85	$ 13,593.85	$23,982.02	Democrat
Hawaii	1,425,157	$19,309	$8,221.29	$ (11,087.71)	$5,768.69	Democrat
Illinois	12,839,047	$105,483	$158,042.27	$ 52,559.27	$12,309.50	Democrat
Maine	1,329,453	$16,078	$7,464.28	$ (8,613.72)	$5,614.55	Democrat
Maryland	5,994,983	$92,987	$63,936.80	$ (29,050.20)	$10,665.05	Democrat
Massachusetts	6,784,240	$75,631	$108,049.21	$ 32,418.21	$15,926.50	Democrat
Michigan	9,917,715	$94,014	$77,948.41	$ (16,065.59)	$7,859.51	Democrat
Minnesota	5,482,435	$44,304	$106,927.81	$ 62,623.81	$19,503.71	Democrat
Nevada	2,883,758	$23,181	$18,450.07	$ (4,730.93)	$6,397.93	Democrat
New Hampshire	1,330,111	$12,414	$11,314.99	$ (1,099.02)	$8,506.80	Democrat
New Jersey	8,935,421	$82,573	$153,917.57	$ 71,344.57	$17,225.55	Democrat
New Mexico	2,080,328	$27,554	$8,969.67	$ (18,584.33)	$4,311.66	Democrat
New York	19,747,183	$195,334	$269,717.00	$ 74,383.00	$13,658.51	Democrat
Oregon	4,024,634	$32,713	$31,219.15	$ (1,493.85)	$7,757.02	Democrat
Pennsylvania	12,791,904	$134,989	$136,108.81	$ 1,119.81	$10,640.23	Democrat
Rhode Island	1,055,607	$11,549	$14,373.32	$ 2,824.32	$13,616.16	Democrat
Vermont	626,088	$6,915	$4,495.28	$ (2,419.72)	$7,179.95	Democrat
Washington	7,160,290	$72,937	$73,334.44	$ 397.44	$10,241.82	Democrat
Wisconsin	5,767,891	$47,735	$51,748.83	$ 4,013.83	$8,971.88	Democrat
Totals	159,147,810	$1,538,588	$1,839,116.64	$ 300,528.64	$11,168.95	

---

[92] Table created from U.S. Census, 2018 National and State Population Estimates, accessed on 7/9/2019, retrieved from https://www.censu-s.gov/newsroom/press-kits/2018/pop-estimates-national-state.html and Department of Treasury, Internal Revenue Service Data Book 2017, Accessed 7/8/2019, Retrieved from https://-www.irs.gov/pub/irs-soi/17databk.pdf

Table 11: Net Chamber Eligibility (Republicans)[93]

State	Population	Rev - Spending	Party	Net Chamber	# of Reps Net Population	%	# of Reps Net Revenues	%
Virginia	8,367,587	$ (57,786.15)	Republican	Ineligible				
Alabama	4,853,875	$ (31,691.74)	Republican	Ineligible				
South Carolina	4,894,834	$ (24,697.74)	Republican	Ineligible				
Arizona	6,817,565	$ (24,674.68)	Republican	Ineligible				
Mississippi	2,989,390	$ (22,839.34)	Republican	Ineligible				
Kentucky	4,424,611	$ (15,318.61)	Republican	Ineligible				
North Carolina	10,035,186	$ (15,170.60)	Republican	Ineligible				
West Virginia	1,841,053	$ (13,942.70)	Republican	Ineligible				
Florida	20,244,914	$ (13,441.51)	Republican	Ineligible				
Idaho	1,652,828	$ (5,353.97)	Republican	Ineligible				
Alaska	737,709	$ (4,850.36)	Republican	Ineligible				
Montana	1,032,073	$ (4,342.90)	Republican	Ineligible				
Oklahoma	3,907,414	$ (3,908.71)	Republican	Ineligible				
Georgia	10,199,398	$ (2,085.40)	Republican	Ineligible				
Louisiana	4,668,960	$ (2,072.85)	Republican	Ineligible				
Iowa	3,121,997	$ (1,913.61)	Republican	Ineligible				
Tennessee	6,595,056	$ (1,799.34)	Republican	Ineligible				
Missouri	6,076,204	$ (1,339.50)	Republican	Ineligible				
Utah	2,990,632	$ (441.28)	Republican	Ineligible				
South Dakota	857,919	$ (292.86)	Republican	Ineligible				
Wyoming	586,555	$ 107.15	Republican	Net Eligible	1	0.33%	0	0.02%
North Dakota	756,835	$ 906.24	Republican	Net Eligible	2	0.42%	1	0.18%
Indiana	6,612,768	$ 2,476.83	Republican	Net Eligible	16	3.70%	2	0.50%
Kansas	2,906,721	$ 2,776.29	Republican	Net Eligible	7	1.63%	2	0.56%
Arkansas	2,977,853	$ 3,994.76	Republican	Net Eligible	7	1.66%	3	0.80%
Nebraska	1,893,765	$ 9,467.77	Republican	Net Eligible	5	1.06%	8	1.89%
Ohio	11,605,090	$ 39,408.15	Republican	Net Eligible	28	6.49%	34	7.89%
Texas	27,429,639	$ 45,445.43	Republican	Net Eligible	67	15.34%	40	9.09%
Totals	161,078,431	$ (143,381.25)		8	133	30.62%	91	20.93%

[93] Table created from U.S. Census, 2018 National and State Population Estimates, accessed on 7/9/2019, retrieved from https://www.censu-s.gov/newsroom/press-kits/2018/pop-estimates-national-state.html and Department of Treasury, Internal Revenue Service Data Book 2017, Accessed 7/8/2019, Retrieved from https://-www.irs.gov/pub/irs-soi/17databk.pdf

Biography

Jordan David Weisinger graduated from the Johns Hopkins University with a M.S. in Data Analytics and Policy, Northwestern University with a M.A. in Public Policy and Administration, and the University of Massachusetts Amherst with a M.B.A in General Management. His undergraduate degree is in Literature from the University of Delaware. Jordan is currently employed as a Business Analyst and spends his days debugging proprietary software for a large organization. This lends itself to designing political systems intended to reform and improve in more conventional political systems.